THE ALGARVE

Forthcoming titles include

Chicago • Corfu • First-Time Round the World
Grand Canyon • Philippines
Skiing & Snowboarding in North America
South America • The Gambia • Walks Around London

Forthcoming reference titles include

Chronicle series: China, England,
France, India • Night Sky

read Rough Guides online

www.roughguides.com

Rough Guide Credits

Text editor: Lucy Ratcliffe
Series editor: Mark Ellingham
Production: Katie Pringle, Zoë Nobes
Proofreading: Amanda Jones
Cartography: Katie Lloyd-Jones, The Map Studio,
Romsey, Hants.

Front (small image) Windmill, Odeceixe © Robert Harding
Back (top) Alvor © Francesca Yorke
Back (lower) Fishing boat, Benfica ©Francesca Yorke

Publishing Information

This first edition published July 2002
by Rough Guides Ltd,
62–70 Shorts Gardens, London, WC2H 9AH

Distributed by the Penguin Group:
Penguin Books Ltd, 80 Strand, London WC2R ORL
Penguin Putnam, Inc. 375 Hudson Street, New York 10014, USA
Penguin Books Australia Ltd, 487 Maroondah Highway,
PO Box 257, Ringwood, Victoria 3134, Australia
Penguin Books Canada Ltd, 10 Alcorn Avenue,
Toronto, Ontario, Canada M4V 1E4
Penguin Books (NZ) Ltd,
182–190 Wairau Road, Auckland 10, New Zealand

Typeset in Bembo and Helvetica to an original design by Henry Iles.
Printed in Spain by Graphy Cems.

© Matthew Hancock 2002
368pp, includes index
A catalogue record for this book is available from the British Library.

ISBN 1-85828-831-2

THE ROUGH GUIDE TO

THE ALGARVE

by Matthew Hancock

With additional accounts by
Amanda Tomlin and Maurice
& Esme Clyde

ROUGH
GUIDES

We set out to do something different when the first Rough Guide was published in 1982. Mark Ellingham, just out of university, was travelling in Greece. He brought along the popular guides of the day, but found they were all lacking in some way. They were either strong on ruins and museums but went on for pages without mentioning a beach or taverna. Or they were so conscious of the need to save money that they lost sight of Greece's cultural and historical significance. Also, none of the books told him anything about Greece's contemporary life – its politics, its culture, its people, and how they lived.

So with no job in prospect, Mark decided to write his own guidebook, one which aimed to provide practical information that was second to none, detailing the best beaches and the hottest clubs and restaurants, while also giving hard-hitting accounts of every sight, both famous and obscure, and providing up-to-the-minute information on contemporary culture. It was a guide that encouraged independent travellers to find the best of Greece, and was a great success, getting shortlisted for the Thomas Cook travel guide award, and encouraging Mark, along with three friends, to expand the series.

The Rough Guide list grew rapidly and the letters flooded in, indicating a much broader readership than had been anticipated, but one which uniformly appreciated the Rough Guide mix of practical detail and humour, irreverence and enthusiasm. Things haven't changed. The same four friends who began the series are still the caretakers of the Rough Guide mission today: to provide the most reliable, up-to-date and entertaining information to independent-minded travellers of all ages, on all budgets.

We now publish more than 150 titles and have offices in London and New York. The travel guides are written and researched by a dedicated team of more than 100 authors, based in Britain, Europe, the USA and Australia. We have also created a unique series of phrasebooks to accompany the travel series, along with an acclaimed series of music guides, and a best-selling pocket guide to the Internet and World Wide Web. We also publish comprehensive travel information on our website: www.roughguides.com.

Help us update

We've gone to a lot of trouble to ensure that this Rough Guide is as up to date and accurate as possible. However, things do change. All suggestions, comments and corrections are much appreciated, and we'll send a copy of the next edition (or any other Rough Guide if you prefer) for the best letters.

Please mark letters "Rough Guide Algarve Update" and send to:

Rough Guides, 62–70 Shorts Gardens, London, WC2H 9AH, or Rough Guides, 4th Floor, 345 Hudson St, New York NY 10014.

Or send an email to mail@roughguides.com
Have your questions answered and tell others about your trip at www.roughguides.atinfopop.com

Acknowledgements

The author would like to thank all the people who helped with the book, especially co-author Amanda Tomlin, and Alex and Olivia for checking out the kids' facilities. Also to Paul and Roberta Dickson for giving me a home to write it up in. For the walks, a special thanks for the legwork put in by Maurice and Esme Clyde, as well as the help of the Wednesday Walkers; Roy and Barbara Porter; and João Santos, President of Almargem and supporter of the Algarve Walkers' development of Via Algarviana. A special mention also to Teresa Ventura at ICEP in London; João Lima and everyone at ICEP in Faro; Cliffors Issler; Daniel Albano at TAP; Enatur; The Ocean Club in Luz and everyone else who helped me out.

At Rough Guides, many thanks to Paul, Martin and everyone who helped set the book up, Sharon Martins for picture research, Katie Pringle for type-setting and especially to Lucy Ratcliffe for her extremely patient and diligent editing.

CONTENTS

MAP LIST

Map Symbols

-----	International boundary	💡	Lighthouse
---- --	District boundary	🦅	Waterfall
--- ---	Chapter divisions boundary	〰	Spring
▬▬▬	Motorway	∴	Ruins
▬ ▬ ▬	Motorway under construction	♙	Castle
════	Main road	⚲	Church (regional maps)
────	Minor road	ⓘ	Information office
▬▬▬	Pedestrianized street	✉	Post office
‖‖‖‖‖	Steps	⊞	Hospital
-----	Footpath	@	Internet access
▬●▬●▬	Railway	✈	Airport
········	River	★	Bus stops
— —	Ferry route	⛺	Campsite
♦	Point of interest	⛳	Golf course
〽	Mountains	▬	Building
▲	Peak	⊞	Church (town maps)
⬇	View point	░	Park
🏛	Cliffs	⣿	Beach

Introduction

"The **Algarve** has always been at variance with itself, more Mediterranean than Atlantic, as much African as European, its Islamic heritage visible in a Christian society. It is altogether, in its 5,000 square kilometres, a contradictory cosmos."

from *The Portuguese* by Marion Kaplan

With some of Europe's best and cleanest sandy **beaches**, picturesque rocky coves and year-round sunshine, this contradictory cosmos has become justifiably the most popular region in Portugal for both overseas visitors and the Portuguese themselves. Popularity has led to heavy development on the central coastal strip from Faro west to Lagos. But even here you can find quiet cove beaches and vestiges of traditional Portugal amongst the panoply of villas, hotels and sports complexes. It is this combination of natural beauty and superb facilities that have made the region popular with celebrities and sports stars from Cliff Richard to the Beckhams.

Development is much less pronounced at the two extremes of the Algarve. Around Sagres and along the

west coast, low-key resorts are close to a series of breath-taking wave-battered beaches, popular with windsurfers. To the **east**, relaxed resorts lie within reach of island sand-banks boasting giant swathes of dune-backed beaches. Away from the coast, **inland Algarve** has a surprisingly diverse landscape, with lush orange groves and wooded mountains offering superb walking territory around **Monchique** and **Silves** to the west and **Serra do Caldeirão** in the centre. In the east, a more wildly beauti-ful landscape marks the border with Spain along the fertile **Guadiana river valley**.

Where to go

International flights call at the coast's main airport at the regional capital **Faro**, a picturesque and historic harbour town lying on the edge of important natural wetlands. These are protected by a series of sandy offshore islets – the *ilhas* – which front the coastline virtually all the way to the Spanish border. The sweeping beaches on the islets can be reached from Faro itself and the ports of **Olhão** and **Fuzeta**.

Just west of Faro lies a series of pupose-built resorts including **Quinta do Lago**, **Vale de Lobo** and **Vilamoura**, each with grand beaches and a brace of golf courses and sports facilities which has led the area to be dubbed Sportugal. North of Faro there are the impressive Roman ruins at **Estói** and the attractive market town of **Loulé**, while further inland lie small villages and walking country round the mountain ranges of the **Serra do Caldeirão**.

The **eastern Algarve** starts at **Tavira** – one of the region's most instantly likeable towns within reach of another glorious offshore island beach – and covers the area

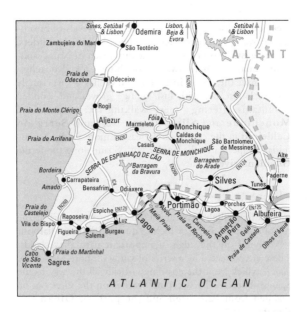

up to the Spanish border at **Vila Real de Santo António**, taking in the smaller coastal resorts of **Cabanas**, **Altura** and **Manta Rota** as well as the high-rise **Monte Gordo**. The verdant Guadiana river valley marks the border with Spain, bolstered by impressive fortresses in the villages of **Alcoutim** and **Castro Marim**. West of here lies some of Portugal's wildest areas, a mountainous barren landscape of small agricultural villages.

Central Algarve includes the region's most popular resorts, as well as one of its largest towns, the functional port of **Portimão**. The coast contains the classic postcard images of the province – tiny bays, broken up by rocky out-crops and fantastic grottoes, at their most exotic around the

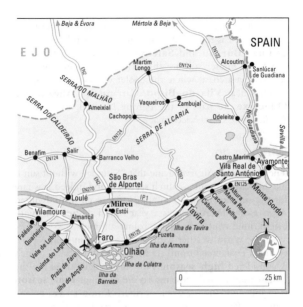

major resorts of **Albufeira**, **Armação de Pera** and **Carvoeiro**. This stretch also contains some of the region's biggest – if most developed – beaches at **Galé**, **Praia da Rocha** and **Alvor**, along with smaller resorts near great cove beaches such as **Ferragudo**, **São Rafael** and **Praia da Marinha**. Inland, the Moorish capital **Silves**, is en route to the **Serra de Monchique**, the highest mountain range in the south, with great walks through the cork and chestnut woods, remote villages and a beautiful old spa village in Caldas de Monchique.

The **western Algarve** embraces **Lagos**, one of the region's liveliest historic towns which lies within reach of more fine beaches; and continues up to the cape at **Sagres**

– site of Henry the Navigator's naval school. In between, development is restricted around the former fishing villages of **Luz**, **Burgau** and **Salema**, each with cliff-backed beaches. Quieter still are the string of villages along the rougher west coast, where the cooler waters of the majestic beaches near **Vila do Bispo**, Carrapateira, **Aljezur** and **Odeceixe** are part of the Parque Natural do Sudoeste Alentejano e Costa Vicentina.

When to go

There is a local Algarve saying that "Saturday without sun is like Sunday without a church service", and indeed it is rare for the sun not to make an appearance even in midwinter. As a result, the Algarve is a year-round destination, with bright, mild winters and long, balmy summers.

Sunny, warm weather with barely a cloud in sight is pretty much guaranteed from late May to early October, which is considered **high season**. Not surprisingly, these are the busiest months and most resorts are bustling. **Peak season** is in July and August, when northern European visitors are joined by Portuguese holidaymakers lured by peak temperatures of 25–30°C, though cooling Atlantic breezes usually make things comfortable.

Golfers ensure that **autumn** remains a busy season, as the cooler breezes off the coast in September and October are ideal for the game. But it is not too cool for beachgoers either, and swimming is tempting well into October (and year round if you're hardy, with water temperatures rarely dropping below 15°C).

In many respects the region is at its best in **spring** or **winter**, with temperatures usually a pleasant 15–18°C, the countryside at its most lush and the resorts delightfully quiet. This is ideal walking weather; only the extreme west of the region round Sagres could be described as cold even in midwinter. Despite the chance of the occasional downpour, most hotels and restaurants stay open, so rooms are easy to find. Indeed, **off-season travel** in the Algarve will get you some of the best deals in the country, with luxury hotels offering discounts of up to seventy percent.

ALGARVE'S CLIMATE

	AVERAGE TEMP (°C)	AVERAGE MONTHLY RAINFALL (MM)	AVERAGE DAILY SUNSHINE (HRS)
Jan	11.5	58	5.6
Feb	12	35	6.7
March	13	68	7.2
April	16	30	8.8
May	16.5	23	10.3
June	20.5	5	11.7
July	22	0	12.4
Aug	23.5	0	11.7
Sept	21	16	9.4
Oct	18.5	43	7.6
Nov	15	56	6
Dec	12	63	5.7

BASICS

Getting there

The most viable way of getting to the Algarve is by flying; flight time from the UK is around three hours. There are scheduled year-round flights to Faro from London and from several regional British airports, including Birmingham, Bristol, Glasgow, Manchester and Stansted. Numerous package companies also sell good value charter flights from a variety of airports, such as Bournemouth, Cardiff, East Midlands, Leeds–Bradford, Luton and Newcastle. Alternatively, if time isn't the most important factor, you can approach the Algarve overland from Lisbon or Spain, to which there are many cheaper, charter deals.

FROM BRITAIN

The budget airline, Go, has scheduled flights from Stansted, Bristol and East Midlands to Faro at around £80 return. However, unless you book well in advance and can be flexible about dates, you're likely to pay £150–200. Other **scheduled flights** (such as British Airways, British Midland, Monarch – who fly from Luton and Manchester – or the Portuguese national airline, TAP) tend to be more expensive, starting from £130–£275 depending on the time of year and length of stay.

Alternatively, you can often get good value **charter deals**, sold either with a package holiday or as a flight-only option. Flights tend to be from London, although regional airports may have one or two a week. Portugália flies daily from Manchester to Faro via Lisbon for around £200, while British Midland fly twice-weekly (Thurs & Sun) to Faro from East Midlands airport for £130–£240.

Airlines

British Airways
Ⓣ 0845/7733377,
Ⓦ www.british-airways.com
British Midland Ⓣ 0870/607
0555, Ⓦ www.flybmi.com
Go Ⓣ 0870/6076543,
Ⓦ www.go-fly.com
Monarch Ⓣ 08700/405040,
Ⓦ www.fly-crown.com
Portugália Airlines
Ⓣ 0870/7550025,
Ⓦ www.pga.pt/atrio
TAP Ⓣ 0845/6010932,
Ⓦ www.tap-airportugal.pt

Flight agents

Eclipse Direct Ⓣ 08705/010
203
Flightbookers Ⓣ 0870/010
7000,
Ⓦ www.flightbookers.com
North South Travel
Ⓣ 01245/608 291,
Ⓦ www.north-southtravel
.co.uk
Portugalicia Ⓣ 020/7221 0333
STA Travel Ⓣ 0870/160 6070,
Ⓦ www.statravel.co.uk

PACKAGE HOLIDAYS

Package holidays start at around £350–400 per person (including flights) for a week in high season, although some companies will take only two-week bookings at this time; in winter, you can pay around £100 less. Specialist holidays come a little pricier, from around £500–700 for a week's golfing holiday based in a four-star hotel.

Specialist operators

Abreu Travel ⓣ 020/7229 9905, ⓔ sales@abreu.co.uk. Portuguese-run agency – good on flights and accommodation.

Caravela Tours ⓣ 020/7630 9223, ⓦ www.caravela.co.uk. Various holidays including stays in *pousadas*, golf packages and fly-drives.

Destination Portugal ⓣ 01993/773 269, ⓦ www.destination-portugal.co.uk. Discount flight-only deals, car rental, villa and manor house lets, bird-watching, sailing and hiking holidays.

HF Holidays ⓣ 020/8905 9558, ⓦ www.hfholidays.co.uk. Walking holidays with flights from Gatwick and Manchester.

Latitude 40 ⓣ 020/7581 3104, ⓦ www.latitude40.net. Flights, car rental, hotels and villas.

The Magic of Portugal ⓣ 020/8741 1181, ⓦ www.magictravelgroup.co.uk. Flights plus villas and hotels.

Mundi Color ⓣ 020/7828 6021, ⓦ www.mundicolor.co.uk. Upmarket packages including golf holidays and fly-drive deals.

Portugala Holidays ⓣ 020/8444 1857, ⓦ www.portugala.com. Villas, hotels, flight only and fly-drive.

Portuguese Affair ⓣ 020/7385 4775, ⓦ www.portugueseaffair.com. High-quality villas and fly-drive.

Something Special ⓣ 08700/270520, ⓦ somethingspecial.co.uk. Flights and villas.

Style Holidays ⓣ 0870/444 4404 or 4414, ⓦ www.style-holidays.co.uk. Flights, car rental and package holidays.

Sunvil Holidays ⓣ 020/8758 4722, ⓦ www.sunvil.co.uk/discovery. Manor houses, hotels and fly-drive.

Travel Club of Upminster ⓣ 01708/225 000, ⓦ www.travelclub.org.uk. Villas and mostly four/five-star hotels, with flights from London, Manchester or Birmingham.

Travellers' Way ⓣ 01527/578100, ⓔ travsway@aol.com. Quality villas plus golfing and riding holidays.

FROM IRELAND

Summer **charter flights** to Faro are easy to pick up from either Dublin or Belfast, while year-round **scheduled** services operate, though these are usually via London and may involve an overnight stop. BA flights from Dublin to Faro (daily services use Aer Lingus via Heathrow or Gatwick) start at €420 in low season. BA flights from Belfast to Faro (via London) start at £187 in low season. British Midland flights are twice weekly from Dublin to Faro via East Midlands airport with prices starting at around €190. You can expect to pay around €200–215 return for summer charters from Dublin to Faro, and around £260 return from Belfast to Faro. Taking a **package holiday** may cut costs, with one week's villa or hotel holiday costing from €400 (from Dublin) or around £500 (from Belfast).

Airlines

Aer Lingus Northern Ireland
Ⓣ 0845/9737 747; Eire
Ⓣ 0818/365 000;
Ⓦ www.aerlingus.ie

British Airways Northern
Ireland Ⓣ 0845/7733377; Eire
Ⓣ 1800/626 747;
Ⓦ www.ba.com

British Midland Northern
Ireland Ⓣ 0870/607 0555; Eire
Ⓣ 01/407 3036;
Ⓦ www.flybmi.com

Go Eire Ⓣ 1890/932 922,
Ⓦ www.go-fly.com

Ryanair Eire Ⓣ 01/609 7800,
Ⓦ www.ryanair.com

TAP (Air Portugal) Eire
Ⓣ 01/679 8844,
Ⓦ www.tap-airportugal.pt

Specialist agents

Abbey Travel Eire Ⓣ 01/804
7100, Ⓔ abbeytvl@indigo.ie.
Charter flights,
accommodation and
packages.

Co-op Travel Care Northern
Ireland Ⓣ 028/90 471 717.
Packages and charters as well
as scheduled flights.

Joe Walsh Tours Eire Ⓣ 01/676
0991, Ⓦ joewalshtours.ie.
General budget fares agent.

Neenan Travel Eire ⓣ 01/606
9900, ⓦ www.neenantrav.ie.
Packages and flights.
Selective Travel Northern

Ireland ⓣ 028/90962010.
Specialists in charter flights
from Belfast.

FROM NORTH AMERICA

There are no direct **scheduled flights** from the US or
Canada to the Algarve, so the best options are to fly to
Lisbon with Air Canada, Continental or TAP, and then
get an onward flight with TAP, or go overland.
Alternatively, you could fly to Faro via London with
British Airways. Fares for all these routes from East Coast
destinations start at US$560–1360/CDN$1300–1800, and
from West Coast destinations at US$850–1650/
CDN$1660–2130.

Airlines

Air Canada ⓣ 1-888/247-2262,
  ⓦ www.aircanada.ca
British Airways ⓣ 1-800/247-
9297, ⓦ www.british-airways
.com
Continental Airlines
  ⓣ 1-800/231-0856,
  ⓦ www.continental.com
TAP (Air Portugal)
  ⓣ 1-800/221-7370,
  ⓦ www.tap-airportugal.pt

Flight agents

Council Travel US
  ⓣ 1-800/226-8624,
  ⓕ 617/528-2091,

ⓦ www.counciltravel.com
**New Frontiers/Nouvelles
  Frontières** US ⓣ 1-800/677-
0720 or 212/986 6006,
  ⓦ www.newfrontiers.com
Skylink US ⓣ 1-800/AIR-ONLY
or ⓣ 212/573-8980; Canada
  ⓣ 1-800/SKY-LINK
STA Travel US ⓣ 1-800/777-
0112 or 1-800/781-4040,
  ⓦ www.sta-travel.com
Travel Avenue US
  ⓣ 1-800/333-3335,
  ⓦ www.travelavenue.com
Travel Cuts Canada
  ⓣ 1-800/667-2887; US
  ⓣ 1-866/246-9762

Specialist agents

There is a list of further travel agents that specialize in holidays to Portugal and the Algarve on Ⓦ atop.org.

4th Dimension Tours
Ⓣ 1-800/877-1525 or 305/279-0014, Ⓦ www.4thdimension.com. Custom-built tours staying in manor house or *pousada* accommodation.

Abreu Tours Ⓣ 1-800/223-1580, Ⓦ www.abreu-tours.com. *Pousada* bookings, tailor-made holidays and land/air packages.

Isram World of Travel
Ⓣ 1-800/223-7460 or 212/661-1193, Ⓔ info@asram.com. Flights, escorted tours, packages and *pousada* accommodation.

Magellan Tours
Ⓣ 215/695-0330, Ⓦ www.magellantours.com. Golfing trips, *pousada* and manor house accommodation, and fly-drive holidays.

Pinto Basto Tours International Ⓣ 1-800/345 0739 or 914/639 8028, Ⓔ info@pousada.com. Fly-drive holidays, packages, flight-only, and customized special-interest trips.

FROM AUSTRALIA & NEW ZEALAND

There are no direct flights from Australia or New Zealand to the Algarve. The most straightforward route is with British Airways: from Australia, via London to Faro (A\$2350–3050) and, from New Zealand, via Los Angeles and London to Faro (A\$2600–3100). You may find it cheaper to buy a budget flight to London from a discount agent then get a scheduled flight with TAP, BA or Go – or a cheap charter flight – on to Faro (see p.3).

Airlines

Air New Zealand Australia
Ⓣ 1300/132476; New Zealand
Ⓣ 1-0800/737000; Ⓦ www.airnz.com

British Airways Australia

ⓣ 02/8904 8800; New
Zealand ⓣ 0800/274 847;
ⓦ www.british-airways.com
Garuda Australia ⓣ 02/9334
9970; New Zealand ⓣ 09/366
1862; ⓦ www
.garuda-indonesia.com
Qantas Australia ⓣ 13 13 13;
New Zealand ⓣ 09/661901;
ⓦ www.qantas.com.au

Flight agents

Anywhere Travel Australia
ⓣ 02/9663 0411,
ⓔ anywhere@ozemail.com.au
Flight Centre Australia
ⓣ 02/9235 3522, ⓣ 131600
for nearest office; New
Zealand ⓣ 09/358 4310;
ⓦ www.flightcentre.com
STA Travel Australia
ⓣ 1300/733035; New Zealand
ⓣ 09/309 0458;
ⓦ www.statravel.com.au
Thomas Cook Australia
ⓣ 131771 or 1800/801002;
New Zealand ⓣ 09/379 3920;
ⓦ www.thomascook.com.au
Trailfinders Australia
ⓣ 02/9247 7666,
ⓦ www.trailfinders.com

Travel.com Australia
ⓣ 02/9290 1500,
ⓦ www.travel.com.au

Specialist agents

Adventure World Australia
ⓣ 02/9956 7766,
ⓦ www.adventureworld
.com.au; New Zealand
ⓣ 09/524 5118,
ⓦ www.adventureworld.co.nz.
Organized tours and
accommodation, plus flights
to Portugal.
European Travel Office (ETO)
Melbourne ⓣ 03/9329 8844;
Sydney ⓣ 02/9267 7727.
Package holidays and
accommodation.
Ibertours Australia ⓣ 03/9670
8388 or 1800/500 016,
ⓦ www.ibertours.com.au.
Pousada and manor house
accommodation, fly-drive
trips and escorted tours.
PFM Travel Australia
ⓣ 02/9550 0788. Flights and
holidays.
Ya'lla Tours Australia
ⓣ 1300/362 844. Holidays to
the Algarve.

GETTING THERE

9

Red tape and visas

EU citizens need only a valid passport or identity card for entry to Portugal, and can stay indefinitely. Currently citizens of the US, Canada, Australia and New Zealand can also enter for up to ninety days with just a passport, but visa requirements do change, and it is always advisable to check the situation before leaving home.

EMBASSIES AND CONSULATES IN PORTUGAL

Australia Consulate Avenida da Liberdade 198, Lisbon ☎ 213 101 500

Canada Consulate Rua Frei Lourenço de Santa Maria 1–1°, Faro ☎ 289 803 757

Ireland Consulate Rua da Imprensa à Estrela 1–4°, Lisbon ☎ 213 929 440

New Zealand Consulate Avenida António Aguiar 122, Lisbon ☎ 213 509 690

UK Embassy Rua de São Marçal 174, Lisbon ☎ 213 929 440, ⓦ www.uk-embassy.pt. Largo Francisco A. Maurício 7–1°, Portimão ☎ 282 417 800

PORTUGUESE EMBASSIES ABROAD

Australia 23 Culgoa Circuit, O'Malley ACT ⓣ 02/6290 1733, ⓦ www.consulportugalsydney .org.au. Plus consulates in Sydney, Melbourne, Brisbane, Adelaide, Darwin and Fremantle.

Britain 11 Belgrave Square, London SW1X 8PP ⓣ 020/7235 5331.

Canada 645 Island Park Drive, Ottawa, K1Y OB8 ⓣ 613/729-0883, ⓔ embportugal @embportugal-ottowa.org. Plus consulates in Vancouver, Montreal and Toronto.

Ireland Knocksinna House, Knocksinna, Fox Rock, Dublin 18 ⓣ 01/289 3375.

New Zealand Consulates: P.O.Box 305, 33 Garfield Street, Parnell, Auckland, ⓣ 09/309 1454; and P.O. Box 1024, Suite 1 1st floor, 21 Marion Street Wellington, ⓣ 04/382 7655.

USA 2125 Kalorama Rd NW, Washington DC 20008 ⓣ 202/328-8610, ⓔ embportwash@mindspring. com. Plus consulates including New York, Boston and San Francisco.

RED TAPE AND VISAS

11

Health and insurance

ortugal poses few health problems for the visitor: the tapwater is safe to drink – although most visitors prefer bottled water – and no inoculations are necessary. Mosquitoes can be a menace in the summer, though December and January are usually mosquito-free. Mosquito-repellent lotion and coils are widely sold in supermarkets and pharmacies. Take care to use a high-factor sun cream as the sun is extemely powerful.

For minor complaints go to a **farmácia** (pharmacy). There's one in virtually every village and English is often spoken. Pharmacists are highly trained and can dispense drugs that would be prescription-only in Britain or North America. **Opening hours** are usually Mon–Fri 9am–1pm & 3–7pm, Sat 9am–1pm. Local papers carry information about 24-hour pharmacies and the details are posted on every pharmacy door.

In the case of serious illness, get the contact details of an English-speaking doctor from the British consular office or, with luck, from the local tourist office, or a major hotel. In an **emergency** dial ⓣ 112 (free).

INSURANCE

Travel insurance is advised for everyone, but in particular for non-EU citizens, who must pay for any medical treatment in Portugal. With insurance, you'll have to pay for

ROUGH GUIDE TRAVEL INSURANCE

Rough Guides offers its own travel insurance, customized for our readers by a leading UK broker and backed by a Lloyds underwriter. It's available for anyone, of any nationality, travelling anywhere in the world.

There are two main Rough Guide insurance plans: Essential, for basic, no-frills cover; and Premier – with more generous and extensive benefits. Alternatively, you can take out annual multi-trip insurance, which covers you for any number of trips throughout the year (with a maximum of 60 days for any one trip). Unlike many policies, the Rough Guide schemes are calculated by the day, so if you're travelling for 27 days rather than a month, that's all you pay for. If you intend to be away for the whole year, the Adventurer policy will cover you for 365 days. Each plan can be supplemented with a "Hazardous Activities Premium" if you plan to indulge in sports considered dangerous, such as scuba-diving or windsurfing. Rough Guides also does good deals for older travellers, and will insure you up to any age, at prices comparable to SAGA's.

For a policy quote, call the Rough Guide Insurance Line on UK freefone ⓣ 0800/015 09 06; US freefone ⓣ 1-866/220 5588, or, if you're calling from elsewhere ⓣ +44 1243/621 046. Alternatively, get an online quote at ⓦ www.roughguides.com /insurance.

HEALTH AND INSURANCE

treatment on the spot, but will be able to claim back the cost as long as you keep the receipts. As an EU country, Portugal has a free reciprocal health agreement with other member states; to take advantage of this, EU citizens need form E111, available from main post offices.

In addition to medical expenses, travel insurance usually provides cover for baggage, money and tickets in case of **theft**; to reclaim from your insurance company, you must register theft with the local police within 24 hours.

Before you buy any insurance, check to see if you are already covered by credit card companies, some of which offer free cover for holidays bought on their account. You may also find medical costs are covered if you have your own private health insurance policy, whilst some personal possessions may be covered by your home contents insurance; check the small print, and make sure you take a copy of contact telephone numbers with you.

If you plan to participate in any water sports or dangerous sports, check the travel insurance policy which may require you to pay a premium.

HEALTH AND INSURANCE

Costs, money and banks

espite being the most expensive region in Portugal, the Algarve remains notably cheaper than northern Europe and North America. There is plenty of choice of accommodation and eating options to suit all budgets, and a broad range of recommendations is given in the text.

A European Under-26 card is well worth having if you're eligible – it'll get you free or reduced admission to many museums and sights, **discounts** on travel, as well as reductions in numerous shops and restaurants (sometimes even hotels). Of much less use is the International Student Identity Card (ISIC), which is rarely accepted. Both are available through STA in Britain and Ireland, Council Travel in the US and Travel CUTS in Canada.

MONEY, BANKS AND EXCHANGE

Portugal is one of the twelve European Union countries to use the **euro** (€). Introduced in January 2002 to replace the escudo, euro notes are issued in **denominations** of 5, 10,

20, 50, 100, 200 and 500 euro, and coins in denominations of 1, 2, 5, 10, 20 and 50 cents and 1 and 2 euro. The exchange rate is around €1.60 to £1 and €1.10 to US$1.

You'll find a **bank** in all but the smallest towns. Standard **opening hours** are Monday to Friday 8.30am to 3pm. In some of the resorts they may also open in the evening. **Changing cash** in banks is easy, and shouldn't attract more than €3 commission.

By far the easiest way to get money in Portugal is to use **ATMs** (called Multibanco). You'll find them in even the most out-of-the-way small towns and you can withdraw up to €200 per day. Check with your bank to see whether you can use your credit or debit card in the Algarve, and remember that you'll be charged interest on credit card withdrawals from day one, in addition to the usual currency conversion fee. Most Portuguese banks will give **cash advances** on cards over the counter and will also charge a currency conversion fee. **Credit cards** are also accepted for payment in many hotels and restaurants.

Watch out if using **travellers' cheques**, as banks charge an outrageous commission for changing them (upwards of €13 per transaction). However, more reasonable fees can be had in *caixas* – savings banks or building societies – and some exchange bureaux. Larger hotels are sometimes willing to change travellers' cheques at low commission. It's probably worth taking a supply in case your plastic is lost, stolen or swallowed by an ATM.

COSTS, MONEY AND BANKS

16

Information, websites and maps

You can pick up brochures and maps, for free, from the Portuguese tourist office in your home country. Once in Portugal, get hold of a copy of the excellent *Turismo do Algarve Guide*, a monthly listings magazine in English and Portuguese, available free from most tourist offices and hotels.

You'll find a **tourist office**, or turismo, in almost every town and village. Details are given in the text; the offices are usually helpful, friendly and English is spoken. There's also an excellent freephone line, Linha Verde Turista ℡ 800 296 296 (Mon–Sat 9am–midnight, Sun & holidays 9am–8pm), the operators speak English and have information on museums, transport, accommodation, restaurants, hospitals, and police stations.

PORTUGUESE TOURIST OFFICES ABROAD

Australia and **New Zealand** No Portuguese tourist offices in Australia or New Zealand, but the website Ⓦ www.consulportugalsydney .org.au has useful information.

Britain 2nd Floor, 22–25A
  Sackville Street, London W1S
  3DW ⓣ 09063/640610,
  Ⓔ iceplondt@aol.com
Canada 60 Bloor St West, Suite
  1005, Toronto, Ontario M4W
  3B8 ⓣ 416/921–7376,
  Ⓔ iceptor@idirect.com
Ireland 54 Dawson Street,
  Dublin 2 ⓣ 01/670 9133,
  Ⓔ info@icep.ie

USA 590 Fifth Avenue, 4th
  Floor, New York, NY 10036-
  4785 ⓣ 212/719–3985 or 719
  4091, Ⓦ www.portugal.org;
  1900 L Street NW, Suite 310,
  Washington, DC 20036
  ⓣ 202/331-8222; 88 Kearny
  Street, Suite 1770, San
  Francisco, CA 94108
  ⓣ 415/391–7080

USEFUL WEBSITES

Ⓦ **www.maisturismo.pt** Search
engine for hotels, mostly
business orientated or at the
top end of the market.
Ⓦ **www.min-cultura.pt**
/Agenda/Agenda.html The
Ministry of Culture's website,
with details of events in major
Algarve towns.
Ⓦ **www.nexus-pt.com** Detailed
site dedicated to the Algarve,
covering everything from
tourist sites to weather and
shopping.
Ⓦ **www.portugal.org**

Government-run site, with an
Algarve section.
Ⓦ **www.portugalvirtual.pt**
Links with extensive hotel and
villa listings, restaurants and
bars, as well as sports
information.
Ⓦ **www.rede-almanaque.pt**
/feiras List of the country's
fairs, *romarias* and events,
though not regularly updated.
Ⓦ **www.rtalgarve.pt** The official
tourist board site. Information
is useful if limited and not
always regularly updated.

MAPS

The Portuguese National Tourist Office and turismos can
provide you with a reasonable **map** of the country

(1:600,000), which is fine for everything except mountain roads. If you're doing any real exploration, however, it's worth investing in a good **road map**. The best available abroad are Michelin's 1:400,000 Portugal (#440); or Geo Centre's Euro Map Portugal and Galicia at 1:300,000. Geo Centre also produces a 1:200,000 map of the Algarve and Bartholomew's Algarve Holiday Map 1:100,000 is good too.

The Geocid **website** is worth a visit at Ⓦ www.geocid–snig.cnig.pt; the site offers high resolution satellite and aerial topographic images. More detailed topographic maps for **walkers** are produced by the Instituto Geográfico do Exercito, Avenida Dr. Alfredo Bensaúde, Olivais Norte, Lisbon (Ⓣ 218 520 063) though ongoing road building in the Algarve means none of them is fully up to date.

MAP OUTLETS

Australia Mapland 372 Little Bourke St, Melbourne, Victoria 3000, Ⓣ 03/9670 4383, Ⓦ www.mapland .com.au

Canada World of Maps 1235 Wellington St, Ottawa, Ontario K1Y 3A3 Ⓣ 1-800/214-8524, Ⓦ www.worldofmaps.com

New Zealand Specialty Maps 46 Albert St, Auckland 1001 Ⓣ 09/307 2217, Ⓦ www.ubdonline.co.nz/maps

UK and Eire Stanfords 12–14 Long Acre, WC2E 9LP Ⓣ 020/7836 1321, Ⓦ www.stanfords.co.uk

USA Rand McNally Ⓣ 1-800/333-0136, Ⓦ www.randmcnally.com

Festivals

Most of the Algarve's traditional festivals revolve around celebrations of the patron saint of the community, and take the form of a church service followed by live music and dancing, food and drink. The biggest of these take place during June, the month of the *santos populares,* or popular, most commonly adopted saints. We've listed the highlights of the festival calendar; the local tourist boards can give a full list of village *festas.* For food festivals, see p.37.

FESTIVALS AND PUBLIC HOLIDAYS

JANUARY

New Year's Day (January 1) Public holiday.

FEBRUARY

Carnival, Loulé. One of the best of the region's lively carnival parades.

MARCH/APRIL

Good Friday Public holiday.

Easter Sunday Aleluia procession, São Brás de Alportel. Most distinctive of the region's Easter processions.

Mãe Soberana, Loulé. The Algarve's biggest religious festival begins when the image of Our Lady of Piety is carried from the hilltop church of Nossa Senhora da Piedade to the Church of São Francisco.

Revolution Day (25 April) Public holiday commemorating the 1974 revolution.

MAY

Atacar o Maio (May 1) Literally 'attacking May', public holiday celebrated with dried figs and *medronho* brandy accompanied by folk music. In Monchique, *medronho* and *mel* (honey) is eaten with *Bolo do Tacho* – pot cake made from corn flour, honey and chocolate.

Pine Cone Festival, Estói (May 2) Pine cones and rosemary are laid at the church of Our Lady of Pé da Cruz, with an evening torchlit procession and fireworks.

Alte Week of Arts and Culture. Live shows, brass bands and folk dancing accompanied by a grand picnic.

Algarve International Cinema Festival, Portimão, Alvor and Praia da Rocha. Screenings of films from Portuguese and international directors.

JUNE

Dia de Camões e das Comunidades (June 10) Public holiday.

Festa de Santo António (June 12–13) Saint's Day celebrating one of the most important of the popular saints. Music, food, drink and all-night dancing in Faro, Tavira,

Quarteira and smaller towns.

Festa de São João (June 23–24) Processions and music throughout the region – especially Lagoa, Lagos, Monchique and Portimão.

Festa de São Pedro (June 28–29) St Peter is the last of the *santos popularos* celebrated with revelry until the small hours.

JUNE/JULY

Feira do Carmo, Faro. The town's big annual fair, with handicrafts and live entertainment. Also celebrated with a parade of boats at Fuzeta.

International Motorcycle Concentration Annual celebration with rock bands playing between Faro beach and Faro airport.

Loulé International Jazz Festival Local and international jazz performers playing at weekends throughout July.

Algarve International Music Festival Biggest cultural event in the south of the country, organized by Fundação Gulbenkian and others. Chamber music, ballet and international artists throughout the region.

AUGUST

Feast of the Assumption (August 15) Public holiday.

Coimbra Serenades Top Coimbra fado is performed throughout the region.

AUGUST/SEPTEMBER

Espectáculos de Folclore Folk performances around the Algarve with a grande finale on Portimão's waterfront.

Conceição de Tavira, Tavira. Folk festival with live music and dancing.

OCTOBER

Republic Day (October 5) Public holiday.

Feira de Santa Iria, Largo de São Francisco, Faro. Second of the big Faro fairs, with a week of craft stalls, bumper cars, music and daily festivities.

NOVEMBER

All Saint's Day Public holiday.

São Martinho (November 11) Saint's day celebrated by eating roasted chestnuts - especially round the mountain village of Monchique - and drinking *agua pé* ('foot water'), the first tasting of this year's wine harvest.

DECEMBER

December 1 Public holiday celebrating independence from Spain in 1640.

Immaculate Conception (December 8) Public holiday.

Christmas Eve (December 24) Traditional *bacalhau* supper after midnight Mass.

Christmas Day (December 25) Public holiday.

New Year's Eve Enthusiastic banging of pots and pans heralds the new year, and live entertainment and fireworks throughout the region.

FESTIVALS

Communication

Recent heavy investment in new technology has shot much of Portugal's telecommunications into the twenty-first century. Post can still be erratic, but satellite TV is the norm and phones generally work like a dream – even public call boxes. Internet access is becoming more widespread, though it's still not generally available outside the main towns.

POSTAL SERVICES

Portuguese **postal services** are reasonably efficient. Letters or cards take three or four days to arrive at destinations in Europe, and a week to ten days to North America. To send a card to Europe or the USA costs €0.55, €0.95 to anywhere else.

Post offices (*correios*) are normally open Monday–Friday 8.30am–6pm, larger ones sometimes on Saturday mornings, too. **Stamps** (*selos*) are sold at post offices and anywhere that has the legend *Correio de Portugal – Selos*.

TELEPHONES

All calls, whether local or international, are most easily

made using card-operated **public phones** called *credifones*, which you'll find in all but the most remote villages. Cards cost €3, €6 or €9, and are available from post offices, newsagents, tobacconists and kiosks.

You'll also find pay phones in bars and cafés (and, increasingly, in turismo offices and newsagents). If you need quieter surroundings you'd be better off in one of the phone cabins found in most main post offices – simply tell the clerk where you want to phone, and pay for your call afterwards. Except in the main resorts, most telephone offices are closed in the evening. The **cheap rate** for inter-national and national calls is Monday to Friday between 9pm and 9am, and all day weekends and holidays.

TELEPHONE CODES AND USEFUL NUMBERS

To phone abroad from the Algarve

Dial 00 + country code (given below) + area code (minus initial zero) + number

Country codes

Australia 61	New Zealand 64
Canada 1	UK 44
Ireland 353	USA 1

To phone Portugal from abroad

Dial the international access code (see below) + 351 (country code) + number (nine digits)

International Access Code

Australia 0011	Ireland 00	UK 00
Canada 001	New Zealand 00	USA 001

COMMUNICATION

25

Reverse charge (collect) calls (*chamada cobrar ao destinatório*) can be made from any phone, dialling ⑦099 for a European connection, ⑦097 for North America, and ⑦098 for the rest of the world. If you encounter difficulties, call ⑦090.

Getting around

Getting around the Algarve by public transport is easier than anywhere else in Portugal, and since the coastline is only 240km long from east to west and around 40km from north to south at its widest point, you can see an awful lot in just a few days. The Algarve rail line runs the length of the region, calling at most major towns en route; buses link all the resorts and main inland villages. Car rental is also worth considering, though you may find you need nerves of steel to drive on some Portuguese roads.

TRAINS

The Algarve rail line runs from Lagos to Vila Real de Santo

António on the Spanish border, but you may have to change at Tunes, Faro or Tavira, depending on your destination. Train **timetables** for Portugal (€3.50) and for the Algarve line are available from information desks at main stations. Always turn up at the station with time to spare as long queues often form at the ticket desk.

Details of train times and routes are online at Ⓦ www.cp.pt.

If you end up on the train without first buying a ticket you could be liable for a huge supplement, payable to the ticket controller. However, smaller regional stations are sometimes unmanned, in which case just hop on and pay the ticket inspector on board.

Children under four go free, under-12s pay half price. Senior citizens (over-60s) can get thirty percent off travel if they produce their passport (or other form of ID proving their age) and ask for a *Bilhete Terceira Idade*.

Lastly, it's as well to note that some train stations are some distance from the town or village they serve and there's no guarantee of connecting transport.

BUSES

It's almost always quicker to go by **bus** than by rail, if you can, though you'll pay slightly more. The two main bus companies are EVA and Frota Azul, which link together in the central Algarve to offer a *Passe Turístico* (valid for three consecutive days €14.50), giving unlimited bus travel between Lagos and Loulé, covering all the main resorts in between (though not Faro). You can buy a pass from any bus station in the region.

Comfortable express buses operate on longer routes, for which you'll usually have to reserve tickets in advance. There's a **long-distance** Linha Litoral express service which connects Lagos to Vila Real/Ayamonte once daily on weekdays, the whole route taking four hours.

Up-to-date information on **routes and times** is available on the internet at ⓦwww.eva-transportes.pt and ⓦwww.rede-expressos.pt/index_uk.htm, which are both available in English, and there's a route map at ⓦwww .rede-expressos.pt/index_uk.htm. Currently there is no website for Frota Azul.

Local bus stations (detailed in the text) are the place to pick up **timetables** and reserve seats, but it's advisable to check first with the local turismo. Note that services are considerably less frequent and occasionally non-existent at weekends.

DRIVING AND CAR RENTAL

Car rental rates are among the lowest in Europe, but **petrol** (*gasolina*), is relatively expensive. Most rental cars run on unleaded (*sem chumbo*), but there is also super and diesel. **Driving licenses** from EU countries are accepted, otherwise an international driving licence is required.

The **east–west coastal road**, the EN125, gets pretty hectic in summer and has one of the highest accident rates in Portugal (which itself has the highest rates in Europe), so for the central and eastern Algarve, it is best to use the fast IP1 which currently runs slightly inland from the Spanish border at Castro Marim to Albufeira (though a new leg to Lagos should be open by late 2002), where it heads north to Lisbon.

On other routes, **road surfaces** are improving, but even major roads are often potholed, narrow and full of dangerous bends. But reckless overtaking is the main problem; even on motorways, you'll need to check your mirror every few seconds.

When **parking** in cities there are usually plenty of car

parks where you pay by the hour, along with pay and display parking bays, for which you'll need exact change, although spaces are often at a premium in high season. You're also likely to see men pointing you to empty spaces; it's best to tip (around €0.50) for this service.

Traffic **drives on the right**: **speed limits** are 50kph in towns and villages; 90kph on normal roads; and 120kph on the motorways. At **road junctions**, unless there's a sign to the contrary, vehicles coming from the right have priority. If you're stopped by the police, they'll want to see your **documents** – carry them in the car at all times and be courteous to the officers (see p.49). If you're taking your own vehicle make sure you have European roadside cover in case you break down.

CAR RENTAL

Car rental agencies can be found in all the major resorts and at the airport in Faro. Local agencies usually charge less than international companies, and contact details for recommended ones are listed in the text. **Rates** are reasonable, from around £30-40 a day to £100–120/US$150–180 a week for the cheapest car with unlimited mileage, though prices are inflated by around thirty percent in high season. You may find it cheaper to organize car rental from home, or arrange car rental in conjunction with your flights.

When picking up your car, check such important details as brakes and insurance coverage. Collision insurance is a good idea and unless you pay a separate supplement the excess may be on your head; if you're given the option of collision damage waiver, take it.

Finally, it can't be stressed enough that foreign and hire cars are comon targets of **theft**. Don't leave anything in an unattended car.

GETTING AROUND

TAXIS

Travelling by **taxi** in Portugal is relatively cheap and is
worth considering for trips across major towns and for
shorter journeys in rural areas. Generally, taxis are metered,
with a minimum **fare** of €1.50. Additional charges are
made for carrying baggage in the boot, and for travelling
between 10pm and 6am and at weekends. Outside major
towns, you can negotiate if you want to hire a taxi for a few
hours.

BICYCLES, MOPEDS AND MOTORBIKES

Bicycles are a great way of seeing the region, though
everywhere much inland from the coast and away from the
Rio Guadiana is hilly and you'll find pedalling hard work.
Unfortunately bikes are not allowed on any trains in the
Algarve. Several special shops, hotels, campsites and youth
hostels rent out bikes for around €10 a day; the major ones
are listed in the text.

You can also rent **mopeds**, **scooters** and low-powered
(80cc) **motorbikes** in many of the resorts, with hire costs
starting at around €25 a day. You need to be at least 18 to
hire these (and over 23 to rent larger bikes over 125cc), and
to have held a full licence for at least a year. Rental usually
includes helmet hire and locks along with third-party insurance.

Accommodation

Most accommodation in the Algarve is fairly modern and there is a phenomenal range to choose from: from luxurious five-star hotels set in their own grounds, simple guesthouses and rooms in private houses to campsites, youth hostels and private villas. It is best to try and reserve in advance if you are travelling in high season – from July to early September.

ROOMS, PENSÕES AND RESIDENCIAIS

Some of the cheapest accommodation consists of **rooms** (*quartos* or *dormidas*) let out in private houses. These are sometimes advertised, or more often hawked at bus and train stations, and they can be good value. The local turismo may also have a list of rooms available. Rates should be a little below that of a *pensão*, say €20 for a double (£13), though in high season, you can expect to pay up to twice this. It's always worth haggling, but ask where the room is before you agree to take it. It is also worth getting the owner to write down the agreed price for you.

ACCOMMODATION PRICE CODES

Nearly all the accommodation prices in this book have been coded using the symbols below. The symbols represent the lowest prices you can expect to pay for a double room in high season. Effectively this means that most rooms in places with a ① or ②category will be without private bath or shower, though there's usually a washbasin in the room. In places with a ③ category and above, you'll probably be getting private facilities; while many of the cheaper places may also have more expensive rooms with bath/shower if you ask.

Price codes are not given for youth hostels and campsites (see p.34 for the rates at those).

① under €25		⑥ €100–125	
② €25–35		⑦ €125–150	
③ €35–55		⑧ €150–200	
④ €55–75		⑨ over €200	
⑤ €75–100			

The main budget travel standby is a room in a **pensão** – officially graded from one to three stars (often, it seems, in a quite random fashion). Many serve meals, but they rarely insist that you take them. *Pensões* that don't serve meals are sometimes called **residenciais** (singular *residencial* or *residência*). Similar to *pensões*, and generally at the cheaper end of the scale, are **hospedarias** or *casas de hóspedes* – boarding houses – which can be characterful places.

HOTELS AND POUSADAS

A one-star **hotel** usually costs about the same as a three-star *pensão*, and is often similar in standard. Prices for two- and three-star hotels, though, see a notable shift upscale, with doubles running from €60 (£40) upwards.

There's a more dramatic shift in rates as you move into the four- and five-star hotel league, where you'll pay anything from €100–300 (£65–200) for a double. *Estalagems* and *albergarias* – **inns** – are other designations of hotels in the same range.

The government-run **pousadas** are a bargain; in summer, a double room in a *pousada* costs around €200 (€100 in winter). Look out for seasonal promotions, however, especially for over-60s, who can receive discounts of around forty percent. At present there are two *pousadas* in the Algarve (see p.97 & 273), but there are plans to open more; for details, contact ENATUR, Av. Santa Joana Princesa 10A, 1749 Lisbon (☏218 442 001, ⓦwww.pousadas.pt).

VILLAS AND APARTMENTS

Virtually every area of the Algarve has some sort of **villa** or **apartment** available for hire, from simple one-room apartments to luxurious five- or six- bed houses complete with gardens and swimming pools. Holiday and tour operators are often the best sources if you want to rent such a place in advance (see p.5). High summer sees the best places booked months in advance; expect to pay at least €50 (£40) a night in high season for an apartment for two people, up to €160 (£100) for a top villa. Outside peak period you should be able to turn up and bag somewhere for around twenty five percent less, and fifty percent less in winter. We have listed some of the better local villa companies in the text.

COUNTRY AND MANOR HOUSES

Country and **manor houses** – phrases commonly used are *Turihab, turismo no espaço rural*, and *turismo rural* – vary from simple farmhouses (*casas rústicas*) offering just two or three rooms on a B&B basis to country manors (*quintas*) and estate houses (*herdades*) with gardens and a pool. In high season in certain areas you might find that stays are for a minimum of three nights. Expect to pay around the same as a three- or four-star hotel. You can book such properties in advance with several of the specialist holiday operators detailed on p.5.

YOUTH HOSTELS

There are five **youth hostels** (*pousadas de juventude*) in the Algarve, most open all year round. Prices run from around €9 for a dorm bed up to around €21 for a double room in high season. Add on a little extra if you need to hire sheets and blankets and for en-suite doubles.

Most have a curfew (usually midnight) and all require a valid Hostelling International (HI) card – available from your home-based youth hostel association.

Youth hostel associations

Australia Australian Youth Hostels Association ℡ 02/9565 1699, ⓦ www.yha.org.au

Canada Canadian Hostelling Association ℡ 613/237-7884, ⓦ www.hostellingintl.ca

England and Wales Youth Hostel Association (YHA) ℡ 01727/845 047, ⓦ www.yha.org.uk

Ireland An Oige ℡ 01/830 4555, ⓦ www.irelandyha.org

New Zealand Youth Hostels Association of New Zealand ℡ 03/379-9970, ⓦ www.yha.co.nz

Northern Ireland Youth Hostels Association of Northern Ireland (YHANI) ℡ 01232/324 733, ⓦ www.hini.org.uk

Scotland Scottish Youth Hostels Association ℡ 01786/890 400, ⓦ www.syha.org.uk

USA American Youth Hostels (AYH) ℡ 202/783-6161, ⓦ www.hiayh.org

CAMPING

The Algarve has countless authorized **campsites**, many in very attractive locations and, despite their often large size (over five hundred spaces is not uncommon), extremely crowded in summer. Most of the bigger campsites have spaces for campervans and caravans and many also have permanent caravans and bungalows for hire. Charges are per person and per caravan or tent, with showers and parking extra; even so, it's rare that you'll end up paying more than €4 a person although those operated by the Orbitur chain (ⓦ www.orbitur.pt) are usually a little more expensive. You can get a fairly complete list from any Portuguese tourist office (see p.17).

There are a few sites in the Algarve for which you will have to produce an **international camping carnet**, available from home motoring organizations like the AA, or, in Britain, from the Camping & Caravanning Club of Great Britain (ⓣ01203/694 995, ⓕ01203/694 886), in the US and Canada from the Family Campers and RVers (FCRV), (ⓣ1800/245-9755, ⓦ www.fcrv.org).

Camping outside official grounds is not allowed in the Algarve, though campervans happily park behind some of the best, out-of-the-way beaches. Be warned, too, that **thefts** from campsites are a regular occurrence.

Eating and drinking

Portuguese food is excellent, good value and served in quantity. All the restaurants listed in the guide have been graded according to the average price of a two-course meal including wine; expect to pay under €12 for those listed as inexpensive; €12–20 at places listed as moderate, and over €20 for those graded expensive.

Portions are generous, undeed you can usually have a substantial meal by ordering a *meia dose* (half portion), or *uma dose* between two. It is worth checking out the good value **ementa turística**, too – not a "tourist menu", but the set three-course meal, including a drink. It's always worth taking stock of the **prato do dia** (dish of the day) if you're interested in sampling local specialities. They're often considerably cheaper than the usual menu fare as well.

Apart from straightforward **restaurantes** you could end up eating a meal in one of several other venues. A *tasca* is a small neighbourhood tavern; a *casa de pasto*, a cheap, local dining room usually with a set three-course menu, mostly served at lunch only. A *cervejaria* is literally a "beer house", more informal than a restaurant, with people dropping in at all hours for a beer and a snack. A *churrascaria* is a restaurant specializing in grilled meat and fish, while a *marisqueria* has a superior fishy menu, especially seafood.

FOOD FESTIVALS

JANUARY
Smoked Sausage Fair, Querença. Celebrates Saint Luís.

MARCH
Smoked Sausage Fair, Monchique. Local produce market and special menus in restaurants.

MAY
Gastronomy Festival, Portimão. Restaurants serve traditional dishes.

JUNE
Week of Portuguese Gastronomy, Lagoa. Gourmets prepare the best of Portuguese food, plus a handicrafts fair.

JULY
Beer Festival, Silves. International beer festival.

Sweet Fair, Lagos. Sculpted egg, almond and fig sweets sold along with other local produce.

Presunto Festival, Monchique. Ham festival.

AUGUST
Festival do Marisco, Olhão. Fish and seafood festival with live music.

Sardine Festival, Quarteira. An enormous grill on the beach cooks 300kg of fish.

Petiscos Festival, Querença. A celebration of small tapas-like dishes accompanied by dancing and music.

Tuna and canned fish festival. Vila Real de Santo.

NOVEMBER
Chestnut festival, Marmelete, Alferce and Vale Silves.

EATING AND DRINKING

Meal times are usually from noon–3pm for lunch, with dinner from 7.30pm onwards; don't count on being able to eat much after 11pm. Simple cafés and restaurants don't charge for service, though there's a cover charge for bread everywhere. You will be charged for every bite of the appetizers that appear on your table as you're waiting to order – tell the waiter to take them away if you do not want them. Each item should be itemized on the menu, so you can see what you're spending. People generally leave just small change as a **tip** in these places, though in more upmarket restaurants, you'll either be charged, or should leave, around ten percent.

BREAKFAST AND SNACKS

Breakfast is not a big meal for the Portuguese, though larger hotels and some cafes will serve substantial continental breakfasts. Locals head for a café or **pastelaria** (pastry shop) for a pastry washed down with a coffee.

You'll often find a whole range of dishes served at a café, but classic Portuguese **snacks** include *rissóis de carne* (deep-fried meat patties); *pastéis de bacalhau* (salted cod fishcakes); and *pastéis de carne* or *pastéis de camerão* (puff pastries stuffed with sausage meat or prawn paste). Some also serve *petiscos*, tapas-like bar snacks, usually consisting of plates of *chouriço* (smoked sausage), *tremoços* (pickled lupin seeds) and *caracois* (snails).

Markets are always good hunting grounds for tasty snacks.

ALGARVE SPECIALITIES

Not surprisingly, the Algarve is best known for its **fish**. Fresh *sardinhas* (sardines) and *atum* (tuna, often grilled with onions) are popular in restaurants, while *cherne* (stone bass), *robalo* (sea bass), *dourada* (bream), *espadarte* (swordfish), *salmonete* (red mullet), *carapau* (mackerel), *esparda* (scabbard fish) and *pescada*

(hake) all feature regularly depending on the season: lobsters, for example, are best from May to September and tuna is best in July and August, while sardines should only be eaten when there is no "r" in the month, so from May to August. Though cod is a cold-water fish not found in Portugal's waters, salted cod (*bacalhau*), remains a favourite dish; there are reputedly 365 ways of cooking it.

Though fresh fish is often best simply grilled – such as *sardinhas no churrasco* (barbecue grilled sardines) – there are several fine fish dishes. The local fish stew is called *caldeirada*, made up of different fish depending on the season. Another speciality is *cataplana*, a kind of fish bouillabaisse named after the dish it is cooked in, the *cataplana*, a circular metal pan that pressure-cooks the fish or seafood. These are nearly always served for a minimum of two people, as is *arroz de marisco*, a bumper serving of mixed seafood served with a soupy rice. Another local speciality is *carne de porco com amêijoas* (pork cooked with clams).

More food vocabulary is detailed on p.329.

Seafood is also excellent and can be relatively inexpensive. Quarteira is rated to have the best prawns in world, while some eighty percent of Portugal's shellfish derives from the salt-flats in the eastern Algarve, and restaurants often feature *mexilhões* (mussels), *ostras* (oysters), *ouriços* (urchins), *santolas* (spider crabs), *sapateiras* (common crabs) and *vieiras* (scallops).

The Algarve is also famed for **meat** such as *presunto* (smoked ham) from Monchique and sausages (*salsicha*) from Querença. Inland, game like rabbit (*coelho*) and wild boar (*javali*) is also common, especially in autumn. Meat is often best simply chargrilled: fried steaks of beef and pork are common, while chicken is on virtually every menu – at its wonderful best when barbecued (*frango no churrasco*).

EATING AND DRINKING

Accompanying most dishes will be potatoes (generally fried so ask if you want them boiled) and/or rice – calorific overkill is a strong feature of Portuguese meal times. Along with rice and chips, a common side dish is *açorda*, a kind of bread sauce. This derives from the staple rural diet – especially for shepherds – who cooked up stale bread with whatever they could find on the land around them, such as wild herbs and birds' eggs. Nowadays garlic tends to be the main ingredient with the bread. Other **vegetables** rarely make an appearance, though you might find sliced fresh tomato served with your fish, and boiled carrots or cabbage and the like accompanying meat stews.

VEGETARIAN FOOD

Despite the superb vegetables available from shops and markets, few of them make it to the tables of Portuguese restaurants. Luckily, most of the larger restaurants in the Algarve have at least one token vegetarian meal, of varying quality. Otherwise, soups such as *sopa de legumes* (vegetable) are good bets, but even *caldo verde* - a popular green soup made with cabbage and potatoes - often has a chunk of ham thrown in for extra flavour. Most restaurants can rustle up a large *salada mista* (mixed salad), but make sure it's clear if you don't want tuna or egg (*ovo*) included.

PASTRIES, SWEETS AND CHEESES

Pastries (*pastéis*) and cakes (*bolos*) are usually at their best in **casas de chá** (tearooms) and in **pastelarias**. Among the best are *pastéis de nata* (delicious little custard tarts). The Algarve's almonds and figs form the basis for marzipan, *tarte de amêndoa* (almond tart) and *Bolos de Dom Rodrigo* (an egg sweet made with almonds and syrup), named after one of the last kings of the Visigoths.

Unfortunately, few of these delicacies are available in restaurants as **desserts**. Instead, you'll almost always be offered either fresh fruit, the ubiquitous Olá ice cream price list, *pudim flan* (crème caramel), *arroz doce* (rice pudding) or *torta da noz* (nut tart).

DRINKS

Portuguese table **wines** are dramatically inexpensive and of a good overall quality. The **best regions** are Bairrada and Dão from the north; Estremadura and Ribatejo near Lisbon; and the Alentejo. **Algarve wines**, however, are highly drinkable. Most come from the Lagoa area, which also produces a fortified wine called *algarseco*. But it's fortified **port** and Madeira that are Portugal's best-known wine exports – and you should certainly sample both.

Beer choices are far less varied, with just two or three national brands and some expensive imports. The most common Portuguese beer (*cerveja*) is Sagres (named after but not produced in Sagres in the Algarve), Super Bock and Cristal. When drinking draft beer, order *um imperial* if you want a regular glass; *uma caneca* will get you a half-litre; a *panaché* is a shandy.

The Algarve offers a wide range of inexpensive, potent **liqueurs**: best known is medronho, a local schnapps-like brandy made from the strawberry tree. Other local spirits include Algarviana, made from almonds; and brandymel, a honey brandy. Look out too for local firewaters known as *aguardente*. **Spirits** are not only cheap – as long as you stick to local (*nacional*) products – but very generous by British or North American standards.

Coffee is invariably fresh and of good quality, and comes in various forms. The most popular type is *uma bica,* a small, strong espresso. *Um galão* is a tall milky coffee in a glass, often little more than flavoured milk. If you want a plain coffee with milk, ask for *uma café grande com leite*. Portuguese *chá* (**tea**) tends to be drunk black or *com limão* (flavoured with lemon rind). Ask for *chá com leite* if you want it with milk.

All the standard **soft drinks** are available. Fresh orange juice is *sumo de laranja* – add *fresca* to ensure you get the real thing. Lastly, mineral water (*água mineral*) is available anywhere, either still (*sem gás*) or carbonated (*com gás*).

Sports and outdoor pursuits

With its superb range of sports facilities, from some of the world's greatest golf courses to year-round tennis and leisure centres, it is not surprising that parts of the Algarve are known as Sportugal. Participatory sports on offer in Portugal include windsurfing, surfing, golf, horse riding and tennis, all of which can be enjoyed pretty much year round. See p.30 for details of cycling.

WATER SPORTS

Equipment and tuition for water sports – including wind surfing and water-skiing – is available on most of the Algarve beaches. The biggest **surfing** destination is the west coast of the region, especially Praia do Amado, where you can have lessons (see p.284), though the winds and currents here require a high level of expertise. **Jet skis** are also for rent from the larger resorts; prices start from around €80 per hour.

Scuba-diving can be rewarding in the clear, sheltered waters close to the coast. Diving sessions cost around €45 for three-hour equipment hire, or you can take four-day PADI open water diving courses from around €345; ask at the local tourist office for details of diving companies.

GOLF

The Algarve has a reputation for containing some of the best **golf** courses in Europe. Exclusivity is the key word at many of the courses, and green fees are rarely under €60 for 18 holes. The best way to guarantee a round is to go on a special golf-holiday package or to stay at one of the hotels or villas attached to golf clubs, which usually charge guests discounted rates. For more information, see the excellent ⓦ www.portugalgolf.pt and ⓦ www .algarvegolf.net.

SPORTS AND OUTDOOR PURSUITS

ALGARVE'S GOLF COURSES

The following is a round up of the main courses, listed according to the nearest main town or resort.

ALBUFEIRA

Pine Cliffs Praia da Falésia ⓣ 289 500 113, ⓕ 289 500 117. No handicap certificate required.

Salgados ⓣ 289 583 030, ⓔ salgados.golf@mail.telepac.pt. No handicap certificate required.

ALVOR

Alto Golf Quinta do Alto do Poço ⓣ 282 416 913, ⓔ golf@altogolf.com. Handicap max 28 men; 36 women.

Penina Golf Club Penina ⓣ 282 420 223, ⓕ 282 420 300. Handicap max 28 men; 36 women.

CARVOEIRO

Gramacho ⓣ 282 340 900, ⓕ 282 340 901. No handicap certificate required.

Vale de Milho ⓣ 282 358 502, ⓕ 282 358 497. No handicap certificate required.

Vale de Pinta ⓣ 282 340 900, ⓕ 282 340 901. Handicap max 27 men; 35 women.

CASTRO MARIM

Castro Marim Golf ⓣ 281 510 330, ⓔ info@castromarimgolfe .com. No handicap certificate required.

MEIA PRAIA

Palmares ⓣ 282 762 961, ⓕ 282 790 509. Handicap max 28 men; 36 women.

QUARTEIRA

Vila Sol Morgadinhos Alto de Semino, Quarteira ⓣ 289 300

505, ℱ 289 300 591. Handicap max 27 men; 35 women.

QUINTA DO LAGO

São Lorenço ℱ 289 396 522, ⓔ sanlourenco@lemeridean-donafilipa.com. Handicap max 28 men; 36 women.

Quinta do Lago/Ria Formosa ℱ 289 390 700, ℱ 289 394 013. Handicap max 26 men; 35 women.

Pinheiros Altos ℱ 289 359 910, ℱ 289 394 392. Handicap max 28 men; 36 women.

SALEMA

Parque da Floresta Vale do Poço ℱ 282 690 000, ℱ 282 695 157. No handicap certificate required.

TAVIRA

Golfe Clube De Tavira Campo de Golfe de Benamor ℱ 281 320 880, ℱ 281 320 888. Handicap max 28 men; 36 women.

VALE DO LOBO

Vale Do Lobo ℱ 289 353 535, ⓔ golf@etvdla.pt. Handicap max 28 men (Ocean Course), 27 (Royal Course); 36 women (Ocean Course), 35 (Royal Course).

VILAMOURA

Laguna (Vilamoura III) ℱ 289 310 180, ℱ 289 310 349. No handicap certificate required.

Millennium ℱ 289 310 188, ℱ 289 310 183. Handicap 24 men; 28 women.

The Old Course (Vilamoura I) ℱ 289 310 341, ℱ 289 310 321. Handicap max 24 men; 28 women.

Pinhal (Vilamoura II) ℱ 289 310 390, ℱ 289 310 393. Handicap 28 men; 36 women.

SPORTS AND OUTDOOR PURSUITS

HORSE RIDING AND TENNIS

There are countless **riding** stables dotted round the Algarve, most of which offer one-hour or full-day rides into the surrounding countryside. Prices start from around €15–20 for an hour's trek, rising to around €80–100 for a full day's trek, which usually includes a picnic lunch. For details of *centros hipicos* (riding schools) in a particular area, contact the local tourist office.

Tennis courts are a common feature of most larger Algarve hotels and villa complexes but there are also numerous leisure centres and specialist **tennis** centres; the best are listed below. All of these can hire out rackets and balls and the larger ones offer tennis coaching (in English) for all ages. Courts cost around €8–13 an hour and stay open year round. For further information contact the Portuguese National Tourist Office.

Tennis and leisure centres

Barringtons Vale do Lobo
Ⓣ 289 396 622,
Ⓦ www.barringtons-pt.com

Burgau Sports Centre Burgau
Ⓣ 282 697 350

Luz Bay Club Rua do Jardim
Ⓣ 282 789 640, Ⓕ 282 789 641

Luz Ocean Club Praia da Luz
Ⓣ 282 789 764,

Ⓔ ocean.club.luz@mail
.telepac

Jim Stewart Tennis Centre
Quinta do Lago Ⓣ 289 398
848, Ⓕ 289 396 695

Rock Garden Sports and Leisure Centre Vilamoura
Ⓣ 289 322 740

Vale do Lobo Tennis Centre
Vale do Lobo Ⓣ 289 396 991,
Ⓕ 289 396 926

WALKING

The Algarve's spectacular coastal paths and unspoilt interior offer exceptional walking. Most of the **walks** are along farm tracks or coastal paths, and none of them are hazardous or unsuitable for inexperienced walkers. They can be tackled all year round, though you'll want to set off early in high summer to avoid the midday heat. We've listed several of the best walks within the guide (see index p.336).

The tourist offices produce some walking **leaflets**, and can usually supply details of local organized tours. The Serra de Monchique is particularly popular. The enviromental NGO, Almargem (☎289 412 959, Ⓔalmargem @mail.telepac.pt) produce a pack of walking leaflets, *Salir, Percursos Pedestres*, available from its headquarters at Alto de São Domingo 14, Loulé (€8), with information about half a dozen way-marked walks in the Salir area. They also produce less detailed, but free, walking leaflets covering a range of inland walks mostly in the central Algarve, available from Loulé's tourist office or from the address above.

Other good sources of **information** are the walking guide books listed on p.323. See also p.5 for tour operators who specialize in walking holidays.

SPECTATOR SPORTS

There are plenty of spectator sports, from the dubious pleasures of bullfighting to top Portuguese soccer to international golfing tournaments.

BULLFIGHTS

The Portuguese **bullfight** is neither as commonplace nor as famous as its Spanish counterpart, but as a spectacle it's marginally preferable. In Portugal the bull isn't killed in the ring, but wrestled to the ground in an elegant, colourful and skilled display. After the fight, however, the bull is always slaughtered.

A *tourada* opens with the bull, its horns padded or sheared flat, facing a mounted *toureiro* in elaborate eighteenth-century costume. His job is to provoke and exhaust the bull and to plant the dart-like *farpas* (or *bandarilhas*) in its back while avoiding the charge. Once the beast is tired the *moços-de-forcado* (or *forcados*), move in, an eight-man team which tries to immobilize it. They line up behind each other across the ring from the bull and persuade it to charge them, the front man leaping between the horns while the rest grab hold and try to subdue it. It's as absurd as it is courageous, and often takes two or three attempts, often resulting with one or more of the *forcados* being tossed spectacularly into the air. The display ends when the bull can no longer continue.

SOCCER

Soccer is the Portuguese national sport, with a long and often glorious tradition of international and **club teams**. The champions are almost invariably one of the big three leading clubs, Benfica and Sporting from Lisbon and FC Porto from the north. **Farense** from Faro are the main Algarve team who have been in the top league for some time (see p.72) and regularly host the top teams. The other Algarve clubs play in the lower leagues, though Portimonense from Portimão have had spells in the top flight. If you want to see a league match, the season runs from September through to May.

Almancil is one of the main venues for the 2004 European Football Championships (see p.75).

For soccer fixtures, match reports and news, visit Ⓦ www.portuguese.soccer.com.

Trouble and police

By European standards, Portugal is a remarkably crime-free country, though there's the usual petty theft in larger resorts. If you are robbed, whatever you do, don't resist.

If you do have something **stolen**, you'll need to go to the police to file a report for your insurance company. Police stations in the major towns are listed in the guide. Showing deference to a police officer is wise: the Portuguese hold respect dear, and the more respect you show a figure in authority, the quicker you will be on your way.

In an emergency, dial ⊤ 112 for the police.

Directory

ADDRESSES Addresses are written with the name of the road first followed by the number. The numbers 1°, 2° etc means first, second floor etc. The ground floor (first floor in US) is marked r/c (*rés-do-chão*). You may also see *d/dto* or *e/esq* after the number, which mean on the right (*direito*) or left (*esquerda*) of the main staircase.

CHILDREN The Algarve is geared up for families and there should be few logistical problems in travelling with children. Most hotels and guesthouses can supply a cot free of charge if given advance notice, and children under eight are generally charged fifty percent of the adult rate if they share their parents' room. International-brand baby foods and nappies are all widely available in supermarkets and chemists, but fresh milk – *leite do dia* – can usually only be bought from larger supermarkets. Take care, though, with the sun; young children should be covered up or in the shade between 11am and 3pm.

DISABLED ACCESS Portuguese people will go out of their way to make your visit as straightforward as possible though special facilities remain limited. There are adapted WCs and wheelchair facilities at the airport and reserved disabled parking spaces in main cities, where the Orange Badge is recognized. National tourist offices can supply a list of wheelchair-accessible hotels and campsites (see p.17–18), some are listed in the text, or contact Wheeling Around the Algarve (℡289 393 636), who organize holiday accommodation, transport and sporting/leisure activities. For the useful booklet, *Accessible Tourism Guide of the Algarve Area*, request at Ⓔsnripd@snripd.mts.gov.pt.

DRUGS In July 2001, Portugal decriminalized the use of all drugs; but drug pushing remains a crime. The use of drugs is unlikely to go down well throughout the Algarve.

ELECTRICITY Portugal uses two-pin plugs (220v). UK appliances will work with a continental adaptor.

EMERGENCIES ℡112 for fire, police and ambulance.

FLIGHT INFORMATION ℡289 800 800

GAY TRAVELLERS Though traditionally a conservative and macho society, Portugal has become increasingly tolerant of homosexuality. The Lisbon-based Centro Comunitário Gay e Lesbica de Lisboa publish gay listings on Ⓦwww.ilga-portugal.org/guia. Reader-vote listings can also be found on Ⓦwww.portugalgay.pt, though the information – in Portuguese – is not updated regularly.

HOSPITALS Hospital Distrital de Faro ℡289 891 100; Hospital Distrital, Rua do Castelo dos Governadores, Lagos ℡282 763 034; Sítio do Poço Secos, Portimão ℡282 450 300.

SHOPPING Monday to Friday 9am–1pm and 3–7/8pm, and Saturdays 9am–1pm. Some supermarkets and larger resort shops open seven days a week, often until 11pm. Credit cards are widely accepted.

SUNBATHING Portugal can be traditional and formal: topless bathing is not common on town beaches, though nudism is on out-of-the-way beaches.

TIME Portugal is on the same time zone as the UK: GMT (late Oct to late March) and BST (late March to late Oct). This is five hours ahead of Eastern Standard Time and eight hours ahead of Pacific Standard Time.

TIPPING Service charges are normally included in hotel bills and in the larger restaurants. Smaller restaurants, cafés and bars do not expect a large tip; simply round up the change or leave ten percent of the bill.

TOILETS There are very few public toilets. However, nearly all the main tourist sights have a public toilet (*casa de banho, retrete, banheiro, lavabos* or *WC*), and it is not difficult to sneak into a café or restaurant. Gents are usually marked H (*homens*) or C (*cabalheiros*), and ladies M (*mulheres*) or S (*senhoras*).

WOMEN will experience few problems travelling alone in the Algarve: they may attract some unwanted attention in the beach resorts but it is unlikely to be insistent or threatening.

THE GUIDE

THE GUIDE

Faro and around

Faro, by far the largest town on the coast and the administrative capital of the region, is one of the Algarve's most likeable towns. The historic centre is considerably more attractive than the concrete suburbs might suggest, and there are some fine beaches and characterful local villages within easy reach. With the Algarve's main airport just west of the centre, it is not a bad place to start or finish a tour of the region. Public transport connections are good either by bus, or the slighter slower Algarve railway line.

The town marks a geographical boundary in the Algarve. West of Faro lie the main Algarve resorts, the majority fronted by the coves or cliff-backed beaches for which the region is famed. The area between Faro and Vilamoura, 25km west, has its own distinct character. Cheap and cheerful Quarteira aside, the sand-fringed coast is lined with purpose-built, low-density resorts sprinkled with leafy villas and first-rate facilities, including marinas, golf links and tennis centres which has led the area to be dubbed Sportugal.

The flat coastline east from Faro, however, is protected by thin stretches of mud flats, fringed in turn by a chain of magnificent long sandbank islands, or *ilhas*. Most are accessible only by boat, so they're usually far less crowded than the resorts to the west. Some of the *ilhas* can be reached from Faro (in season) and throughout the year from **Olhão**, a fishing port with a Moorish flavour, and the small neighbouring town of **Fuzeta**. Ornithologists should take binoculars as the shores are teeming with wading birds in winter and spring, with some of the most interesting species to be seen from the **Quinta Marim** ecology centre near Olhão.

The area covered in this chapter is shown on map 3, at the back of the book.

Inland also offers rewarding diversions from the beach, especially the Roman remains and palace gardens at **Estói** and the lively market towns of **Loulé** and **São Brás de Alportel**, each set in gently rolling countryside. To the north, the **Serra do Caldeirão**, dotted with cork forests and rural villages, marks the boundary between the Algarve and the Alentejo region.

Faro

FARO has been transformed from a sleepy provincial town into a centre of tourism-based trade and commerce within three decades. However, although the international airport delivers visitors right to its door, the town has a job holding on to them, as most are immediately whisked away to the beach resorts on either side. This is a little unfair: there's a handful of **museums**, some fine **churches**, an attractive **harbour** backed by a bustling, pedestrianized shopping area, and boats and buses run out to a couple of excellent local **beaches**. In summer, too, there's lively **nightlife**, as thousands of travellers pass through on their way to and

FARO

ACCOMMODATION

Adelaide	3
Alameda	8
Algarve	2
Eva	7
Madalena	4
Oceano	6
Pinto	5
Samé	10
São Filipe	1
Youth hostel	9

RESTAURANTS

Aliança	F
Adega Dois Irmãos	D
Cidade Velha	M
Gardy	H
Faro e Benfica	K
Fim do Mundo	E
O Gargalo	G
Ginásio Clube Naval	J
Mesa dos Mouros	N
Adega Nova	B
Piramides	I
Adega Rocha	L
Sol e Jardim	C
Taska	A

EN125 Lisbon, Lagos & Airport

RUA ABOIM ASCENSÃO

RUA INFANTE D. HENRIQUE

LARGO DE S. SEBASTIÃO

R. DE S. SEBASTIÃO

R. CONSELHEIRO SEBASTIÃO TELES

RUA DA ROAVISTA

Igreja do Carmo

LARGO DO CARMO

R. AMEL BOMBARDA

R. TOMÁS RIBEIRO

R. SEPPA PINTO

PR. SILVA PORTO

RUA CRUZ DOS MESTRES

RUA DO ALPORTEL

RUA DO SOL

R. DA HORTA MACHADO

LARGO DA ESTAÇÃO

RUA FRANCISCO BARRETO

R. TEOFILO DE BRAGA

Igreja de São Pedro

R. DA CONCEIÇÃO

LARGO DAS MOURAS VELHAS

R. DO JUSTINO CIMIANO

Train Station

RUA DE LEANS

R. DO FORNO

R. DA MADALENA

LARGO DO S. PEDRO

R. DE S. PEDRO

RUA JOSÉ ESTEVÃO

R. BAPTISTA LOPES

LARGO DO SOL POSTO

RUA DA LETHES

RUA F. F. HORTA

RUA DO CRUZ

R. DA BARQUETA

AVENIDA DA REPUBLICA

R. COMPROMISSO

RUA DE S. PEDRO

RUA DE PORTUGAL

RUA DE MOTA

RUA DA LETHES

RUA DE LIMES

Bus to Campsite & Airport

Bus Terminal

PR. D. FRANCISCO GOMES

R. CONSELHEIRO BIVAR

RUA ALDE CASTRO

PR. FERREIRA DE ALMEIDA

R. VASCO DA GAMA

PR. DE LIBERDADE

Museu Marítimo

R. D. F. GOMES

R. TEN VALDIM

LARGO D. S. NOBRE

R. DE S. ANTÓNIO

Museu Regional

Doca (harbour)

Jardim Manuel Bivar

R. DE DEZEMBRO

RUA REBELO DA SILVA

RUA CASTILHO

PR. ALEXANDRE HERCULANO

RUA MONTEIRO

R. ALEXANDRE HERCULANO

RUA V. D'ALMEIDA

RUA DO BOCADE

N

RUA DA MISERICÓRDIA

Arco da Vila

RUA DO MUNICIPIO

RUA COM FRANCISCO MANUEL

RUA DO ALBERGUE

R. DE S. FRANCISCO

R. DE S. FRANCISCO

RUA RASQUINHO

RUA DE CAÇADORES

R. D. T. RAMALHO ORTIGÃO

0   200 m

Bishop's Palace

CIDADE VELHA

PR. AFONSO III

LARGO DA SÉ

RUA DO TRIPO

Sé

LARGO DO CASTELO

RUA DO ARCO

Museu Arqueológico

LARGO DE S. FRANCISCO

Igreja de São Francisco

Centro Ciência Viva

Ferries to Farol & Ilha Deserta

Jetty

FARO

from the airport. The town's bustling commercial life also ensures that the array of restaurants and cafés rely on Portuguese locals as much as tourists, keeping the quality up and the prices down.

Some history

Faro's Roman predecessor was 8km to the north, at Ossonoba (see p.99); the present city was named by the Moors around the eleventh century, under whom it became a thriving commercial port, supplying the regional capital at Silves (see p.187). Following the town's conquest by the Christians under Afonso III in 1249, the city experienced a chequered few centuries, surviving a series of conquests and disasters. Sacked and burned by the Earl of Essex in 1596 when Portugal's occupation by the Spanish made it an enemy of the British, like much of the region, the town was devastated by the Great Earthquake of 1755. However, Faro was less affected than the then regional capital, Lagos, and so took over the role in 1776. The opening of the Lisbon to Faro railway line in 1889 was a boost to the local economy and the town's population quickly grew. In the early twentieth century, Faro's cafés became the fashionable hangout for famous writers such as Pessoa and Sá-Carneiro, but it was not until the opening of the airport in 1965 that the town took off as a centre of tourism. These days it is also the most important administrative and business centre in the south of Portugal.

ARRIVAL, ORIENTATION AND INFORMATION

The **bus terminal** is located on Avenida da República, just across the harbour from the old part of town. The **train station** faces Largo da Estação, a few minutes' walk further northwest of the bus terminal up the *avenida*.

Faro's historical buildings lie within a compact area, north and west of the walled *Cidade Velha* (Old Town) to

FARO AIRPORT

Faro's modern international **airport** lies 6km west of the town centre. From June to October there is an **Aerobus** service operated by EVA (from the airport Mon & Wed–Sun hourly from 9am–8pm; from Faro/town bus station Mon & Wed–Sun hourly 8.15am–8.15pm), which takes fifteen minutes. The bus runs between the airport and the town bus station and is free to flight-ticket holders – simply show your ticket when boarding. Two local **buses** also run from the airport to the centre, a twenty- to twenty-five-minute ride costing €1: the #16 (8am–8.30pm, July to mid-Sept until 11pm roughly every 45min) and the rather less frequent #14. Both stop outside the bus terminal in town and further on at the Jardim Manuel Bivar by the harbour.

One of the quickest ways of getting into the centre is by **taxi**, a ten- to fifteen-minute ride which should cost about €8, plus €1.50 for any luggage that goes in the boot; there's also a twenty percent surcharge between 10pm and 6am, and at weekends.

The airport has various standard **facilities** – a bank with an ATM machine, post office, police and first-aid post and a tourist office (daily 10am–midnight; ☏ 289 818 582), but there is little in the way of shops or restaurants except a poor, over-priced self-service canteen. A number of **car rental** companies (see p.71) also have offices at the airport. Most use a special car park right opposite the terminal, though some use a less convenient dropping off point ten minutes away; check with the company when you collect your car.

the south of the harbour. Away from here, a series of mostly pedestrianized roads and small squares stretch north to Largo do Carmo and east to Praça de Liberdade, beyond which spreads the newer town. The town centre is simple

FARO: ARRIVAL, ORIENTATION AND INFORMATION

59

to negotiate on foot, and all the accommodation and places to eat are extremely central. There is a **town bus service**, but you'll need it only to get to the airport (see p.59) and the beach (see p.73).

Faro's main **turismo** is close to the harbourfront at Rua da Misericórdia 8 (May–Sept daily 9.30am–7pm; Oct–April Mon–Fri 9.30am–5.30pm, Sat & Sun 9.30am–12.30pm & 2–5.30pm; ☎ 289 803 604). They can provide maps of the town, help with accommodation and there are noticeboards with comprehensive information on local and long-distance bus, boat and train timetables too. The regional tourist office – **Região de Turismo do Algarve** – north of the old town at Avenida 5° Outubro (Mon–Fri 9.30am–12.30pm & 2–5.30pm; ☎ 289 800 400, ⓦ www.rtalgarve.pt) is another good source of information on the area as a whole.

If you need the **internet**, there are several terminals at PapaNET, Rua Dr Justino Cúmano 38 (Mon–Sat 10am–2pm & 3–7pm; ☎ 289 804 338, ⓔ mail@papanet.pt; €2/hr), en route to the market building in the northeast of town.

ACCOMMODATION

Like most of the Algarve, Faro's **accommodation** is stretched to the limit in summer. If you fly in without a reservation, it's worth asking the airport tourist office to help book you a place – though it's not officially part of their job and you'll have to pay for any calls they make on your behalf; otherwise the main turismo can give you an idea of where to look for **rooms**. Most of the city's **pensões** and **hotels** are concentrated in the area just north of the harbour. There's also a decent **youth hostel** around 2km north of the centre and the nearest **campsite** is on Praia de Faro, near the airport (see p.73).

Casa de Hóspedes Adelaide

Rua Cruz das Mestras 7–9
ⓣ 289 802 383, ⓕ 289 826 870
The friendly owner offers very basic, clean rooms, several en suite. Communal kitchen and lounge. Avoid the front ground floor room or you'll feel you're sleeping on the street. ❸

Residencial Alameda

Rua Dr. José de Matos 31
ⓣ 289 801 962, ⓕ 289 804 218
In the modern part of town, this *residencial* is a bit removed from the action but tidy, if small, rooms all come with en-suite facilities and some boast balconies facing a small park. Price does not include breakfast. ❸

Residencial Algarve

Rua Infante Dom Henrique 52
ⓣ 289 895 700,
ⓔ reservas@residencialalgarve. com
Just north of the train station, this new *residencial* is by far the most comfortable in town. Spruce rooms have spotless bathrooms and cable TV; breakfast is served in a little patio in summer. Good value, though the front rooms can be noisy. ❺

Hotel Eva

Avda da República 1
ⓣ 289 803 354, ⓕ 289 802 304
This large, modern block is the town's best hotel occupying a superb harbourfront position. Rooms have balconies overlooking the old town or the marina. There's a rooftop pool and a courtesy bus to the local beach. Disabled access. ❼

Pensão Madalena

Rua Conselheiro Bivar 109
ⓣ 289 805 806,
ⓕ 289 805 807
A mixed bag of rather characterless rooms – many of which are somewhat gloomy – but all are en suite, with TVs. It's also very central, and just about far enough from the Rua Conselheiro Bivar's nightlife not to be too noisy. ❸

Pensão-Residencial Oceano

TrAvda Ivens 21–1°

Ⓣ 289 823 349, Ⓕ 289 805 590
Centrally located, this clean, bland *pensão* is ideally placed for the town's nightlife although not too close to be noisy. The poky rooms have bathrooms, but don't live up to the promise of the *azulejos*-lined stairway. Price does not include breakfast.

Residencial Pinto
Rua 1º de Maio 27
Ⓣ 289 807 417
Recently renovated, this welcoming *residencial* offers characterful rooms with marble floors, high ceilings and polished furniture. Communal bathrooms; price does not include breakfast.

Residencial Samé
Rua do Bocage 66
Ⓣ 289 824 375, Ⓕ 289 804 166
This clean, modern hotel offers small rooms in a block just outside the old town. Some have balconies and all come with bathrooms and TV. There's an appealing communal lounge downstairs.

Pensão São Filipe
Rua Infante Dom Henrique 55–1º
Ⓣ & Ⓕ 289 824 182
Clean, reasonable rooms with high ceilings, wooden shutters and TVs; shared bathroom. A little out of the centre, north of the train station, on a fairly busy through-road; price does not include breakfast. ❸

Youth hostel
Rua da Policia de Segurança Pública (PSP)
Ⓣ 289 826 521, Ⓕ 289 801 413
Located in a quiet spot to the north of the old town, next to the public gardens. Prices are €10 for beds in dorms of four or six people, or €21 for a double room, €23 en suite. You'll need a hostel card, and should book well in advance. Disabled access.

CIDADE VELHA

The oldest and most picturesque part of Faro is the **Cidade Velha** (old town), on the southern side of the harbour: an oval of cobbled streets and brightly painted buildings – some housing, shops, cafés and galleries – are set within a run of sturdy walls. The main entrance is through the nineteenth-century town gate, the **Arco da Vila**, next to the turismo. The Neoclassical arch, often capped by a stork's nest, was built by the Italian architect Francisco Xavier Fabri, who also designed the church in Estói (see p.98), on a commission by the Algarve's bishop, Francisco Gomes do Avelar, whose memorial sits in an alcove inside the arch. From here, Rua do Município leads up to the majestic Largo da Sé, lined with orange trees and flanked by the cathedral and a group of palaces – including the former bishop's palace. The **Sé** itself (Mon–Sat 10am–12.30pm & 1.30pm–5pm, Sun open for Mass at 10am & noon; €1) is a squat, white mismatch of Gothic, Renaissance and Baroque styles, all heavily remodelled after the 1755 earthquake. It's worth looking inside for the fine eighteenth-century *azulejos*, though the main appeal is its clock tower, which you can climb up for superb views over the old town and the surrounding coastland.

Museu Arqueológico

May–Sept Mon & Sat 2.30–6pm, Tues–Fri 10am–6pm; Oct–April Mon & Sat 2–5.30pm, Tues–Fri 9.30am–5.30pm; €2

Housed in the sixteenth-century Convento de Nossa Senhora da Assunção in Praça Afonso III, the **Museu Arqueológico** is the Algarve's oldest museum, first opened in 1894, while the beautiful internal cloister is one of the oldest in the country. The most striking of the museum's exhibits is a superb third-century AD Roman mosaic of Neptune surrounded by the four winds, unearthed near the train station. Other items include a fine collection of Roman statues from the excavations at Estói (see p.99), exquisite Moorish lamps, vases and bowls and beautiful Naive sixteenth-century multicoloured tiles. Unfortunately parts of the museum are undergoing virtually permanent restoration and it's rarely all open to the public. An upstairs room houses temporary exhibits, usually of distinctly average local art.

THE HARBOUR AND AROUND

The **harbour** is Faro's most vibrant area: the town gardens and a cluster of outdoor cafés overlook the rows of sleek yachts and at the end of the day, much of Faro gathers to promenade here. Head round to the right of the harbour, as you face the sea, for a couple of the town's best restaurants (see p.68). You'll also pass the small **Museu Marítimo** (Mon–Fri 2.30–4.30pm; free), a modest maritime museum with engaging displays of model boats and local fishing techniques.

BOAT TRIPS TO BEACHES

Ferries shuttle from the jetty just south of the Centro Ciência Viva by the town wall, through narrow marshy channels to a couple of superb sandbar beaches between Faro and Olhão. They depart, either to **Farol** (see p.106) on the Ilha da Culatra (info ☏ 917 634 813; June to mid-Sept 4 daily, first boat 9.30am, last return 7pm; €3.50 return); or to the so-called **Ilha Deserta** (info ☏ 917 811 856; June to mid-Sept 4 daily; €10 return), part of the Parque Natural da Ria Formosa and the most southerly point of mainland Portugal. The name is actually a misnomer, as there are cafés and plenty of other sun worshippers for company; the island's official name is Ilha da Barreta.

Heading southwards on Rua Comandante Francisco Manuel, along the foot of the harbour, you can follow the railway line for an attractive walk along the seafront, with the town walls on one side and the mud flats on the other; a small arch through the old town walls offers another approach to the Cidade Velha (see p.63). From the jetty opposite here, ferries depart to the local sandspit beaches (see p.64).

Centro Ciência Viva

July to mid-Sept Tues–Sun 4–11pm; mid-Sept to June Tues–Fri 10am–5pm, Sat & Sun 3–7pm; €2, under 12s €0.50, students half price on Thurs; ☎ 289 890 920

On the waterfront Rua Comandante Francisco Manuel lies the **Centro Ciência Viva**, the Centre for Living Science, a good wet weather spot, especially for kids. Set in the town's former electricity generating station, with an attractive roof terrace at the back, there are several low-tech interactive exhibits that explain scientific principles. Exhibits change, but permanent displays include a rock pool and a flight simulator. Most of the displays are labelled only in Portuguese.

THE REST OF THE TOWN

A block back from the harbour, on the mosaic pedestrianized backstreets around **Rua de Santo António** lie most of the town's bars, restaurants and shops. At the eastern end of the street, on Praça de Liberdade, is the most likeable of Faro's museums, the **Museu Regional** (Mon–Fri 9am–noon & 2–5pm; €2), which has a display of local crafts and industries, including reconstructions of cottage interiors and models of the net systems still used for tuna fishing. There are also black and white photos of the town and local beaches before tourism took hold.

From the Museu Regional it is a five-minute walk north-west to Largo de São Pedro, where the sixteenth-century **Igreja de São Pedro** is one of the town's most attractive churches with a finely decorated altar (to the left of the main altar) whose central image is a gilded, wooden *Last Supper*.

Igreja do Carmo

Mon–Fri 10am–1pm & 3–6pm (until 5pm Oct–April), Sat 10am–1pm, Sun only for Mass at 9am; free, chapel of bones €1

By far the most curious sight in town, just beyond the Igreja de São Pedro, lies in the twin-towered, Baroque **Igreja do Carmo**, on the Largo do Carmo. A door to the right of the altar leads to the sacristy where you can buy a ticket for the macabre **Capela dos Ossos** (Chapel of Bones), set in an attractive garden. Like the one at Alcantarilha (see p.178), its walls are decorated with human bones as a reminder of human mortality – in this case disinterred in the nineteenth century from the adjacent monks' cemetery.

EATING

The pedestrianized area on either side of Rua de Santo António offers innumerable **restaurants**, **cafés** and **bakeries** – the latter stocked with almond delicacies, the regional speciality. One of the best is the takeaway branch of Gardy, opposite the café (see below), which does superb croissants and fresh bread. Most of the pavement restaurants have similar menus and prices.

For picnic, souvenir or self-catering food, there are several supermarkets round town – including one on Rua 1 de Maio and another opposite the bus station – or try the Saturday and Sunday covered **market**, east off Rua General

Teófilo da Trinidade. Also recommended is Rui Garrafeira, Praça Ferreira de Almeida 28 (Mon–Sat 8am–8pm), a deli-cum-off-licence selling sweets, cheeses, ports and wines.

CAFÉS

Café Aliança
Rua Dr Francisco Gomes 6–11
Daily 8am–midnight.
Inexpensive
This 1908 coffee house is said to be the oldest in Portugal, though the decor dates from the 1920s. Once the favoured haunt of the literary set, including Simone de Beauvoir, Fernando Pessoa and Mário Sá Carneir, it remains wonderfully atmospheric. There are tables outside, and a full menu of salads, omelettes, pastries and ice cream.

Gardy
Rua de Santo António 16
Daily 8am–midnight.
Inexpensive
Cavernous and popular local *pastelaria* with a counter piled high with cakes and savouries. Tables spilling out onto the main pedestrianized street and a side alley make this one of the best places in town to watch the world go by.

Café Piramides
Jardim Manuel Bivar
Daily 8am–midnight.
Inexpensive
All-purpose pre-payment kiosk with tables in the attractive gardens facing the harbour; a fine place to enjoy anything from breakfast and coffee to pizzas, ice creams and beers.

RESTAURANTS

Adega Dois Irmãos
Largo Terreiro do Bispo 13–15
Daily noon–11pm.
Moderate–expensive
This attractive tile-lined place, opened in 1925 by two brothers (*irmãos*) in a former welder's shop, is one of the oldest of the city's fish restaurants. Its window display heaves with the day's catch and the *pratos de dia* are usually better value.

FARO: EATING

Marisqueira Faro e Benfica

Doca de Faro

Mon & Wed–Sun 10.30am–2am.

Moderate–expensive

One of the best choices in town for a splurge on fish and seafood, with tables facing the town across the harbour. Specialities include *cataplanas, feijoada* and various rice dishes.

Fim do Mundo

Rua Vasco da Gama 53

Wed–Sun 11am–3pm & 6–11pm, Tues 6–11pm.

Inexpensive

Bustling place filled with locals enjoying good-value grilled fish and meats – the *frango piri-piri* is the house speciality.

O Gargalo

Largo Pé da Cruz

Mon & Wed–Sun 12.30–3pm & 7.30–11.30pm. **Moderate**

Smart Italian restaurant serving well-cooked antipasto, and a good range of pasta and pizza in a cavernous room just north of the old town.

Restaurante Ginásio Clube Naval

Doca de Faro

Tues–Sun noon–3pm & 7–11pm. **Moderate**

On a raised terrace right on the harbour, this is one of the few places in town where you can dine on fish and grilled meats with fine views over the mud flats. It also has a simple downstairs café offering inexpensive drinks with views over the marina.

Mesa dos Mouros

Largo de Sé. ☎ 289 878 873

Mon–Fri 12.30–3.30pm & 7.30–11pm, Sat 7.30–11pm.

Moderate–expensive

Tiny place – so best to reserve for a meal – right opposite the Sé serving cakes, drinks and refined cuisine including seafood and tasty chickpea salads. A few outdoor tables sit on the broad Largo de Sé itself.

Adega Nova

Rua Francisco Barreto 24

Daily 9am–midnight.

Inexpensive

Near the train station, this great barn of a place is an

FARO: EATING

old-fashioned *adega* with Portuguese food and jugs of wine. Turn up early as the benches get packed, especially at weekends. Good value if you steer clear of the more pricey seafood.

Sol e Jardim
Praça Ferreira de Almeida 22–23
Daily noon–11pm.
Moderate–expensive
Standard Portuguese grills served in a junk shop-turned-restaurant, with flags, stuffed turtles, and baskets suspended from the ceiling. There is also a huge jungle-like patio hung with creepers. Live folk music at weekends.

Taska
Rua do Alportel 38
Mon–Sat noon–3pm & 7–11pm.
Moderate
Friendly place serving traditional Algarve fare to a mostly Portuguese crowd. House specialities include *gambas* (prawns) accompanied by an excellent range of Portuguese regional wines.

DRINKING AND NIGHTLIFE

Faro has a vibrant **nightlife** for both tourists and the local inhabitants. Most of the late-night action is concentrated along two or three cobbled, pedestrianized streets – in particular the wide **Rua Conselheiro Bivar** with its café-bars with outdoor tables, and the parallel **Rua do Prior** and nearby **Rua da Madalena**, where many of the bars and clubs feature guest DJs, live bands and video screens. Things get going around midnight and, as the bars fill up, drinkers spill out onto the cobbled alleys to party. Some of the larger clubs have a "minimum consumption" charge of around €25. This means you must consume drinks to at least this value or you'll be charged the balance on exit, basically a ploy to stop people dancing all night without buying drinks (as many locals, at least, would happily do).

Faro also occasionally hosts big-name rock and pop **gigs** at the football stadium – check posters around town, or ask at the turismo.

O Cofre
Rua Conselheiro Bivar 54
Daily 9am–midnight
Café-*pastelaria* by day, youth hangout by night with the tables hogged by lively locals gearing up for a night at the nearby bars.

Columbus
Jardim Manuel Bivar, corner with Rua João Dias
Tues–Sun 9.30pm–2am
Jazzy local haunt with seats outside under the arcades opposite the harbourfront gardens. There's a dartboard inside too.

Conselheiro
Rua Conselheiro Bivar 72–78
Daily 10pm–4am
Disco bar with a minimum consumption of €25 most nights; indoor tables, swirling lights and occasionally some good tunes.

Diesel Bar
Travessa São Pedro
Wed–Sat 11pm–5am
Chilled disco bar in a small, dark street off Ruo do Prior with Aztec-style decor and glitzy lights. Offers a wide selection of cocktails and Mexican shots.

Gothic
Rua da Madelena 38
Mon–Sat 11pm–4am
Goths are alive and still looking unwell at this suitably darkened club with cheap beer and wicked shots.

Kingburger Bar
Rua do Prior 40
Wed–Sat 11pm–4am
A small, relaxed bar with a mixed clientele; one of the first to open along this stretch.

Millenium III
Rua do Prior 21
Thurs–Sun 11pm–5am
Large industrial club playing all the latest sounds, good DJs and performances by local bands. One of the better venues in town.

O Prior
Ruo do Prior 41
Wed–Sat 11pm–4am
Run by the same management and with a similar clientele as *Univercidade*, but the venue is smaller and the music less cheesy.

Univercidade
Rua de São Pedro 19–23
Wed–Sat 11pm–4am
At the end of Rua do Prior, regular live bands and cheap beer make this a popular student hangout.

Upa Upa
Rua Conselheiro Bivar 51
Daily 9pm–4am
Laid-back and relatively early-opening music bar with a mixed clientele; tables outside on the pedestrianized street.

Versailles
Rua Ivens 7–9
Daily 8am–midnight
Restaurant, *pastelaria* and bar that's good for a drink post-restaurant/pre-club, with outdoor seating and, later on at least, a youthful Portuguese crowd.

LISTINGS

Airlines British Airways (airport ☎289 818 476); Lufthansa (airport ☎289 800 751); TAP, Francisco Gomes 8 (☎289 800 200).

Airport Flight information ☎289 800 800.

Bus terminal Avda da República 106 (☎289 899 700 or 706). There's an English-speaking information office inside the terminal, though it is not always staffed.

Car rental Auto Jardim (airport ☎289 800 881); Avis (airport ☎289 810 120); Europcar (Avda da República 2 ☎289 823 778, airport ☎289 818 777); Hertz (Rua Infante D. Henrique 91A ☎289 803 956, airport ☎289 810 150).

Cinema Cinema Golden City (☎289 820 308) has four

small screens in the giant Faro shopping complex on the airport road (EN125).

Consulate Canadian: Rua Frei Lourenço de Santa Maria 1–1°; ☎289 803 757.

Hospital Hospital Distrital de Faro (☎289 891 100), behind Farense football stadium.

Left luggage At the bus terminal (Mon–Fri 9am–1pm & 2–6pm; €2.50 per item per day).

Police Rua da Policia de Segurança Pública 32 (☎289 822 022).

Post office Largo do Carmo.

Railway station ☎289 803 090.

Soccer The Algarve's top soccer team, Farense (see p.48), play at the Estádio São Luís (☎289 894 020), in the north of Faro. Tickets (from €15–20) can be purchased on match days from the office at the back of the stadium. Advance tickets for big games (against Benfica, Sporting etc) can be bought from the Loja Farense on Praça Ferreira de Almeida 14 (Mon–Fri 9.30am–12.30pm & 2.30–7pm, Sat 9.30am–1.30pm & 3.30–6.30pm).

Taxis There's a rank in Praça Dr. Francisco Gomes, by the town gardens, or phone ☎289 822 275 or 289 895 795.

Telephones See post office above.

Travel agencies Abreu, Avda da República 124 (☎289 870 900, ✉faro@abreu.pt); Top Tours, Edificio Hotel Eva, Doca de Faro (☎289 895 349, ✉faro@toptours.pt).

PRAIA DE FARO

Faro's town beach – **PRAIA DE FARO** – is typical of the sandspit *ilha* beaches of the eastern Algarve; a long sweep of beautiful sand with both a sea-facing and a more sheltered lagoon-facing side. It's less characteristic in being both overcrowded and overdeveloped, with bars, restaurants, villas and a campsite jammed onto a sandy island almost too narrow to cope in the height of summer. Still, if you just want a few hours away from the centre of Faro, it's more than adequate and out of season you'll probably have the sands to yourself. For quieter beaches, head west along the Praia de Faro towards Quinta do Lago (see p.77) where after a kilometre of so, the crowds thin out.

Practicalities

Lying just 3km from the airport, Praia de Faro makes a good base for a first or last night in the country. The beach is situated on the Ilha de Faro (also called Ançao), southwest of the town. **Buses** #14 and #16 run from the harbour gardens in central Faro, or the stop opposite the bus station, calling at the airport en route (daily 8am–8.30pm, until 11pm from July to mid-Sept, every 45 minutes; €1), stopping just before the narrow bridge to the beach itself. There are timetables posted at the bus stops; buy tickets on board.

Accommodation is available year round at the basic **campsite** (☎289 817 876, ⊕289 819 101; €0.40/person, €0.40/tent) ten minutes' walk east of the main beach car park. It is very cramped, however, and usually full in summer, with tents and caravans wedged onto a sandy dune. Make sure you phone ahead to book; there are reductions out of season, when it is a more attractive bet. Alternatively, the modern *Estalagem Aeromar* (☎289 817 542, ⓔaeromar@net.sapo.pt; ❺), right by the bridge over to the sand-spit, is a good choice for anyone with an early flight the next day. Adjacent to the inner harbour, above a decent restaurant, it offers clean, comfortable rooms, some with small balconies.

There are plenty of reasonable places to **eat and drink** strung along the seafront. By far the best of these is *Camané* (Tues–Sun 12.30–3.30pm & 8–11pm; ☎289 817 539), just east of the campsite and facing the inner harbour, rated one of the Algarve's top restaurants. Sumptuous (and expensive) dishes include *lagosta* (lobster), *fondue de tamboril e gambas* (monkfish and prawn fondu), *cataplana* and *caldeirada*. For something simpler, the moderately priced *Restaurante Paquete* (May–Sept daily 10am–10pm; Oct–April Mon, Tues & Thurs–Sun 10am–8pm), is one of the beach's best-positioned café-restaurants, just west of the campsite, with a sunny terrace facing the waves. It offers everything from toasted sandwiches and salads to decent, full Portuguese meals.

Sportugal

The coast immediately west of Faro is unremitting holiday village territory, with most accommodation in the form of international-style hotels and rented villas. **Almancil** contains one beautiful church, but otherwise this is territory for those into **Sportugal** – as the tourist board promotes the area. What you do get, however, is sports facilities that are second-to-none, plus international restaurants and bars. **Quinta do Lago** and **Vale do Lobo** are relatively small, upmarket resorts with a plethora of sports facilities, while **Vilamoura** is a giant, low-density conglomeration of restaurants, apartments and golf courses. All the resorts, set amongst neatly tended semi-tropical gardens and lawns, front superb beaches, but accommodation is limited for independent travellers or for those on a budget. A better bet is high-rise **Quarteira**, a more downmarket coastal resort with another fine beach. Alternatively you can easily stay in Faro and see the places below by **bus**; departures are roughly hourly throughout the day to all the resorts except Vale de Lobo, for which you'll need a car.

ALMANCIL

Around 12km northwest of Faro, **Almancil** offers easy access to much of Sportugal, as it's a short ride from Quinta do Lago, Vale do Lobo and Quarteira, but it is an undistinguished town blighted by through traffic. At its eastern edge, however, the church of **São Laurenço** (Mon 2.30–6pm, Tues–Sat 10am–1pm & 2.30–6pm; €1) comes as a surprise amid the development. Built in the eighteenth century, it survived the earthquake of 1755 and retains its superb fully tiled interior (see box on p.76) depicting the life of São Laurenço (St Lawrence), in particular, panels of his martyrdom showing his death in graphic detail. They were painted in 1730 by Policarpo de Oliveira Bernardes, considered one of the country's best artists.

Otherwise there is not much reason to hang around, though that situation may change with the building of a brand new 30,000 capacity Faro-Loulé **soccer stadium** just northwest of Almancil at Vale de Judeu. This will be the Algarve's only base and one of just seven venues for Portugal's European Championships in 2004. Once the competition is over, it will also host athletics meetings, concerts and conferences.

ALMANCIL

AZULEJOS

Azulejos are the distinctive glazed tiles used throughout the country to decorate everything from the outside of houses, railways, and fountains to the interiors of churches and cafés. The best places to see *azulejos* in the Algarve are in Almancil (see p.75), at the Palácio do Visconde de Estói (see p.98) and in churches throughout the region, especially the parish churches of Luz de Tavira (see p.129), Estômbar (see p.215) and Monchique (see p.226).

The word azulejo derives from the Arabic *al-zulecha*, small stone – which was introduced to Iberia during the Moorish occupation in the eighth century. Early Portuguese tiles were produced using Moorish techniques, with thin ridges of clay used to prevent the lead-based colours from running into each other. The Koran prevents the representation of living beings – hence the typical geometric Moorish designs – but the ridges hindered the Catholic Portuguese from creating more figurative designs and it was not until tile-making techniques became more advanced around the mid-sixteenth century that Portuguese *azulejos* developed their own style. A new Italian method allowed images to be painted directly onto the clay using a tin oxide coating which prevented running. At first, religious imagery was favoured but during the seventeenth century, colourful, decadent images became the rage: the wealthy commissioned large *azulejo*-panels displaying battles, hunting scenes and fantastic images influenced by tales from the New Worlds.

ALMANCIL

Regular buses make the 13km run to Almancil from Faro throughout the day. The main through-road is lined with cafés and restaurants all with similar menus. Should you wish **to stay**, *Pensão Santa Teresa* on Rua do Comércio 13 (☎289 395 525, ⑤289 395 364; ❹) is a central *pensão* which offers pleasant rooms with en-suite facilities and satellite TV.

Later that century new Dutch Delftware techniques allowed individual tiles to be decorated in immense detail, with tiny figures of birds, boats and flowers. The most common patterns at this time were religious ones commissioned by the Church; known as *tapetes* (rugs), they covered whole church walls, resembling giant Persian carpets. Around this time, Dutch tile makers began producing tiles in blue and white only, a form influenced by Chinese pottery. By the late seventeenth century, these blue and white tiles were the most popular among Portugal's aristocracy – who favoured images of flowers and fruit – while the Church also began to use this style to portray the lives of the saints, such as St Lawrence in Almancil (see p.75). The early eighteenth century saw trained masters producing highly decorated multicoloured ceramic mosaics.

After the Great Earthquake, the fireproof and insulation properties of the tiles were prized above their decorative effect and they were often used for facades. By the mid-nineteenth century, *azulejos* were being mass-produced in factories to decorate shops and industrial buildings. Today, though, there are individual artists maintaining the hand-painted tradition but the majority of today's tiles are less impressive mass-produced items, pale imitations of the old figurative or geometric designs.

QUINTA DO LAGO

Around 8km south of Almancil, **Quinta do Lago** is the first, most pleasant and most exclusive of the sports resorts. A sprawling, luxury holiday village linked by miles of roads and roundabouts, it boasts top-class golf courses (see p.45), a sports complex and opulent hotels set amongst rolling grassland, waterways and pine forest. At the edge of the complex there's an **information office** (Mon–Fri 9.30am–1pm & 2.30–6pm; ☎289 396 097) which can give out maps of the area. Head down Avenida André Jorge, the main drag, and you reach a car park opposite the beach. Here, a long wooden bridge crosses the Ria Formosa and dunes to the splendid sandspit **beach**, a huge swathe that is a continuation of Praia de Faro (see p.73). The area around the wooden bridge gets pretty packed in high season, but just walk for ten minutes or so in either direction and you can find plenty of empty sand.

The sandspit also protects the eastern extremity of the **Parque Natural da Ria Formosa** (see box p.108), an important wetland area for birds and wildlife. The fresh water lagoon at Ludo just to the east is one of the few places in Portugal where you can see the purple galinule, one of the country's rarest species of bird. Two well-used **nature trails** are signed from next to the bridge. The longer and marginally more appealing one, the São Lourenço *trilho*, heads southeast for an easy-to-follow 3.3km return walk past bird hides to a Roman pillar. The shorter 2.3km return walk, the Quinta do Lago *trilho*, heads northwest to a small lake where flamingos sometimes feed.

VALE DO LOBO AND AROUND

Heading west from Quinta do Lago, just before Vale do Lobo, a sign points to "Julia's Beach", where there is a cluster of more down-to-earth beach cafés facing another fine stretch of dune-backed sands at **Praia de Ançāo**. Here you don't have to enjoy an enormous salary to make the most of the facilities, which include sun lounges and pedaloes.

Vale de Lobo has an information line on which you can book villas directly on ☎ 289 393 939.

A couple of kilometres further west, **Vale de Lobo**, 6km west of Quinta do Lago, means "Valley of the Wolves", but there is little in the way of wildlife left here. It is similar to Quinta do Lago, with serious-money hotels, low-density upmarket villas, golf courses, a riding school, and tennis centre. Like Vilamoura (see p.81), Vale do Lobo is something of a prototype village which recently won a Green Globe award, a tourist industry prize for environmental awareness. **Accommodation** here is in the form of rented villas and upmarket hotels; you'll need to book in advance all year round and, with very few buses, you'll definitely need your own **transport**. However, the beach, **Praia de Vale do Lobo**, is magnificent.

QUARTEIRA

The first proper town west of Faro is **Quarteira**, 22km away, and around 7km southwest of Almancil. Once a small fishing village, this is a good weekly market (Monday to Saturday) by a small fishing harbour to the west end of town. Stick to the area round the market, the palm-lined seafront promenade and the attractive stretch of beach – Praia de Quarteira – and it's a pleasant enough destination. But head a little back inland and you're surrounded by rows of tower blocks. In the town's favour, however, it remains Portuguese in character, and prices are moderate in comparison with the resorts on either side.

Around 5km inland from Quarteira, on the crossroads between the EN125 and the road to Loulé at Quatro Estradas, the **Parque Atlântico** water park (May–Sept daily 10am–6pm; €10; ☎ 289 397 282) makes a fun excursion especially for those with kids; in high season it some-times features high-divers from Acapulco.

Practicalities

The **bus terminus** (☎289 389 143) is a couple of blocks back from the beach, on Avenida Dr. Sá Carneiro, with the **turismo** on Praça do Mar by the beach (May–Sept Mon & Fri–Sun 9.30am–1pm & 2–5.30pm, Tues–Thurs 9.30am–7pm; Oct–May Mon & Fri–Sun 9.30am–1pm & 2–5.30pm, Tues–Thurs 9.30am–5.30pm; ☎289 389 209). They should be able to help with finding **rooms** if the places below are full. In summer, a **toy train** trundles along the seafront to Vilamoura marina (see p.81) and back every hour or so (daily 10.15am–1pm & 3pm–midnight; €1.80).

ACCOMMODATION

There's a well-equipped **campsite** (☎289 302 821, ⓕ289 302 822; €4.20/per-son, €3.50/tent), 1km east of town; any bus to or from Faro stops right outside. They also let out rickety-looking two-tiered wooden bungalows with their own bathrooms and kitchenettes sleeping two or four people from around €31 per person.

Pensão Miramar
Rua Gonçalo Velho 8
☎289 315 225, ⓕ289 314 671

Just off the seafront, this is much the best budget choice in town. Rooms are plain but spotless with private bathrooms and TVs. Some have sea views, others face a charming plant-lined internal terrace. There's also a great communal roof terrace. ❹

Pensão Romeu
Rua Gonçalo Velho 38, ☎289 314 114
Up the road from the *Miramar* and almost identical in terms of its rooms and layout, though it lacks the sea views. ❸

QUARTEIRA

EATING AND DRINKING

- - - - - - - - - - - - - - - - - - -

O Jacinto

Avda Sá Carneiro ☎ 289 301 887

Tues–Thurs 10.30am–7pm, Fri 10.30am–6pm. **Expensive**

On the north side of the main road, despite its relatively humble appearance, this is one of the best restaurants in the Algarve. Superbly cooked fish and seafood specialities include Quarteira prawns (around €70 a kilo). Reservations necessary.

Rosa Branca

Marginal ☎ 289 314 430

Daily 10am–midnight. **Moderate**

The best positioned of a cluster of café-restaurants at the market end of the beach, with decently priced fish and grilled meats served on outdoor tables facing the sands.

VILAMOURA

Three kilometres from Quarteira and based around Europe's largest marina stands **Vilamoura**, a purpose-built and constantly expanding resort, with a bewildering network of almost 200km of roads. The resort was created in the 1970s as an upmarket extension of Quarteira, and has been carefully designed to cater to all tastes, with around 100 restaurants and shops, and specially constructed trails for walking, cycling and running. Beyond the marina, the development radiates outwards with a series of low-density hotels and over a thousand villas set in sub-tropical grounds. Vilamoura is due to expand further, with a series of environmentally-friendly resorts, a Lakeside Town, an equestrian village and a new sports centre.

- -

A toy train runs from Vilamoura marina to Quarteira in high season; see p.80.

- -

VILAMOURA

The beach and the marina

The town beach, **Praia da Marina**, is stunning, with some two miles of Blue Flag sands, and, if you're not bothered by the crowds – which get overwhelming in high season – enjoyable enough. The stretch north of the marina – **Praia da Falésia** – tends to be slightly quieter as it involves a short walk via a wooden footbridge over an inlet to get there. Just back from here, west of the marina, a tethered **balloon** (May–Sept daily noon–8pm; Oct–April 10am–6pm; every 15min, weather permitting; €15) offers a fun way to peer over the town and beach from a height of 150m.

Vilamoura boasts four highly exclusive **golf courses**, with a fifth one in the pipeline. See p.45.

Bristling with high-tech power boats and sleek yachts, the **marina** makes for a mildly interesting stroll or you can settle down at a café and watch the leisured set fooling around on their boats. At the northwest end, various stalls offer **boat trips** which range from dolphin-watching excursions to fishing trips; prices start from around €25 for a two-hour trip to €50 for a full-day excursion. The boat trips are a great way to see the surrounding coastline.

Just to the northwest of the marina, the **Museu Cerra da Vila** (May–Sept Tues–Sun 10am–1pm & 3–8pm; Oct–April until 5pm; €4) is an archaeological site displaying the vestiges of a late Roman, Visigothic and Moorish colony. You can make out the foundations of a Roman mansion, baths and a fish-salting tank, together with well-preserved Roman mosaics laid out in a scrubby field. There is also a small exhibition hall on the site giving information about the history of the site. Generally, however, the site is less impressive than the remains at Milreu (see p.99).

VILAMOURA

Practicalities

Regular buses from Faro, Quarteira and Albufeira drop you next to the casino, one block from the Praia da Marina. Most **accommodation** consists of villas but the majority are block-booked by package companies. Of the handful of hotels, *Vilamoura Marinotel* (☎289 389 988, ✉marino-tel@mail.telepac.pt; ❾), is a modern concrete and glass hulk dominating the south side of the marina, but undoubtedly the top place to stay in town. There are nearly 400 rooms, most with superb views over the neighbouring beach or marina, and facilities include indoor and outdoor pools.

For **food** or **drink**, take your pick from row upon row of bland international cafés round the marina, each of them overpriced and underwhelming but perfectly placed for people-watching. If you want to blow some money, there's a **casino** just south of the marina. It also hosts a fairly tacky disco (June–Sept nightly; Oct–May Thurs–Sun 11pm–6am) and lays on regular cabaret-style dance shows and exhibitions. *Kadoc* (Fri–Sat midnight–6am), on the outskirts, opposite the Mobil garage on the Vilamoura–Albufeira road is the Algarve's biggest **club**, which pulls in up to eight thousand revellers a night, often with international guest DJs.

WEST OF VILAMOURA

Four buses daily depart from Vilamoura and Quarteira to Aldeia das Açoteias, a bewildering chalet and villa complex just back from **Praia da Falésia**, 10km east of Albufeira. The beach here, one long tremendous stretch of sand backed by unbroken red *falésias* (cliffs), is a continuation of Vilamoura's beach, but though the sands are superb, the area around Falésia is a mess of apartments and cafés with no real shape or focal point. Much of the coastal stretch is fenced off to shelter the vast **Pine Cliffs Resort**, which embraces the flash *Sheraton Algarve* (☏ 289 500 100, ✉ sheraton_algarve@sheraton.com; ⓪). Set in a wooded complex of villas and sports facilities just back from sea cliffs – with its own lift down to the beach – this is one of the classiest and priciest hotels in the Algarve. The huge, rooms have enormous bathrooms – the best, with balconies facing the sea, will set you back a cool €450 in high season. There are two outdoor pools and an indoor one along with a gym, tennis courts and discounts for the neighbouring golf course (see p.44) plus disabled access.

West of here, the coast changes and the expansive beaches become smaller sandy bays backed by ochre-red cliffs, all reached on local buses (roughly hourly) from Vilamoura and Albufeira. One of the nicest of the beaches is **Olhos de Água**, 8km west of Vilamoura and 6km west of Praia de Falésia. Its name, which translates as "eyes of the water", derives from the freshwater springs that bubble up under the sands. An erstwhile fishing village, it has a small beach and the highly rated *La Cigale* **restaurant** (daily 10.30am–midnight; ☏ 289 501 637), an expensive place right on the beach with a lovely terrace and great seafood.

At low tide you can walk the 2.5km from Olhos de Água along the beach to **Praia da Oura**, just 2km from Albufeira (see box p.163), which is also served by the regular Vilamoura–Albufeira bus. This beach, though, has been extensively developed and is less alluring than Albufeira's own town beach (see p.162).

North of Faro

Though most people visit the Algarve for its beaches, it is well worth venturing inland to see some of the variety the region has to offer. **Loulé**, an easy 18km ride northwest of Faro, has a fascinating archaeological museum set in the remains of its castle, though it is better known as the venue for one of the Algarve's best Saturday markets. Further north, unspoilt countryside dotted with cork woods and olive and citrus groves stretches up into the mountainous **Serra do Caldeirão**. This countryside is beautiful terrain for a walk or picnic, especially around the tiny villages of **Salir**, with the remains of another Moorish castle, **Benafim** and **Penina**. A little northeast, **Ameixal** is another interesting agricultural town close to the border with the neighbouring Alentejo region. Heading northeast out of Faro, it is just 17km to **São Bras de Alportel**, a sleepy market town with an attractive *pousada* and a quirky museum, via the town of **Estói**, a fairly nondescript village which nevertheless boasts the beautiful gardens of the Palácio de Estói and the fascinating Roman site of **Milreu**.

LOULÉ

LOULÉ, 18km inland from Faro and served by a regular bus service, is a thriving market town, and though its suburbs are beginning to sprawl across the surrounding hillsides, its compact centre makes an interesting half-day visit. The sites of interest mostly lie a short walk from the remains of its Moorish castle, now a museum, and the thirteenth-century Gothic Igreja Matriz church.

Arrival and information

The **bus terminal** (☎289 416 655/6) is on Rua Nossa Senhora de Fátima, a couple of minutes' walk north from the old town (head down Alto São Domingos to reach the tourist office); there are daily services from Quarteira, Albufeira and Faro. The **turismo** (May–Sept Mon 9.30am–1pm & 2–5.30pm, Tues–Fri 9.30am–7pm, Sat 9.30am–3.30pm; Oct-April Mon 9.30am–1pm & 2–5.30pm, Tues–Fri 9.30am–5.30pm, Sat 9.30am–3pm; ☎289 463 900) is inside the castle walls next to the archae-ological museum, at Largo Dom Pedro I.

Accommodation

There is not a great deal of choice of accommodation in Loulé, but the tourist office has details of a few **private rooms** to supplement the following **hotel** options. Virtually opposite the tourist office, on the main road through town, *Casa Beny* (☎289 417 702; ❸), is a tastefully renovated town house offering neat, slightly flowery rooms, with their own TV and bathrooms. There is also a roof ter-race with great views over the bustle. Down the hill close to the dried fruit museum, on Praça Manuel de Arriaga 23, is the attractive *Loulé Jardim Hotel* (☎289 413 094, ☎289 463 177; ❸), with small but well-decorated rooms with cable TV and private bathrooms. There's also a bar and a small pool in the grounds.

The town

Loulé's most interesting streets lie around the **Igreja Matriz** church just southwest of the centre – take any turning southwest off Praça da República – a grid of whitewashed cobbled lanes that house numerous **handicraft** shops where you're free to watch the craftsmen at work. Lacemaking and copper work, in particular, are flourishing local industries. On Saturdays, the town is transformed as the whole region seems to arrive en masse for a busy **market,** selling a motley collection of clothes, ceramics, agricultural produce and general goods. At other times, just off Largo Gago Coutinho, you'll find a wonderful covered fruit and veg-etable market (Mon–Sat 8am–3pm), set in a red onion-domed building with Moorish key hole-style windows. Close by, on Avenida Marçal Pacheco, one block beyond the market, it is worth stopping to see the Manueline coiled rope twirls on the facade of the **Misericordia** church.

Loulé hosts an annual Jazz Festival featuring top international musicians who perform on July weekends.

Loulé's most curious sight, however, is the beehive-shaped **Nossa Senhora da Piedade**, on a hilltop around 1km west of town, in the direction of Boliqueime. At Easter, the church is the starting point of a procession into town for Mãe Soberana, one of the Algarve's most impor-tant religious festivals (see p.21).

Museu Arqueológico and the castle
Mon–Thurs 9am–5.30pm, Sat 10am–2pm; €1.80

The remains of Loulé's castle enclose a mildly interesting **Museu Arqueológico**, housing a range of Roman, Moorish and early Portuguese finds from Loulé and the surrounding area. There are second-century amphora, ninth-century pots from Salir castle (see p.92) and the foun-dations of a twelfth-century Moorish house, *in situ* under a glass floor. The largest exhibit is a giant sixteenth-century stone urn, retrieved from the castle itself.

The entry price to the museum allows access to the **castle walls** from where you can peer down over the old town.

The entrance is up the steps to the side of the museum, via a room set out in traditional Algarvian style, complete with pots, pans and straw dummies in traditional dress. Sneak a look, too, through the door opposite into the Municipal Archives, lined with a row of ancient typewriters.

The ticket to the Museu Arqueológico also covers entry to the **Polo Museológico dos Frutos Secos** at Rua Gil Vicente 14 (Mon–Fri 9am–5.30pm, Sat 10am–5.30pm), five minutes' walk downhill via the pedestrianized Rua 5 de Outubro. This dried fruit museum is only really worth the effort if you're interested in early twentieth-century industrial machinery or dehydrated apricots.

Eating and drinking

There's a good range of **places to eat** in Loulé to suit all budgets. For an inexpensive lunch, there are countless cafés along the pedestrianized Rua 5 de Outubro, or you could put together a tasty picnic from the covered market (see p.87).

Bica Velha
Rua Martim Moniz 17
Mon–Sat 6.30pm–midnight.
Moderate–expensive
Highly regarded, slightly formal restaurant downhill from the tourist office. The Portuguese food is always good but the atmosphere can be rather subdued.

Café Calcina
Praça da República
Mon–Sat 8am–11.30pm.
Inexpensive

A great traditional café with marble table tops and black-and-white photos of old Loulé on the walls. The perfect spot for *pastéis de nata* (custard cream tarts), *rissóis de bacalhau* (dried cod rissoles) or a beer with *tremoços* (pickled lupin seeds).

A Muralha
Rua Martim Moniz
Mon & Tues 7–11pm, Wed–Sat noon–3pm & 7–11pm.
Moderate–expensive

LOULÉ

With a flower-filled patio and *azulejo* panels of old Loulé decorating the interior, this is one of the most popular tourist spots in town. Grills are unexceptional, but the more elaborate meat and seafood dishes such as *arroz de marisco* and meat fondues are good bets. There's also a children's menu.

Museu do Lagar
Largo da Matriz 7
Tues–Sun noon–4pm & 7–11pm. Moderate
Opposite the Igreja Matriz, this cavernous *marisqueira* has its own fountain and bubbling fish tanks. A good range of well-prepared dishes include *arroz do pato* (duck rice) and shellfish.

Speed Squad Bar
Rua Dr Joaquim Nunes Saraiva 21
Mon–Fri 1.30pm–2.30am, Sat & Sun 9pm–2.30am.
With its car-influenced decor and loud music, this is where the young things of Loulé hang out; friendly and fun.

Os Tibetanos
Rua Almeida Garrett 69
Mon–Sat 12.30–2.30pm & 7.30–10pm. Inexpensive
Small vegetarian canteen and shop serving decent if unexciting dishes such as tofu curry, salads and *rissóis de queijo cabra* (goat's cheese rissoles).

THE SERRA DO CALDEIRÃO

The **SERRA DO CALDEIRÃO**, around 16km north of Loulé, is a series of superb, gently rolling hills that separate the Algarve from the neighbouring region of the Alentejo. Much of the area is agricultural land – often subsistence farming – with the fields and orchards worked as they have been for centuries. Most of the Serra forms part of the *Rede Natural 2000*, an EU category which classifies the area as being of environmental importance. The categorization

THE SERRA DO CALDEIRÃO

CORK

The inland Algarve and neighbouring region of Alentejo produce over fifty percent of the world's supply of **cork**. The material has been a major Portuguese export since the late nineteenth century when São Brás de Alportel became the main centre for the industry.

Cork (*quercus suber*) consists of a layer of spongy cells called phellogen that appear under the bark during the first year of the tree's growth. As the tree grows, the cells grow radially outwards to form the durable, impermeable material with excellent thermal insulation. These qualities enable the cork to act as a barrier against pests, fire and extremes of temperature, allowing the tree to thrive even in these barren landscapes. Young cork tends to crack as the tree trunk grows underneath it, so this form of virgin cork is harvested for cork agglomerates, ground up to make cork tiles or flooring.

Perhaps the most important property of a cork tree is its ability to regenerate itself when a layer of cork is destroyed. Not just once but throughout the life cycle of the tree, new layers replace those that are cut off, continuously producing thicker layers than the previous one. Cork farmers therefore strip away the cork layer without harming the tree in any way. This highly skilled task is performed by carefully separating the rectangular sheets of cork from the trunk by hand using a curved axe. Around the harvesting months of July and August, you'll see the peeled trunks and piles of curved cork through-

is designed to encourage member governments to look after these zones, though there is nothing legally binding to guarantee the area protected status.

With your own transport, there are several small villages dotted round the hills that make a rewarding excursion from Faro or the surrounding area. The easiest out the inland region. Each tree is harvested every nine years or so, allowing the cork to grow to a thickness of 4–6cm – traditionally thick enough to make wine corks. The white numbers painted on the trees throughout the region show the year when they are next due to be harvested. Most trees survive for over a century, though one tree in the Alentejo known as the Whistler Tree is nearly 220 years old.

Cork trees in Portugal have enjoyed protected status for over 700 years since the reign of Dom Dinis. They are not allowed to be stripped for cork until they are 25 years old, while pruning the trees' branches is also strictly regulated. As a result, the areas where they grow have become superb, protected habitats for wildlife including wild boar and the Iberian lynx, considered the rarest wild cat in the world. Few forms of cultivation are as self-sustaining as cork, yet this ancient method of farming is under threat from plastic cork substitutes.

Until recently, almost ninety percent or the world's wine corks came from this region, but the growing popularity of plastic wine stoppers is threatening the livelihood of the cork farmers and the environment they work in. Fans of plastic corks claim they avoid the problem of corking when bacteria from the natural cork infects the wine. Plastic corks also tend to be less expensive. If the cork harvests prove to be unprofitable and farmers seek a more viable crop, an ancient, environmentally important, sustainable lifestyle will be destroyed.

approach is from Loulé, where it is a short drive north to Salir via Querença. Heading west from Salir along the EN124, it is 13km to the attractive town of Alte via the picturesque villages of Pena and Benafim. Alternatively, the same road heading east joins the N2 at Barranco Velho, from where it is a highly scenic route north to the

THE SERRA DO CALDEIRÃO

Alentejo district border just beyond the sleepy village of Ameixial.

Querença to Salir

Ten kilometres northwest of Loulé, **Querença** is an unexceptional village that comes alive in January for a Smoked Sausage Fair (see p.37). On the EN396 just south of Querença, around 7km northeast of Loulé, *O Moinho ti Cozinha* (Tues–Sat 12.30–3pm & 7.30–10pm, Sun 12.30–3pm; ☎ 289 438 108, reservations essential) makes a good lunch spot. This rural **restaurant** set by an old mill is famed for its traditional cuisine, in particular tapas-like *petiscos*, grilled meat dishes and, in autumn and winter, game.

A further 12km northwest, 14km from Loulé, the village of **Salir** makes a more interesting stop. Set on a hilltop facing rolling countryside, the attractive agricultural village retains the vestiges of a Moorish **castle**. To visit, park by the diminutive Ermida de Pé da Cruz church from where it is a short stroll along a cobbled track to what's left of the castle – a few low walls and stumps of turrets. Though the ruins are no great shakes, they're in a gorgeous position, the path passing white flower-decked houses with great views over Salir and the valley beyond. On the way to the castle you'll pass *Mouro Bar Castelo* on Rua dos Muros do Castelo 1 (Tues–Sun noon–10pm), a simple **restaurante-bar** serving solid Portuguese nosh at decent prices with a dining room commanding superb views over the valley.

The Loulé tourist office (see p.86) has leaflets detailing walks, mountain bike routes and horse riding possibilities throughout the region.

THE SERRA DO CALDEIRÃO

West to Benafim

Six kilometres west of Salir, the backstreets of **Benafim** are a delightful maze of whitewashed houses and narrow streets lined with geraniums and colourful pot plants. The village, which has a handful of cafés, is similar to Alte, 5km west (see p.175), marginally less well kept but totally free of tourists. For a real taste of rural Algarve, take the signed back road from Benafim, which leads to Penina before rejoining the main road at the village of Pena – a short drive or a superb eight-kilometre-round **walk**, returning to Benafim along the main EN124. En route you'll pass through cork and olive groves dotted with traditional wells.

Penina itself is a simple agricultural village where some of the elderly inhabitants still wear traditional dress. A good drink stop is *Café Cacadores* (open daily), close to the main shop. To get here by public transport, there is one daily bus departing from Loulé at 8.25am (continuing to Alte; see p.175). The bus returns to Loulé at 2.50pm.

Beyond Penina, the road continues alongside the foot of **Rocha da Pena**, a craggy limestone hill protecting rare flora and fauna, including mongoose, eagle owls, buzzards and Bonelli eagles, though you'll need to walk to the hill itself for a likely chance to see any of these (see box below). Another 2km beyond Penina lies another totally unspoilt tiny agricultural village, **Pena**.

Rejoin the main road just south of Pena, from where you can return to Benafim and on to Alte to the west, or back to Salir to the east.

North to Ameixial

Some 12km east of Salir lies **Barranco Velho**, another traditional village sitting on the crossroads of the road to Cachopo – one of the most scenic routes in the Algarve

THE SERRA DO CALDEIRÃO

A WALK UP ROCHA DA PENA

The mini table mountain of Rocha da Pena lies in the heart of the Algarve and has its own micro-climate supporting an array of flora and fauna. This 1hr 45 (4.5km) round walk offers superb views over the interior of the region and is relatively unstrenuous, even though it passes right over a small mountain. The walk is signed anti-clockwise from its eastern end close to Pena, but this description is in the opposite direction starting in Penina, as the clockwise climb to the Rocha da Pena trigonometry point (TP-479m), negates a tricky descent. As a result it's easier to start at the *fonte*-cum-shrine in Penina (see p.93). Close by are the village shop for supplies and the *Café dos Caçadores,* where you can order lunch or a snack for your return. From the café, head northwest along the narrow streets through a small square, Largo das Lades, where there is a water-tap for filling up waterbottles. The paved road soon turns into a stony track as it starts to climb into the countryside.

The track soon reaches a water tank, where you'll see international yellow and red waymarks or *pequenas rotas*; these are angled for anti-clockwise walkers. Continue climbing as the track swings northeast, then east with wonderful views behind you to the west. As the track levels, look for waymarks on your right indicating a path that takes you up to the Trig. Point (25min; 1.5km). In spring, tread warily so as not to destroy wild pink peonies. At the summit by the Trig. Point there are magnificent views over the coastline from Lagos to the west almost to Faro in the east.

Return to the main track and turn right (east) and descend to a plateau. Cross over an overgrown pasture to locate yellow/red waymarks upon rocks (to the southeast) and follow a well-trodden, rocky path (45min; 2km), that takes you close to the cliff edge. Along the path ahead, you can see a barrier of weathered limestone thought to be the defensive wall for a pre-Moorish settlement. Continue along the rocky track with stunning views around you until you pass the wall's southern end (60min; 2.5km) where, in spring, various varieties of wild flowers – including a miniature daffodil – flourish away from the northerly winds.

Follow the track as it rises a little, then descends to a path with a left-hand fork. This is a detour leading to caves in which Moors hid from Crusaders – take great care as the entrance is steep and prone to landslips. Return back to the fork and continue along the main path eastwards. You are now above Pena village and can see Salir with its white water tower in the distance to the southeast. Your well-waymarked path becomes rockier as it descends, bringing you to a clearing where you should ignore the waymarks to your left and ahead and take the sharp right turn west for your return (70min; 3km) towards Penina.

Halfway down the slope on your right you'll see a popular rock-climbing spot just before your track swings left (southeast). Wild peonies abound here in spring: remember that these are an important part of the local ecosystem and picking them is damaging to the environment. At the bottom of this rough track a café lies on your left (80min; 3.5km) and in front of you, Fonte da Pena (a spring, now fed through a tap) and a display board illustrating the boundaries of the protected area around Rocha da Pena.

Turn right (west) on to an undercliff path that is part of Via Algarviana (see p.175) for your mostly level return to Penina (145min; 4.5km).

A WALK UP ROCHA DA PENA

(see p.150) – and the EN2. The latter, originally Roman, is one of the oldest roads in Portugal, and links Faro via São Bras de Alportel (see below) with Chaves in the Trás-Os-Montes district in the extreme north of Portugal. The stretch from Barranco Velho north is delightful, a narrow road winding through superb countryside.

The last village in the Algarve before the road enters the Alentejo district is **Ameixial**, 20km further north, a drowsy place with a tiny Monday to Saturday morning market. There's nothing else to the village itself, but it's a wonderful drive here nonetheless.

In April, villages throughout the area celebrate the Festival de Serra do Caldeirão with displays of handicrafts, and gastronomy.

SÃO BRÁS DE ALPORTEL

Sixteen kilometres north of Faro, and 13km south of Barranco Velho, **São Bras de Alportel**, on the western edge of the Serra de Monte Figo, makes a good stop to stretch your legs. Just east of the main square, on Rua Dr. José Dias Sancho, the **Museu Etnográfico do Trajo Algarvio**, at no. 61 (Tues–Fri 10am–1pm & 2–5pm, Sat & Sun 2–5pm; €0.80), housed in an old mansion, is quite the best reason to come to São Brás, its alcoves and corridors full of traditional costumes. At the back, a series of buildings round a courtyard shelter cork cutting equipment, ancient donkey carriages, saddles, bull carts and an old loom. Occasional demonstrations of the machinery take place and, outside in the courtyard, you can walk down steps to the bottom of a traditional well which has been partly excavated.

From the museum, cut down Rua Nova de Fonte and

you'll reach the **Jardim da Verbena** (May–Sept 8am–8pm; Oct–April 8am–5pm; free), a wonderful little garden with an open-air **swimming pool** (hours as park; free). Just west of here lie the narrow streets of the oldest part of town, clustered round the church of **Senhor dos Passos** (signposted *Igreja Matriz*), from where there are lovely views of the surrounding valleys.

Practicalities

Regular **buses** from Faro pull into the main square, a fairly dull space with a couple of banks and a tourist booth that seems to have shut down for good. There is not much reason to stay in São Bras, unless you're tempted by one of the Algarve's two *pousadas* which is just to the north.

ACCOMMODATION

Pousada de São Brás
ⓣ 289 845 171,
ⓔ enatur@mail.telepac.pt
Two kilometres north of town, this terracotta-tiled building was, in 1942, the second *pousada* to open. The views from the balconies of the comfortable rooms are splendid, and there's a pool, tennis courts, games room and (expensive) restaurant. Advance booking essential in summer; rates tumble in winter. ❼

Residencial São Brás
Rua Luís Bivar 27
ⓣ & ⓕ 289 842 213
Superb town house, a couple of minutes' walk west of the main square, swathed in *azulejos* with an ornate stairway. Sadly the large, musty rooms don't live up to the communal areas and bathrooms are shared. ❸

EATING AND DRINKING

Pousada de São Brás
ⓣ 289 845 1712

Daily noon–2.30pm &
7.30–9pm. **Expensive**
The *pousada* restaurant
commands superb views over
the surrounding valleys.
International and Portuguese
cuisine is well prepared and
not too outrageously priced
(unlike the wine list), though
the overly formal service and
atmosphere is rather off-
putting. Book ahead in
summer.

Savoy
Rua Luís Bivar 40
Mon–Sat noon–11pm, Sun
noon–8pm. **Moderate**
Past the *Residencial São Brás*,
this good-value option serves
old-fashioned international
cuisine such as prawn
cocktail, spaghetti bolognaise
and pork with apple sauce.
There's also a kids' menu.

ESTÓI

ESTÓI, 11km north of Faro, has a long main street, a little
square and an attractive Igreja Matriz, designed by
Francisco Xavier Fabri, the Italian architect who was commissioned to replace the original church that was destroyed
in the Great Earthquake of 1755. Just off the main square is
the delightful peach-coloured **Palácio do Visconde de
Estói**, a diminutive version of the Rococo palace of
Queluz near Lisbon, built by the Visconde de Carvalha at
the end of the eighteenth century. At present, only the
attractive **Jardim** (garden), reached down a palm-lined
avenue, is open to the public (Tues–Sat 9am–12.30pm &
2–5.30pm; free). The grounds spread down below a terrace
dotted with statues of Portuguese literary figures – Camões,
Herculano and Garrett – along with the Marquês de
Pombal. The stairs from the terrace are lined with eigh-
teen-century *azulejos* of plants and tropical birds. The
palace is earmarked to become a *pousada*.

Milreu

Tues–Sun: April–Sept 9.30am–12.30pm & 2.30–6pm; Oct–March
9.30am–12.30 & 2–5pm; €1.30

The main reason for visiting Estói, however, is the Roman
site at **MILREU**, a ten-minute walk downhill from the
main square. Known to the Romans as Ossonoba, the town
predated Faro and was inhabited from the second to the
sixth century AD. The site is relatively small and it's easy to
find your way around. Archaeological excavations are on-
going, but you can clearly make out the remains of a peri-
style villa to the north of the site, dominated by the apse of
a temple a little to the south, which was converted into a
Christian basilica in the third century AD, making it one of
the earliest known Christian churches in the world. The
other recognizable remains are of a bathing complex southwest of the villa, which had underfloor heating, with fragments of fish mosaics; and the *apodyterium*, or changing
room, with its stone benches and arched niches below for
clothes. Many of the busts from the site – including those
of Hadrian and Empress Agrippina Minor – are on display
in Faro's archaeological museum (see p.63).

Practicalities

There is no accommodation in Estói, but this hardly matters as regular **buses** (daily 4–7) make the twenty-minute
journey from Faro; it is also only 7km north to São Bras
(which is served by the same bus). Buses drop you in the
main square, a minute's walk from the Jardim. There's good
food at *Casa do Pasto Victor's*, Rua Vasco da Gama 41
(Mon–Sat noon–3pm & 7–10pm), just off the square on
the Olhão road, a cheap and cheerful grill house where
you'd be hard pushed to spend more than €8 a head.
There are also no fewer than eleven **café-bars** around the

ESTÓI

main street; all are of a similar standard, though most people settle at one of the two with outdoor seating on the main square.

Olhão and around

Linked by the fast EN125, **Olhão**, 8km to the east of Faro, is a characterful, large fishing port retaining a kernel of Moorish-style houses and with a great market. It also has a year-round service to two superb sandbank *ilhas*, **Culatra** and **Armona**, both of which boast tremendous and relatively uncrowded beaches. The latter island can also be reached from **Fuzeta**, a lively fishing town and a stop on the Faro to Tavira railway line. The *ilhas* also protect a marshy lagoon, part of the Reserva Natural da Ria Formosa, which can be visited from **Quinta da Marim**, an environmental centre that's home to bizarre, web-footed aquatic poodles.

OLHÃO

OLHÃO is the largest fishing port in the Algarve and an excellent base for visiting the surrounding sandbank *ilhas*. There are no historic sights to speak of, but with its vibrant market, attractive riverfront gardens and atmospheric backstreets, it makes a great place to visit for a day-trip, or to stay for a few nights.

Arrival, orientation and information

Olhão's waterfront Avenida 5 de Outubro, with its market, gardens and ferry terminal to the islands, marks the southern side of the old town, a complex network of narrow alleys. Take Rua M. Albuquerque, the road heading northwest opposite the market buildings, and you will reach Rua do Comércio (on your left) and Rua Vasco da Gama (on your right), both of which converge on Avenida da República, the main shopping street running north into the new town.

Arriving at the **train station**, you will find yourself at the northeastern edge of town, off Avenida dos Combatentes da Grande Guerra some ten to fifteen minutes' walk from the waterfront. To reach the centre, turn left out of the station and then right down Avenida da República. The **bus terminal** (℡289 702 157) is a few minutes away on Rua General Humberto Delgado. To reach the centre from the bus station, which takes around five minutes, turn right out of the exit then right into Avenida da República. At the parish church, the avenue forks: keep to the left of the church along Rua do Comércio, and at the fourth on the right you'll find the **turismo** at the top of Rua Olhanense (June to mid-September Mon–Fri 9.30am–5.30pm; mid-September to May Mon–Fri 9.30am–1pm & 2–5.30pm; ℡289 713 936), which can provide a town map, advice on accommodation and boat times to the *ilhas*.

For **internet access**, the post office on the main Avenida da República (Mon–Fri 8.30am–6pm), has a *Netpost* terminal; prepaid cards can be bought from the counter.

Accommodation

Accommodation can be hard to find in the height of summer, despite a fair scattering of **pensões**. Served by regular bus, the local **campsite**, *Camping Olhão* (℡289 700 300, ℮sbicamping@mail.telepac.pt; €3.20/person, from

OLHÃO

€2.60/tent), is at Pinheiros de Marim, 3km east of town next to Quinta da Marim (see p.107). The upmarket site is set in substantial grounds with its own pool, kids' playground, tennis courts, mini market, restaurant and bars; there is even live music some nights.

B & B City Lodge
Rua da Verdade 6
ⓣ 289 706 607, ⓕ 289 723 709
Off the riverfront *avenida*, this small, friendly B&B in a modern building has large rooms with balconies overlooking the market; there's also a communal kitchen and bathroom. ❷

Pensão Bela Vista
Rua Teófilo Braga 65–67
ⓣ & ⓕ 289 702 538
The best option in town, so be sure to book ahead. A spotless reception sets the tone for the bright rooms, most en suite, arranged around a tiled, flower-filled courtyard. From the turismo, turn left, then left again, and it's directly opposite. ❸

Pensão Bicuar
Rua Vasco da Gama 5
ⓣ 289 714 816
Near the waterfront, pleasant rooms, some with their own balcony, but no ensuites. Price does not include breakfast. ❸

Pensão Boémia
Rua da Cerca 20, off Rua 18 de Junho
ⓣ & ⓕ 289 714 513
Neat place offering en-suite rooms with balconies; handy for the bus station. Slightly out of the centre, near the post office. ❸

Hotel Ria Sol
Rua General Humberto Delgado 37
ⓣ 289 705 267, ⓕ 289 705 268
Standard two-star hotel just up from the bus station. Rooms are en suite with TVs and the price includes a buffet breakfast. ❹

Suiss Brito
Avenida 5 de Outubro 98, 1°e
ⓣ 289 715 562
Characterful town house, with a mixed bag of simple

OLHÃO

rooms, some gloomy, some large and airy. The best have balconies facing the front. Communal showers; breakfast not included. ❷

Pensão Vasco da Gama
Rua Vasco da Gama 6

☎ 289 702 785
Cheap and cheerful place opposite the *Pensão Bicuar*, with simple rooms, some with balconies. Shared bathrooms and price does not include breakfast. ❷

The Town

Once through the built-up outskirts, Olhão is quite an attractive town. There are no sights as such, but the flat roofs, stairways and white terraces of the old town give a striking North African feel to the place. Indeed, Olhão has centuries-old trading links with Morocco, as well as a small place in **history** for its uprising against the French garrison here in 1808 when Napoleon's troops occupied Portugal. After the French were forced out, local fishermen sent a small boat across the Atlantic to Brazil to transmit the news to the exiled king, João VI. After the king's restoration to the throne, the journey – completed without navigational aids – was recognized by the town being rewarded with a royal charter.

The best view of the whitewashed cube-houses is from the bell tower of the unspectacular seventeenth-century parish church of **Nossa Senhora do Rosário** (Tues–Sun 9.30am–noon & 3–6pm), right in the centre of town. Outside, at the back of the church, an iron grille protects the chapel of **Nossa Senhora dos Aflitos**, where townswomen traditionally gathered to pray for their menfolk when there was a storm at sea. Nowadays curious wax models of children and limbs sit amid candles as *ex voto* offerings for fertility and to cure ailments.

The other obvious focus of the town is the **market**

OLHÃO

(Mon–Fri 7am–2pm, Sat 6.30am–3pm), held in the two modern red-brick turreted buildings on the harbour at the bottom of town. There's meat, fruit and vegetables and cheeses on one side, fish on the other. The fish hall is full of such delights as octopus, scabbard fish whose eyes pop out during decompression, and the ubiquitous sardine.

Either side of the market lie the **riverside gardens** where you can cool off in summer under the shade of exotic plants. There are also a couple of kids' play areas to keep children entertained and, by the ferry terminal, east of the market, a miniature aviary.

Eating and drinking

There are plenty of inexpensive **cafés and bars** around the market buildings, while the riverfront Avenida 5 de Outubro is lined with more expensive **fish restaurants**. Up by the ferry stop lie another clutch of budget cafés and fast-food restaurants.

Café Al-Hain
Centro Comercial Al-Hain, Avda da República
Daily 8am–midnight.
Inexpensive
Lively *pastelaria*-cum-café/bar with frequent live soccer on TV, and a good range of snacks.

Restaurante Bela Vista
Rua Dr Teofilio Braga 59
Mon–Sat 8am–11pm.
Inexpensive
Close to the tourist office, this simple, low-ceilinged café-restaurant with blue *azulejos* is a cosy and inexpensive place for generous portions of grilled meats and fish.

A Bote
Avda 5 de Outubro 122
Mon–Sat noon–10pm.
Moderate
This local joint, close by the fish market, serves grilled fish and moderately priced meat, accompanied by stacks of potatoes and salad.

OLHÃO

Café Gelvi
Mercado, Avda 5 de Outubro
Tues–Sun 8am–midnight.
Inexpensive
Pastelaria and *croissanteria* in
the corner of the fish market,
with outdoor seats facing the
water.

Pizza Mar
Avda 5 de Outubro
Mon, Tues & Thurs–Sun
11.30am–3pm & 6.30–10.30pm.
Inexpensive
One of a cluster of inexpensive
restaurants at the ferry end of
the *avenida*, with a fair range of
acceptable pizzas.

THE ILHAS: CULATRA AND ARMONA

Olhão's harbour is protected by the middle two of the six
sandspit islands that lie parallel to the coast between Quinta
do Lago to the east and Manta Rota to the west. **Ilha da
Culatra**, a thirty-five-minute ferry ride southwest of
Olhão, is the more populated of the two, with a regular
ferry service from Olhão and a summer service from Faro
supporting two sizeable communities: the villages of
Culatra to the east and Farol to the west. Originally fishing
villages facing the more sheltered inner lagoon, the wooden
fisherman's shacks are now outnumbered by holiday chalets
and cafés that spread south across the narrow island to a
wonderful Atlantic-facing sandy beach. Just to the east of
Ilha da Culatra, facing Olhão, **Ilha da Armona** is a much
narrower island with a similar fishing-village-cum-holiday
settlement. The rest of the island is virtually deserted, consisting of mud flats facing inland and a superb Atlantic-facing beach that stretches all the way to Praia da Fuzeta two
hours' walk to the east. Separate **ferries** leave for the *ilhas*
from the jetty at the eastern end of Olhão's municipal gardens, five minutes' walk from the market. There's a
timetable posted at the ticket kiosk; if it isn't open, you can
buy tickets on the ferries (see below for details).

Ilha da Culatra

The **ILHA DA CULATRA** is the most populated of the sandspits, its northern, land-facing shore dotted with a series of fishermen's huts between the two main centres at either end of the island, Culatra and Farol. In summer the island's population swells to around 3000, well supported by a mini market, medical centre and a cluster of seasonal cafés. The easternmost of the settlements is the ferry's first port of call, **Culatra**, the larger of the two, a fairly untidy collection of huts and holiday homes. Ten minutes west by boat, **Farol**, the second stop, is far more agreeable. A network of narrow paths links low-rise holiday homes and fishermen's huts clustered round a tall *farol* (lighthouse). Farol (like Culatra) is edged by beautiful tracts of beach on the ocean side, though the mainland-facing beach is grubby. In winter the villages are almost deserted.

Ferries from Olhão depart to the Ilha da Culatra throughout the year (June & Sept 6 daily; July & Aug 7 daily; rest of year 4 daily; €1 to Culatra, €1.20 to Farol return), calling at Culatra (35min) and Farol (45min). In summer, an additional service runs between Farol and Faro (see p.64). If you want to stay, ask around at the cafés for **private rooms**; camping on the island is not encouraged. For **food and drink** in Farol, *À-do-João* (daily 9.30am–3pm & 7–11pm), up by the seafront just west of the lighthouse, serves some fine seafood dishes as well as less pricey sandwiches, salads and *tostas* (toasted sandwiches). In summer, the nearby *Zé Pinto* (May–Sept noon–10pm), is a bustling grill house with an outdoor barbecue and a roof terrace offering fine sea views.

Ilha da Armona

Ferries drop their passengers at the northern end of the single settlement on **ILHA DA ARMONA** – a long, crowded strip of holiday chalets and huts that stretches right across the island on either side of the main path. Follow the path and it's a fifteen-minute walk to the ocean-facing beach, which stretches out into the distance; a short walk will take you to attractive stretches of sand and dune – the further you go, the greater the privacy.

Boats ply the fifteen-minute ride from Olhão to the island all year round (June & early Sept 9–11 departures daily; July & Aug first departure 7.30am, then hourly 9am–8pm; late Sept–May one daily, three on Saturdays; €0.90 return). There are a few **bar-restaurants** by the jetty, though most close out of season when it is best to stock up on supplies from Olhão's market. Accommodation is scarce; there are no *pensões* or hotels on Armona and camping on the beach is frowned upon, but *Orbitur* (April–October only; ℡289 714 173; ❸) operates a series of holiday **bungalows** on the island – though you will need to book ahead in high season.

You can walk along usually deserted beach from the Olhão end of Armona to the eastern end opposite Fuzeta in about two hours. For details of Praia da Fuzeta, see p.110.

QUINTA DA MARIM

Daily 9.30am–12.30pm & 2.30–5.30pm; €1.50

Three kilometres east of Olhão, just off the EN125 Olhão-Tavira road (and served by regular bus from Olhão and Fuzeta), **Quinta da Marim** is an environmental educational centre lying just beyond the campsite (see p.101) within the Parque Natural da Ria Formosa (see p.108), in an area of scrubby dunes and mud flats dotted with pines and gorse. It's a lovely quiet spot well worth a half-day's visit.

THE PARQUE NATURAL DA RIA FORMOSA

The **Parque Natural da Ria Formosa** was created in 1987 to encompass 1840 square kilometres of land behind the unique system of barrier islands that stretch from Praia de Ancão, near Quinta do Lago, to Manta Rota, some 60km to the east. The six sandspit islands of Ancão (or Faro), Barreta, Culatra, Armona, Tavira and Cabanas help protect a system of salt marshes, tidal flats and channels, which are considered such important natural sites that they were defined by the Ramsar Convention on Wetlands in the late 1980s as of "International Importance".

The environmental issues are a challenge to the park's organizers. This is a rare habitat for some unusual wildlife (see p.316) but there is also a resident population of 7500 who are dependent on gleaning a living from the area's natural reserves. Fishing and shellfish collection are a traditional mainstay but there is also money to be made from the increasing number of visitors attracted by the relatively undeveloped beaches and natural beauty of the area. Several industries, including salt extraction (see p.125) and sand dredging, pose problems for the vulnerable ecosystem, but even more worrying, are the rash of illegally constructed buildings scattered around the area and the growing number of golf courses encroaching on the park (see p.133).

The reserve is best known for being the refuge for bizarre **aquatic poodles**, web-footed dogs that were bred to dive into the water to help chase fish into the fishermen's nets. Unfortunately, the aquatic poodles were abandoned for more modern methods in the 1950s, though the shaggy dogs still thrive here in their pure-bred form. The poodles can be seen as part of a three-kilometre-long **nature trail** that leads from the car park past various signed highlights: a salt marsh, freshwater pond where you sometimes can spot rare birds – including, if you are lucky, the purple ganilule (see p.317) – a bird hospital and the remains of Roman salting tanks, used for preserving fish.

The area is also home to one of Portugal's last working *moinhos de maré* – **tidal mills**. Once common throughout the country, these use the movement of the tide to grind corn by damming water at high tide and releasing it at low tide to move the mill. There's a **visitor centre** with models of traditional fishing boats, fossils, a small aquarium of native fish and a decent **café**. You can also explore the lagoon in a restored **tuna fishing boat**. Departures are fairly regular in summer, though at other times of year they leave only when there are enough people around to make it worthwhile.

If you want **to stay** in rural solitude, book well in advance (☎289 704 134) for either beds in a simple dormitory close to the car park, or for a more comfortable villa lying among pines further within the park. Simple dorm beds (for up to thirty people) cost €5 per person, or are free if you volunteer to do a half day's work at the reserve. The villa sleeps up to eight people, with its own kitchen and TV (**⑤**), with two separate double rooms (**③**).

FUZETA

Around 10km east of Olhão, the fishing town of **FUZETA** (or Fuseta) consists of a straggle of backstreets on a low hill facing the lagoons, sheltered by the eastern extremity of Ilha da Armona. Its waterfront of modern shops and apartments, faces broad gardens largely taken over by the town's campsite. Beyond this lies a **river beach**, a fine bendy stretch of white sands weaving up to a wooden lifeboat house. In summer many people splash about in the calm waters of the river, though more exhilarating and cleaner waters can be had over the river at Praia da Fuzeta on the Ilha da Armona, reached by a regular ferry from the fishing quay behind the campsite.

Fuzeta is not the most beautiful town in the Algarve, but it does retain its character as a working fishing village. Indeed its daily routine revolves round the fishermen – whose colourful boats line up on the river alongside town – and, in summer, the campsite and its lively community of backpackers and campervanners. Much of the daily catch finds its way to the small covered **market** on Largo 1° de Maio, the road running parallel to the river; the quayside behind the building is often lined with drying octopus. On Saturdays the market expands into a weekly **flea market** that lines the adjacent Rua Tenente Barrosa. Continue up this road to reach the town's little palm tree-lined central **square** and the main shopping street, Rua da Liberdade.

Praia da Fuzeta

Regular **ferries** (April–October roughly every 15 minutes; Nov–March four daily; €1 return) shuttle from the fishing quay at the back of the campsite across the lagoon to **PRAIA DE FUZETA** on the eastern end of the Ilha da Armona (see p.106). The **beach** immediately opposite the ferry stop gets fairly crowded in high summer, but you only have to walk ten minutes or so either way from the holiday beach huts to have beautiful, low dune-backed sands all to yourself. If you're feeling energetic you could also walk the two hours up the beach to the western end of the island, where there are cafés and regular summer ferries to Olhão (see p.100).

Practicalities

Fuzeta is served by up to 18 **buses** daily from Olhão; buses pull up at the waterfront opposite the campsite. It is also on the main Faro to Vila Real **train** line; the station is ten-minutes' walk from the waterfront, at the northern end of Rua da Liberdade, the main shopping street.

Accommodation is limited in Fuzeta, although this has helped the town retain its character. The waterside **campsite**, *Parque de Campismo da Fuzeta* (☎289 793 459; €1.80/person, from €1.80/tent), is beautifully positioned under trees and has its own mini market, but it gets pretty chock-a-block in high summer. Otherwise options are limited to **rooms** in private houses, or the very basic *Pensão Liberdade*, on Rua da Liberdade 130 (☎289 793 297; ❷), which has seen better days, close to the train station. There is a mixed bag of rooms: the worst are gloomy dungeons with communal bathrooms (❶), the best larger with their own showers. The price does not include breakfast, but you get what you pay for and this certainly has rock-bottom rates.

Eating and drinking
The riverfront at the back of the campsite by the ferry stop is lined with **bars** and **cafés** in little wooden chalets (most close November–March).

Bar Beira Mar 18
Mon–Sat 7am–midnight.
Inexpensive
Opposite the ferry stop, this wooden shack with a few outdoor tables is where the fishermen enjoy their Super Bock beers from the early hours. Always lively and usually packed with locals.

Restaurante Caetano
Praia da Fuzeta, Ilha de Armona
Daily: May–Sept 9.30am–10pm; Oct–April 9.30am–5pm.
Moderate
Praia da Fuzeta's only restaurant; just by the ferry stop this is a friendly place with superb salads and well-priced fish and meat dishes. Also serves snacks on a small shady outdoor terrace.

Restaurante Skandinavia
Rua Tenente Barrosa 10
Mon & Wed–Sun

FUZETA

10am–midnight. Closed
Nov–March. **Moderate**
The best place for moderately
priced grilled meats and fish,
all prepared on a huge
barbecue by the front terrace.
It's on the road leading from
the main square to the
market.

Café das Taças
Rua da Liberdade 33
Daily 8am–midnight.
Inexpensive
In a great building with a
Moorish key hole-shaped door
and window, this characterful
place serves superb coffee and
big doughy croissants; outdoor
tables on the main street.

FUZETA

Praia de Faro

Grilled sardines

Tavira

Tiled stairway, Palácio de Estoi

Salt pans, Ria Formosa

Parade, Loulé

MATTHEW HANCOCK

Rio Guadiana

JOHN MILLER

Cork trees

The eastern Algarve

T he eastern Algarve has largely escaped the full-scale development suffered by the central swathe of the region, perhaps in part because of the relative inaccessibility of its most spectacular beaches, which lie offshore on the sandspit islands of **Ilha de Tavira** and **Praia de Cabanas**. The sandspits end at **Manta Rota**, though the impressive beaches continue from here right up to the Spanish border at **Monte Gordo**. The accessibility of these sands mean a corresponding level of development in an area that has always been popular with Spanish day-trippers.

This is perfect territory for those who want to spend some time on the sands, with pristine and relatively uncrowded beaches served by regular ferry services from **Tavira**, one of the Algarve's most attractive towns. Birdwatchers are drawn here too as the islands protect a system of lagoons forming part of the Parque Natural da Ria Formosa (see p.108). However, with no fewer than seven new golf courses in the pipeline, the eastern Algarve has plenty to offer those looking to combine the sun with some sport.

Away from the coast, the scenery around the **Serra de Alcaria** remains wildly beautiful, though the area has recently been put on the tourist map with a new golf course and mining theme park round **Vaqueiros**. Northeast of Monte Gordo, the beautiful **Rio Guadiana** marks the border with Spain and tour boats ply up from Vila Real to the picturesque village of **Alcoutim**.

The area covered by this chapter is shown in map 3, at the back of the book.

Tavira and around

Situated 30km east of Faro, **Tavira** is one of the most attractive towns in the Algarve and, with a wide range of accommodation and restaurants, makes the best base in the east. Its local beach is on the **Ilha de Tavira**, one of the most beautiful and extensive of the sandspit beaches that can be reached by ferry, or by toy train from the neighbouring holiday village of **Pedras d'el Rei**. A more traditional village lies even closer in the picturebook fishing port of **Santa Luzia**, a couple of kilometres to the west, rightly famed for its excellent seafood. In summer Tavira attracts a mixed bag of holidaying families and backpackers, while in autumn a sportier set moves in, attracted by the new **golf course** at nearby Benamor (see p.45). Tavira is well served by buses and also lies on the main Faro to Vila Real rail line.

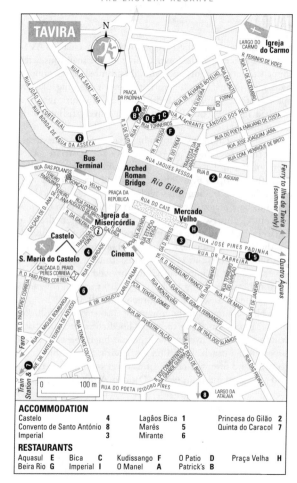

ACCOMMODATION

Castelo	**4**	Lagâos Bica	**1**	Princesa do Gilão	**2**
Convento de Santo António	**8**	Marés	**5**	Quinta do Caracol	**7**
Imperial	**3**	Mirante	**6**		

RESTAURANTS

Aquasul	**E**	Bica	**C**	Kudissango	**F**	O Patio	**D**	Praça Velha	**H**
Beira Rio	**G**	Imperial	**I**	O Manel	**A**	Patrick's	**B**		

۱RA

Set on both sides of the gently flowing Rio Gilão, **TAVI-RA** is a graceful little town of fine white mansions with hipped terracotta roofs and wrought-iron balconies, topped by a neat little castle. There is the inevitable ring of new apartments radiating outwards, but the old centre retains a decayed nobility complemented by the lively fishing trade along the riverfront.

The earliest remains – including parts of the pedestrianized bridge over the river – date from the **Roman** settlement of Balsa. The town's current name, however, derives from the Moorish title Tabira, and it was the **Moors** who established the trading links with North Africa that led the town to be a major commercial port until well into the seventeenth century. Tavira lost importance when the Rio Gilão began to silt up, and much of the town was flattened by the Great Earthquake of 1755. The graceful old town was rebuilt at the end of the eighteenth century, but Tavira never regained its importance and survived mainly as a centre for the tuna fishing trade (see p.120) until tourism took over as the main source of income in the 1970s.

Fishing continues to be important, however, and fish dinners at restaurants along the palm-lined river are a justifiable reason to stop. However, most people linger because of the superb island beach at the **Ilha de Tavira**. Ferries shuttle out to the island from the centre of town in summer (see p.126), and all year round from nearby **Quatro Águas** (see p.125).

Arrival and information

Most of Tavira's important buildings lie on the west bank of the Rio Gilão, though there are plenty of good restaurants and bars on the east bank. The **bus terminal** (☎281 322 546) is on the west side by the river just north of the centre, two minutes' walk to the pedestrianized bridge and the main square, Praça da República. In front of here lie the riverfront gardens leading up to the main road bridge and the old market building, now a cultural centre. Beyond, fishing boats line the riverfront up to a third bridge, a fly-over taking traffic east; for Quatro Águas, head under the flyover and follow the river.

The **train station** is 1km north of the Praça da Republica, straight up the Rua da Liberdade, at the end of Avenida Dr. Mateus Teixeira de Azevedo. Up the steps just off Praça da República is the **turismo**, at Rua da Galeria 9 (May–Oct Mon & Fri–Sun 9.30am–1pm & 2–6pm, Tues–Thurs 9.30am–7pm; Nov–April Mon–Fri 9.30am–1pm & 2–5pm; ☏ 281 322 511).

For access to the **internet**, head to *Café Bela Fria*, Rua das Polanos 1 (Mon–Sat 9am–11pm; €1/15min), opposite the bus station.

Accommodation

Tavira has relatively few upmarket hotels, but there are a fair smattering of inexpensive guesthouses. However, places are at a premium during the summer season; but the tourist office can also help with **private rooms**. The nearest **campsite** is on the Ilha de Tavira (see p.127).

Pensão do Castelo
Rua da Liberdade 22
☏ 281 320 790, ☏ 281 320 799
Rambling place, very centrally located, offering enormous clean rooms all with marble floors, TVs and bathrooms; front rooms can be noisy. Disabled access.

Rates drop out of season. ❸

Convento de Santo António
Rua de Santo António
☏ 281 321 573, ☏ 281 325 632
Book ahead (fax only) for one of the 7 double rooms, or the superior chapel room,

TAVIRA

in this elegant sixteenth-century convent with roof terrace. There's also a swimming pool and breakfast is served in the tranquil courtyard. Minimum stay of 4 nights in summer; 2 in winter. Closed Jan. ⑧

Residencial Imperial
Rua José Pires Padinha 24
Ⓣ & Ⓕ 281 322 234
Small *residencial* with attached restaurant; avoid the noisy street-facing rooms and ask for one of those overlooking the gardens and river. All rooms have TV and shower. ⑥

Residencial Lagâos Bica
Rua Almirante Cândido dos Reis 24
Ⓣ 281 322 252
Characterful place on the northside of the river with small, simple en-suite rooms clustered round a patio. There's also a communal roof terrace. Price does not include breakfast. ⑥

Residencial Marés
Rua José Pires Padinha 134–140
Ⓣ 281 325 815,

Ⓔ maresresidencial @mail.telepac.pt
Twenty-four superb rooms with air conditioning, TVs, *azulejos* and balconies over the river or old town. There's a great roof terrace and a communal sauna too. Rates drop in the winter. ⑤

Residencial Mirante
Rua da Liberdade 83
Ⓣ 281 322 255
This characterful town house with a faded tiled facade has large high-ceilinged rooms with their own bathrooms. Some of the rooms overlooking the street are a bit noisy. ⑥

Residencial Princesa do Gilão
Rua Borda d'Àgua de Aguiar 10–12
Ⓣ & Ⓕ 281 325 171
A modern, white building with *azulejo*-decorated interior, this friendly *residencial* stands right on the quayside. Rooms are tiny but have their own shower rooms and small balconies. Go for a room at the front with a balcony overlooking the river. ⑥

TAVIRA

Quinta do Caracol
℡ 281 322 475,
✉ quintacaracol@netc.pt
Set in lawned grounds north of the train station, this lovely farmhouse offers self-catering apartments sleeping 2–5 people in tastefully converted outbuildings. There are tennis courts, a tiny plunge pool, children's play area and bikes for rent. ❺

The castle and around

From the arcaded **Praça da República** by the river, it's a short climb up into the oldest part of town around the castle. Ahead of you stands the graceful, if weathered, facade of the **Igreja da Misericórdia**. Built between 1541 and 1551 by André Pilarte, the mason who worked on Belém's famous Jeronimos monastery in Lisbon, its once fine (now badly worn) carved stone doorway depicts a series of mermaids, angels and saints, including Peter and Paul, though the most visible carvings are a couple of lute-playing figures in the doorframe. Inside there's a striking *azulejo* interior showing scenes from the life of Christ, below a wooden vaulted ceiling.

From the Igreja da Misericórdia it's a couple of hundred metres up the cobbled Travessa da Fonte to the ruins of the **Castelo** (Mon–Fri 8am–5pm, Sat & Sun 9am–5.30pm; free), half hidden amid landscaped gardens on a low hill in the centre of town. There has been a fort here since Phoenician times, though the current structure dates back to the thirteenth century, and parts were rebuilt in the seventeenth century. From the walls you can look down over the curved terracotta rooftops and the town's many churches.

Adjacent to the castle, the whitewashed **Santa Maria do Castelo** is open daily. Built in the thirteenth century and restructured in the eighteenth century in Renaissance style, it contains the tomb of Dom Paio Peres Correia, who reconquered much of the Algarve from the Moors, includ-

TAVIRA

ing Tavira itself in 1242. Fittingly, the church stands on the site of the former mosque.

A toy train trundles from the main Rua da Liberdade up to the castle, along the riverfront and out to Quatro Águas (see p.125), every hour or so between 10am–9.30pm (until midnight in July and Aug) for €2 per person.

Along the riverfront

With its tranquil vistas and leafy, palm-lined gardens, the riverfront is the best part of Tavira for a wander. Gardens lined with cafés run from south of Praça da República as far

TUNA FISHING

Tuna (*atum*) was once the mainstay of the local fishing community and continues to be the speciality in many of Tavira's fish restaurants. The Moors were the first to take advantage of the large numbers of tuna, developing specially adapted fishing boats which used a combined netting system known as an *armação* (giving the name to the town of Armação de Pera; see p.179), which continued to be used until recently. During the nineteenth century, around forty of these boats would set off in a special formation designed to guide the giant fish – which can be up to three metres long – into the centre of the nets where they were harpooned by the fishermen. The best ever catch was in 1881, when 42,000 tuna were caught off the coast here. Nowadays, modern fishing techniques and dwindling tuna stocks have seen the town's importance as a tuna fishing centre decline and most fish is caught from Olhão, Portimão and Vila Real, which help supply some twenty percent of Portugal's total catch. With their more plentiful supply, sardines have overtaken tuna as the most important fish off the Algarve's coast.

as the **old market** (*mercado velho*) building, which has been converted into a "cultural and shopping centre" - actually a handful of small boutiques and appealing waterfront cafés. The old market walls are also used for temporary exhibitions, usually the works of local artists and photographers.

Beyond the market, fishing boats dock as far as the new flyover; along this stretch of river lie restaurants or more basic fishermen's bars, most of which serve up decent meals, generally involving big tuna steaks. Just before the flyover, **ferries** depart for the beach in high season (see p.126). Head under the bridge and you'll see the large new town **market** (Mon–Sat 8am–1.30pm), housed in a dull concrete box but still retaining a bustling interior filled with an array of vegetables and sea creatures of all shapes and sizes.

Eating

Tavira is generously endowed with **restaurants**, most of which serve decent food at moderate prices. Tuna is the local speciality, though for top quality seafood head out to the restaurants at Quatro Águas (see p.127) or to Santa Luzia (see p.128).

Aquasul
Rua Torneiros 11–13
Tues–Sat 7pm–midnight.
Closed Dec–Feb. **Moderate**
Brightly decorated French-run place with a limited but refreshing menu of healthy pastas and salads.

46–48
Daily 6pm–10pm. Closed
November. **Inexpensive**
This riverside bar-restaurant, with tree-shaded tables, is an attractive venue for pizza, pasta and salads, with a good range of vegetarian dishes.

Beira Rio
Rua Borda da Àgua de Assêca

Bica
Rua Almirante Cândido dos

TAVIRA

Reis 22–24

Daily noon–3pm & 7–10pm.
Inexpensive
Excellent-value meat, fish, *cataplanas* and omelettes, served with a TV for company. The tourist menu is a bargain at €7.50.

Imperial

Rua José Pires Padinha 22
Daily noon–3pm & 7–11pm.
Moderate
Just back from the riverside gardens and recently renovated, the *Imperial* is well known for clams and tuna.

Kudissango

Rua Dr Augusta da Silva Carvalho 8
Mon–Wed & Fri–Sun noon–2am, Thurs 7pm–2am. **Moderate**
Excellent spot to sample cuisine from Portugal's former colonies. There is a good range of vegetarian food, as well as the speciality, boiled mandioca fish with *escabeche* or *mufete*, an Angolan dish of boiled beans with palm oil and grilled fish.

O Manel

Rua Almirante Cândido dos

Reis 6

Mon & Wed–Sun 12.30–3pm & 6.30–11pm. **Moderate**
Decent if unexciting grill house specializing in *espetada de lombinho com camarão* (pork and shrimp kebabs).

O Patio

Rua Dr. António Cabreira 30
Mon–Sat 6–11.30pm. **Expensive**
Pricey French-influenced restaurant with formal service and an attractive summer roof terrace.

Patrick's

Rua Dr. António Cabreira 25–27
Mon–Sat 6pm–2am. Closed Nov. **Moderate**
Welcoming *adega*-style, English-run bar-restaurant. The speciality of the house is the mouthwatering *piri-piri* prawns; otherwise there's a daily menu that includes curries, and one vegetarian option. Full English breakfasts served until 3pm.

Marisqueira Praça Velha

Mercado Velho
Mon & Wed–Sun noon–3pm & 7–10pm. **Expensive**
One of the more classy new

places round the old market, serving tasty seafood and *cataplanas.* There is a neat little inside room along with pleasant outdoor tables spreading onto the square.

Drinking and nightlife

Tavira is not really king when it comes to nightlife, though north of the river, there is a series of lively bars and a disco. The town is better supplied with cafés, where you can get a decent *bica* or an *imperial* throughout the day.

Anazu
Rua Jacques Pessoa 11–13
Daily noon–10pm. Closed November
Large bar-restaurant on the riverfront – a good place for sunset.

Arco Bar
Rua Almirante Cândido dos Reis 67
Tues–Sun 10pm–2am
Unusually for the Algarve this is a gay-friendly place, attracting a laid-back crowd; great for those into retro music.

Bar Malfado
Rua Dr Augusta da Silva Carvalho 22
Mon–Sat midnight–3am
Late-night bar where, fuelled by inexpensive drinks, you can get down to African and Brazilian sounds till 3am.

Ref' Café
Rua Gonçalo Velho 23
Thurs–Sun 9pm–3am
Jazzy bar serving potent cocktails and catchy sounds to a largely local clientele.

Ribeirinha
Mercado Velho
Mon–Wed & Fri–Sun 9am–9pm
One of the livelier cafés on the river side of the old market building, serving drinks and snacks.

Tavirense
Rua Marcelino Franco 19
Daily 8am–midnight
Big, old-fashioned, *azulejo*-lined *pastelaria* opposite the

TAVIRA

cinema, serving great breakfasts, cakes and pastries.

UBI

Rua Almirante Cândido dos Reis

May–Sept Tues–Sun midnight–6am; Oct–April Fri and Sat only

On the eastern outskirts of town, Tavira's only disco is housed in a huge, metallic warehouse and plays a mix of house, Latin and techno grooves; the locals warm up with a few pre-clubbing drinks in the *Bubi Bar* in the same building (open from 10pm).

Café Veneza

Praça da República 11

Daily 8am–midnight. Closed Nov

Old-style café with tables spilling onto the main square; this is where the locals read their papers and sip their bedtime coffees.

AROUND TAVIRA

South and east of Tavira lie the flat, open marshlands of the Parque Natural da Ria Formosa. Due south along the Rio Gilão valley it is a short ride – past the distinctive salt basins – to **Quatro Àguas**, where the river meets the sea. The shore here is sheltered by the offshore sandspit of **Ilha de Tavira**, with one of the best beaches in the Algarve – large enough to absorb the crowds even in high summer.

You can also reach the Ilha de Tavira from the holiday village of **Pedras d'el Rei** just east of Tavira. Here, a year-round toy train ferries passengers across the marshland to another part of the beach at **Barril**. On the way to Pedras d'el Rei, you'll pass the palm-lined riverfront of **Santa Luzia**, a charming fishing village with a row of neat fish restaurants.

Rent-a-Bike, at Rua do Forno 22 (☎ 281 321 973,
@ exploratio@hotmail.com), on the north side of the river in
Tavira rents bikes and organizes cycling tours to the nature
reserve of Ria Formosa and the countryside around Tavira.

Quatro Àguas and Ilha de Tavira

Quatro Àguas is little more than a huddle of cafés and
restaurants next to the ferry terminal, though it's a pleasant
place to stop for a coffee and admire the views. You'll want
to spend most of your time, however, on the fantastic
beaches on the **Ilha de Tavira** opposite. The island
stretches southwest from Tavira almost as far as Fuzeta,

SALT EXTRACTION

Between Tavira and the Ilha de Tavira you will see large, rectangular basins cut into the marshy soil. These are **salinas**,
salt extraction plants, which cover nearly one hundred square
kilometres of land around Tavira and Ludo, Olhão and Fuzeta
and supply Portugal with fifty percent of its salt. The system
used today is similar to that used in Roman times, with the sun
and the tides the only forms of energy required to transform
brackish water into high-quality salt. The basins are designed
so that salt water flows from one to another, with evaporation
increasing the salinity of the water until the last basin, where
the salt crystallizes at the bottom. Despite the industrial look of
the rod-straight basins, their shallow waters act as a useful
source of food for migrating birds. In some places, the *salinas*
have been converted into fish farms used to breed gilthead,
bass, sole, seabream, eel and cockles.

AROUND TAVIRA

some 14km away. For most of its length, the landward side of the island is a dank morass of mud flat, but at the eastern tip the mud gives way to an expanse of sand and sea. The beach is enormous, backed by tufted dunes, and its growing popularity has led to a certain amount of development. At the end of the main path, which runs from the jetty through a small chalet settlement, there are water sports facilities, beach umbrellas and loungers, and half a dozen bar-restaurants. Rather than spoiling things, however, this has fostered something of a good-time feel at the beach.

You can walk west up the beach for around 3km to the beachside café-restaurant at Barril. From here a toy train takes you back to the mainland at Pedras d'el Rei, where you can get a bus back to Tavira.

In July and August the crowds can get overwhelming around the cafés, but you can always walk west to escape the crowds. Here you'll find nudism pretty much the norm, though if you're around out of season you'll probably have the place entirely to yourself. Alternatively, pick up an attractive path heading west from the ferry stop, parallel to the coast alongside picnic tables dotted under fragrant pines.

Practicalities

Buses (July to mid-Sept Mon–Fri roughly hourly from 7.50am, last back 7.45pm) leave from the bus station in Tavira, for the ten-minute trip to the jetty at Quatro Àguas. You could also choose to walk the half-hour from town (along the river, past the old market, and just keep going), or get a taxi.

From July to mid-September, **ferries** from Tavira to the island depart roughly hourly from the quayside near the fly-over (daily 8am–7.30pm, last return 8pm; €1 return). At other times of the year you have to pick up a ferry from Quatro Àguas, 2km east of town. The ferries from Quatro Àguas to the island (every 15min: June 8am–10pm; July & Aug 8am–midnight; April, May & Sept 8am–9pm; roughly hourly: Oct–March 9am–dusk; €0.75 return) take just five minutes – out of season, check with the ferryman what time the last boat returns.

Most visitors to the island base themselves in Tavira, but if you want to stay, the **campsite** on the *ilha* (T 281 324 455; April to mid-Oct), set under trees a minute from the sands and with a well-stocked mini market, draws a youthful crowd. There's a kids' play area and ATM too, and it all gets very full in July and August.

Despite Portugal's forward-thinking attitude to drugs (see p.51), some of the cafés on the island have been in trouble with the police for an over-tolerant attitude to drug-taking. Any blatant use of drugs is a bad idea and can get both yourself and the cafés into trouble.

There are half a dozen **cafés and bars** serving slightly pricey drinks and meals on the island itself, the best bet is the *Sunshine Bar* (daily: July–Sept 9am–11.30pm; April–June & Oct 9am–10am; rest of year in good weather only), an Irish-Portuguese-run café serving tasty tuna steak, sardines, full breakfast plus vegetarian options. World music and jazzy sounds accompany the beach views. There are also a couple of fine if expensive **restaurants** by the ferry terminal in Quatro Águas; the more famous of the two is *Restaurante Quatro Águas* (Tues–Sun noon–3pm & 7–10pm), which is a highly rated seafood restaurant specializing in dishes such as *açorda* and *cataplana de marisco* (seafood stews) and *bife de frango com molho roquefort* (chicken with roquefort sauce). Also serving good quality fish and seafood, at moderate prices, is *Portas do Mar* (Mon &

AROUND TAVIRA

Wed–Sun 12.30–3pm & 6.30–10.30pm), which has a little terrace facing the waters.

Santa Luzia

West along the coastal road from Tavira is **SANTA LUZIA**, a small fishing village with a growing number of seafood restaurants catering to day-trippers attracted by its palm-lined waterfront and small but lively fishing harbour. Having admired the octopus traps on the jetty and the bright whitewashed buildings, most people settle for a leisurely meal. In summer, however, (usually Tues and Thurs), it's worth enquiring at Safari Boats (☎933 683 237, ⓔsafariboat@clix.pt), who run **river trips** up the Ria Formosa from just east of the fishing jetty. Most trips last for two or three hours and pass wading and seabirds with stop-offs for swimming at quiet beaches. Advance bookings are essential for the trips to Tavira, Ilha de Tavira, and sometimes up to Cacela Velha.

Accommodation in Santa Luzia is limited to private villas or rooms; look around for signs advertising *quartos* if you want to stay. Ten weekday **buses** (three on Sat) make the 3km run from Tavira, some of the buses continuing on to Pedras d'el Rei (see p.129). The waterfront is the spot to head for **restaurants**; the best place for moderately priced seafood is *Baixa Mar* (Tues–Sat 12.15–2.30pm & 7–9.30pm, Sun 12.15–2.30pm), right opposite the jetty. Octopus is the local speciality, served with rice or as *bicha de polvo e camarão na grelha* (octopus and prawn kebab). Just east of *Baixa Mar*, with a spacious, *azulejo*-lined interior and an outdoor terrace, *Marisqueira Capelo* (Mon–Tues & Thurs–Sun noon–2am) is a tad more upmarket (and pricey), with a long menu of well-prepared fish and seafood.

Pedras d'el Rei and Praia de Barril

A further kilometre west from Santa Luzia, 4km west of Tavira lies **PEDRAS D'EL REI**, served by six buses daily from Tavira's bus station (Mon–Fri only). Most of Pedras d'El Rei consists of a fairly upmarket holiday complex, but it also offers access to another stretch of the Ilha da Tavira at Barril.

Four kilometres northwest of Pedras d'El Rei, on the main Tavira to Olhão road, the church at Luz de Tavira boasts a superb Manueline door, one of the best in the region.

From the bus stop next to Pedras D'El Rei, cross the causeway to the terminal of a rather ancient-looking black and red **miniature train** (daily, except in bad weather, 8am–dusk, roughly every 30min; €0.80 single). This shuttles across the mud flats - sending thousands of fiddler crabs scuttling about - to the beach of **BARRIL** on the Ilha de Tavira. A few minutes' walk right or left of the terminus and there are miles of beautiful, peaceful, dune-fringed beach. Take your own food and drink, though, since the relative isolation means high prices in the couple of café-bars around the train stop.

The only **accommodation** is the tasteful holiday apartments and larger villas at *Pedras d'El Rei* (⊕ 281 380 600, ⓔ pedrasdelrei@mail.telepac.pt; ❺), on a leafy hillock above the waterfront. All accommodation has its own balcony or terrace, and the village has a pool, shop, restaurant, tennis courts and children's club.

The minor EN397 winding north of Tavira to Cachopo is a highly picturesque road across the Serra de Alcaria, linking with the inland route described on p.150.

AROUND TAVIRA

East to Monte Gordo

Six kilometres east of Tavira - past the new golf course at Benamor (see p.45) - lies **Cabanas**, another erstwhile fishing village which is developing into a resort in its own right thanks to its excellent sandspit beach, the Praia de Cabanas. This spit can also be reached from Fabrica further east (see p.133), below **Cacela Velha**, (not to be confused with Vila Nova de Cacela, 2km inland), one of the prettiest villages in the Algarve and, for the time being at least, barely touched by tourism.

Beyond Cacela Velha, the sandspit starts to thin out, merging with the shoreline beach at Manta Rota, 12km away. Predictably **Manta Rota** and **Altura** have both been heavily developed, although the beaches at both the resorts are splendid, if rather crowded in summer; there are more alluring sandy stops at **Praia Verde** and **Monte Gordo**, the latter a lively resort and the last beach stop before the border.

CABANAS

CABANAS is a long line of fairly nondescript, low-rise shops, cafés and bars facing the river estuary. Moored fishing boats testify to the village's former mainstay, though nowadays the economy is largely driven by tourism thanks to the glorious sands on **Praia de Cabanas** over the estuary, and a series of hotel complexes are scattered around the outskirts of the town.

Cabanas' other attraction is the **Quinta Alegre**, or the Happy Farm (Mon–Sat 10am–dusk, Sun 2pm–dusk; adults €5, children €2.50), reached by going through the Golden Club west of the town. What was once an ostrich farm has become a substantial theme park, ideal for kids of any age, complete with a mini zoo, donkey rides, crazy golf, bumper cars and Portugal's largest bouncy castle.

Practicalities

Eight weekday **buses** (2 on Sat) run from Tavira to Cabanas (which is just 1km south of Conceição on the Tavira to Vila Real **railway** line), pulling up at the west end of the waterfront. There is no tourist office in Cabanas but you can access the **internet** at *@Benson's* on Rua Jornal Povo Algarvia 16b, one block back from the front (Mon, Tues & Thurs–Sat 10am–2pm & 5–8pm).

To reach the beach, there are two ferry services, one from the east of town, the other from the west. Ten minutes' walk east of the bus stop, **ferries** shuttle passengers to the beach every fifteen minutes or so (May–Sept only; €1 return). Five minutes' walk west of the main riverfront, an all-year ferry service is also operated by the Golden Club resort (May–Sept daily every 15min; Oct-April 4 daily; €0.80 return, free to hotel guests).

Accommodation

Accommodation options are mainly limited to apartments and villas, although you can always ask at bars and cafés for private **rooms**. *Pastelaria Jerónimos*, opposite the eastern ferry jetty on Avenida 28 de Maio (℡281 370 649; ❹) rents out decent apartments with sea-facing balconies, while on the sloping main road into town, *Pedras da Rainha* (℡281 370 181, ✉pedrasrainha@mail.telepac.pt; ❺), has apartments and villas (sleeping up to ten) clustered round pleasant lawns, tennis courts and a large pool, all with disabled access. Just to the west of town is the *Golden Hotel* (℡281 370 972, ✉goldenreservas@mail.telepac.pt; ❹), part of the Golden Club resort, a large tourist complex with apartments in and around a central hotel block. There's a

CABANAS

pool and entertainment programme but the grounds are spoilt by on-going development.

Eating and drinking

Cabanas has a high number of **cafés**, **bars** and **restaurants** spreading along the riverfront and a block or two inland. A good bet opposite the main bus stop, is *Cobacabana* (April–Oct daily noon–11pm), a smart place on two floors with a sprawling menu featuring pizzas, burgers and average-priced Portuguese staples. The upper floor has fine views over the water. Right opposite is *Quasimodo* (daily 8pm–2am), a low-ceilinged bar specializing in loud music and cocktails, with "no coffee" as a warning sign. A little further east, by the eastern ferry stop at Avenida 28 de Maio, is the *Restaurante A Rocha* (April–Oct daily 12.30–3pm & 7–10pm), an attractive place with a breezy terrace where you can enjoy mid-priced omelettes, salads and fresh fish.

CACELA VELHA

Ten kilometres east from Tavira, **CACELA VELHA** is a tiny whitewashed village perched on a rocky bluff overlooking the sea. Surrounded by olive groves, and home to an old church and the remains of an eighteenth-century fort, it is spectacularly pretty – a reminder of how the Algarve must have looked half a century ago. Get there while you can, as the idyllic nature of the village looks set to change with the planned construction of two golf courses, a luxury hotel and a tourist complex on the green fields immediately to the east. To get here, you need to get the Tavira–Vila Real **bus** to set you down on the highway, just before Vila Nova de Cacela, from where it's a fifteen-minute walk down a signposted side road to the village.

Naturally enough, the hamlet is short on facilities, but it has a little restaurant and a couple of **cafés** where you can ask about private **rooms**, though these are snapped up quickly in the summer.

The **beach** below the village, a continuation of Praia de Cabanas, is a delight. To get to it, follow signs to **Fabrica**,

GOLF AND THE ENVIRONMENT

The success of the purpose-built **golf** resorts such as Vilamoura and Vale do Lobo in the central Algarve have persuaded the authorities that golf courses are the perfect way to lure more visitors to the region. Projects underway are set to increase the number of golf courses by over fifty percent, no doubt with the inevitable entourage of luxury hotels, villas and pools. The advantages are clear: such developments are great for the economy, while the pro-golf lobby argue that the courses offer areas of wilderness and lakes that are ideal for wildlife. The upmarket, leafy surroundings are also less intensive than large-scale package tourist development. The new course at Vaqueiros (see p.151), for example, looks likely to breathe new life into a largely barren area.

Environmentalists, however, are worried. More water is used to green a golf course than to supply an entire town, and overuse of bore holes can lead to salination and contamination of drinking supplies. Although some courses use recycled water for irrigation, the fertilisers and pesticides used to keep the greens weed free are environmentally harmful. In addition, the traditional, relatively environmentally sensitive mixed agricultural system risks being abandoned if land can be sold off to lucrative golf developers. The area under greatest threat is the Parque Natural da Ria Formosa. The new courses planned for Cacela Velha, for example, lie close to highly sensitive bird sanctuaries.

CACELA VELHA

just west of the village, around a kilometre downhill. Here a ferry man can take you over to the beach for around €1 return; daily in summer but only during good weather the rest of the year. Fabrica also has a couple of good **restaurants**, best of which is *O Costa* (May–Sept daily noon–3pm & 7–11pm), serving moderately priced fish and grilled meats on a broad terrace facing the waters.

MANTA ROTA

MANTA ROTA, 2km further east from Cacela Velha along the coast, is the first place east of Tavira where the beach is accessible by land. And it's a superb, wide stretch of beach too, though the village that backs it is a characterless splodge of villas and modern apartments. If you want to stay, ask around for **private rooms**. Eating options are more encouraging: *Praia Mar* (daily: May–Sept 9am–9pm; Oct–April 9am–5pm) is the best-positioned beachside **café**, with a large outdoor terrace, decent bar snacks and drinks. For a **full meal**, *Restaurante Restinga* (April–Oct daily noon–10pm), is a better bet for Portuguese staples, well prepared and decently priced, in an attractive building just back from the beach with an outdoor terrace.

From Manta Rota you can **walk** along the beach all the way to the eastern edge of Portugal: from Manta Rota it's around thirty minutes to Alagoas, another twenty minutes to Praia Verde, and forty more on to Monte Gordo.

There are no direct **buses** to Manta Rota from Tavira; the only services are from Vila Real (or Monte Gordo). Alternatively, ask to be let off any bus from Tavira to Vila Real at the Manta Rota turning on the highway, and walk the 2km down the side road.

ALTURA AND PRAIA DE ALAGOAS

Three kilometres or so east of Manta Rota, **ALTURA** is a large modern resort spreading inland from another fine beach, **Praia de Alagoas**. Here, there's a line of beach umbrellas, bars and water sports on hand, along with the high-rise *Eurotel Altura* **hotel** (☏281 956 450, ☏281 956 371; ❻), a towering three-star which dominates the beach-front. Views from the top-floor rooms are stunning, and with 135 large rooms you can usually find space here. Rooms have disabled access and come with bath, TV and minibar and there's also an inside and outside pool, games room and tennis courts. Rates more than halve in low season.

If you're in the mood for a splurge, try the *Bate que eu Abre* in Urbanizição Rota do Sul (☏281 956 656; Mon, Tues & Thurs–Sun 12.30–3pm & 7.30–11pm), a highly rated if pricey **restaurant** tucked away in a residential part of Altura. Dishes include meat fondue, *feijoada* and *bacalhau*. There is no shortage of less expensive restaurants and **cafés** around the seafront. The best-positioned of these is *Restaurante das Mares* (May–Sept Mon & Wed–Sun 10am–3pm & 7–11pm; Oct–April 10am–3pm), serving moderately priced seafood, salads and omelettes right on the sands.

PRAIA VERDE

It's another 4km along the main road from Altura to the point on the hillside directly above the sands at **PRAIA VERDE**. Despite the densely packed cubes that make up the *Real Village* holiday complex on the wooded hill above, this remains the least-developed beach along this stretch, with just a couple of seasonal **beach cafés** and one **restaurant**, *Pezinhos* (Feb–Nov daily 10am–2am), selling slightly overpriced snacks and grills in a superb position right on the unspoilt sands.

The walk to or from Praia Verde's car park, at the top of the hill, will reward you with a splendid panoramic view from the lookout at the top. Further east, towards Monte Gordo, the beach becomes more unkempt, backed by scrubby dunes, but the sands are much less likely to be crowded in summer.

There are no **buses** to Praia Verde; if you're relying on public transport catch any bus going to Vila Real and get off on the highway and walk down the side road.

MONTE GORDO

MONTE GORDO is the last resort before the Spanish border and the most built-up of the eastern holiday towns. It is unashamedly high-rise, with new buildings still shooting up from the ground either side of the seafront casino. But though its name – which means "fat mountain" – is appropriately ungainly, the high-rises are relatively set back from the beach and the seafront road is partly pedestrianized. The **beach**, popular with Spanish day-trippers, is wonderfully broad, scattered with a café-restaurants offering studiously similar menus and inflated prices. There are also water sports and hot and cold showers.

Walkers can head east up the beach to the mouth of the Rio Guadiana, from where you can stand at the most southwesterly point of Portugal and peer over the border into Spain.

Practicalities

Buses from Vila Real and Tavira pull up on Rua Pedro Álvares Cabral, by the parish church. From here it is a short walk down the main Avenida Vasco de Gama to the seafront and the casino. Just east of the casino is the **turismo** (May–Sept Mon–Fri 9.30am–7pm; Oct–April 9.30am–1pm & 2–5.30pm; ⓣ281 544 495), which can hand out town maps and give details of **private rooms**. These are also advertised at various bars in town. Out of season, it's also worth checking on discounts at the hotels with the turismo. Monte Gordo is the site of the last – and largest – **campsite** on this stretch (ⓣ281 510 970, ⓕ281 511 932; €2.50/person, from €2/tent), a huge place set under pines out on the Vila Real road, a short walk from the beach.

ACCOMMODATION

Pensão Monte Gordo
Avda Infante Dom Henrique
ⓣ281 542 124, ⓕ281 542 570
Set back from the main drag just west of the casino, this pleasant modern *pensão* offers large rooms with their own showers. ❹, rooms with sea-facing balconies ❺.

Hotel Vasco da Gama
Avda Infante Dom Henrique
ⓣ281 510 900,
ⓔvagamahotel@mail.telepac.pt
If you want to stay on the beach, then this high-rise is your best bet; a nice place with balconies in some rooms, tennis courts, kids' play areas, bar and restaurant. All rooms have TVs and en-suite bathrooms ❻, or rooms with sea-facing balconies ❼.

EATING AND DRINKING

Restaurante O Firmo
Daily noon–9pm. **Moderate**
On the beach in front of the casino, this laid-back restaurant offers slightly pricey grills and salads, but its terrace can't be faulted.

Restaurante do Jaime
Daily 9am–7pm. **Inexpensive**
Simple beach café-restaurant facing the jumble of fishing boats west of the casino. The Portuguese food is nothing

MONTE GORDO

special but the prices are good.

Restaurante Mota
Daily 10am–10pm. **Moderate**
Just east of the casino right on the sands, this is the best place to eat on the front, a big place specializing in *cataplanas*, *arroz* dishes, *feijoada* and seafood.

Along the Guadiana and into the Serra de Alcaria

The broad **Rio Guadiana** marks the Algarve's eastern border with Spain. Until the 1990s, the main route from the Algarve into Spain was via **Vila Real**, a historic border town which marks the end of the trans-Algarve railway line. Then, all train, car or bus passengers had to hop onto a ferry to **Ayamonte** over the river for onward connections. The ferry remains the most fun way of visiting Spain, but nowadays a modern road bridge to the north whisks cars and buses straight over the permanently open border.

North of Vila Real, **Castro Marim**'s historical role as a frontier town is still evident in its two spectacular forts, while further border fortifications are also evident at the picturesque town of **Alcoutim**, 40km to the north. The minor road hugging the river valley in between these two towns is a delight, while spectacular mountain scenery can be enjoyed inland from Alcoutim across the wild **Serra de Alcaria**, where virtually the only form of development is near **Vaqueiros**, with a brand new golf course and a mining village theme park, **A Corvo dos Mouros**.

ALMOND BLOSSOM

The blossoming of the almond trees in late January and February have become one of Portugal's most famous sights. The blossom is known as the Snow of the Algarve after the legend of a Moorish king, who fell in love with and married a Swedish girl. But the girl grew gradually more depressed with the passing of each snow-free winter in the sunny Algarve. The king duly imported hundreds of almond trees and planted them round the land. The following winter, the king proudly pointed to the white almond blossom, declaring "Look, the snow of the Algarve", and they lived happily ever after. Today the almond tree continues to supply many of the Algarve's delicacies, including salted almonds and marzipan.

VILA REAL

The border town and harbour of **VILA REAL DE SANTO ANTÓNIO** has suffered a marked change in character since the completion of the bridge across the Rio Guadiana in the early 1990s, 4km to the north of town. Fewer cars and tourists now clog the streets in summer since anyone bound for Spain can now bypass the town and drive (or catch a bus, see p.144) straight there. You may want to call in anyway, not least because, once past the modern suburbs, it's one of the more architecturally interesting towns on the Algarve. The original settlement was demolished by a tidal wave at the beginning of the seventeenth century, and the site stood empty until it was revived in 1774 by the Marquês de Pombal. Eager to apply the latest concepts of town planning, Pombal used the same techniques he had already pioneered in the Baixa quarter of Lisbon and rebuilt Vila Real on a **grid plan**. The whole project only took five months – a remarkable achievement,

VILA REAL DE SANTO ANTÓNIO

RUA DE AYAMONTE

Train Station, Faro & Castro Marim

Bus Stop

Ferries to Ayamonte

RUA DR. MANUEL ARRIAGA

RUA JOSÉ BARÃO

AVENIDA DA REPÚBLICA

RUA CÂNDIDO DOS REIS

RUA DR DE SOUSA MARTINS

RUA A. CAPA

RUA DA PRINCESA

Rio Guadiana

RUA C.F. RAMIREZ

❶

Marina

❷ Ⓐ

RUA TEÓFILO BRAGA

Ⓑ ⓘ Ⓒ

Centro Cultural

Ⓔ António Aleixo

PR. MARQUÊS DE POMBAL

Ⓓ

RUA 5 DE OUTUBRO

N

RUA 1 DE MAIO

❸

RUA GENERAL HUMBERTO DELGADO

RUA DO BRAZIL

0   50 m

R. C. DA GRANDE GUERRA   Monte Gordo

ACCOMMODATION

Felix	1
Guadiana	2
Youth hostel	3

CAFÉS & RESTAURANTS

Os Arcos	A
Arenilha	E
Cantinho do Marquês	C
Caves do Guadiana	D
O Coração da Cidade	B

but a startling waste of resources, as it transpired that the hewn stone that Pombal had dragged all the way from Lisbon could have been quarried a couple of miles up the road.

Arrival and information

Vila Real is the eastern terminal of the Algarve railway, and **trains** pull up at the station five minutes' walk north; turn left out of the station to get to the riverfront. **Buses** (℡281 511 807) stop right on the riverfront itself or at the terminus just north of the train station. The **turismo** (Mon–Fri 9.30am–1pm & 2–5.30pm; ℡281 542 100) is situated in a corner of the old market building just north of the main square on Rua Teófilo Braga, the pedestrianized drag leading inland from the riverfront Avenida da República.

Accommodation

If you're heading on to Spain (or elsewhere in Portugal come to that), you really shouldn't need to stay, though the town makes a reasonable base from which to explore Castro Marim or Ayamonte. West of the bus terminal, at Rua Dr. Manuel Arriaga 2, the eager-to-please owners of *Residência Felix* (℡281 543 791; ❶) oversee basic little rooms with wooden floors and a clean communal bathroom; price does not include breakfast. Two blocks south, overlooking the river on the Avenida da Republica, the *Hotel Guadiana* (℡281 511 482, ℻281 511 478; ❺), is a national monument, with a grand exterior and fine Art Deco touches, including a fine dining room. Sadly the high-ceilinged rooms are showing their age, and despite the TVs and en-suite bathrooms, they fail to live up to the promise of the communal areas. For tighter budgets, the town's **youth hostel**, at Rua Dr. Sousa Martins 40 (℡ & ℻281 544 565; reception closed noon–6pm; open all year), is a characterful if cramped place set in an old town house. The pleasant communal areas include a bar, and there are a handful of doubles and twins (from €19) and various dorms of three, four or six beds (from €8.50).

The Town

The grid focuses on the handsome central square, ringed by orange trees and low, white buildings, a couple of wl pleasant outdoor cafés. Just north of the square Teófilo Braga, the old market building has been the **Centro Cultural António Aleixo** (10am–1pm & 3pm–7pm; free), an innovative spac

BOAT TRIPS UP THE GUADIANA

Various companies offer day **cruises** up the Guadiana departing from Vila Real harbour. Some go as far as Alcoutim (see
p.148), around 40km away, others to Foz de Odeleite, around
half that distance. Either trip is idyllic, passing through rolling
countryside. Prices start at around €40 per person, which
includes lunch and sometimes swimming stops. Try Turismar
(℡281 513 504) who sell tickets at the Ayamonte ferry ticket
office; Rio Sul, Rua Tristão Vaz Teixeira, Monte Gordo (℡281
510 200); Transguadiana, Rua Diogo Cão, Monte Gordo
(℡281 512 997); or Mega Tur, Rua Conselheiro Bivar 80, Faro
(℡289 808 489).

temporary exhibits, installations and occasionally even films.
The centre also embraces the **Museu de Manuel Cabanas**,
displaying the works of a local painter and wood engraver.

The surrounding streets have a certain low-key charm,
bristling with linen shops, electrical retailers and grocers
catering to the Spanish day-trippers who filter over the
border. Head down, too, to the riverside **gardens**, where
there are several cafés and fine views across the marina to
the splash of white that is Ayamonte in Spain.

Eating and drinking

There's a line of half a dozen similarly priced **places to eat**
along the riverfront Avenida da República, all with outdoor
seats overlooking the river. There are also a couple of
worthwhile points of call in and around the central Praça
Marquês de Pombal.

Os Arcos
Avda da República 45
Tues–Sun 12.30–3pm &

7.30–11pm. **Inexpensive**
South of the main square, this
neighbourhood restaurant

serves reliable, if unspectacular, Portuguese nosh.

Churrasqueira Arenilha

Rua Cândido dos Reis

Daily noon–3pm & 7–11pm.

Inexpensive

Opposite the market building, the attractive interior is lined with old black-and-white photos of Vila Real. The Portuguese food is nothing special but prices are low and the atmosphere bustling.

Café Cantinho de Marquês

Praça Marquês de Pombal

Mon–Sat 8am–11pm

Busy café with tables spilling out onto the main square under fragrant orange trees. The perfect drink stop.

Restaurante Caves do Guadiana

Avda da República 90

Mon–Wed & Fri–Sun noon–3pm & 7–10pm. **Moderate–expensive**

This has long been considered the best restaurant in town. It's got a nice tiled, vaulted interior and offers a long list of fish, grilled meats and omelettes.

O Coração da Cidade

Rua Dr Teófilo Braga

Daily 7.30am–10pm. **Moderate**

On the corner of Rua Almirante Cândido dos Reis, just north of the market building, this all-purpose café-restaurant sells everything from snacks and drinks to full meals. Always lively downstairs, though the upstairs restaurant can be too quiet.

INTO SPAIN: AYAMONTE

A fun half-day's excursion is to take the ferry over to **Ayamonte** in Spain (every 40mins from 9am, last return 7pm, which is 8pm Spanish time; €1 each way). The crossing takes twenty minutes, a lovely ride across the Guadiana with the forts of Castro Marim visible to the west and the impressive bridge to the north.

PUBLIC TRANSPORT CONNECTIONS TO SPAIN

Two daily buses (9.10am & 5.15pm) run from Vila Real across the bridge to Ayamonte in Spain (15min), continuing on to Huelva for connections to Sevilla; the total journey takes around four hours. Coming from Spain, two similarly timed services from Ayamonte run through Vila Real and on to Tavira and Faro. There are timetables posted at the bus terminus in Vila Real. Remember that Spanish time is one hour ahead of Portuguese.

Ferries stop at Ayamonte's dull waterfront, but head 200m or so inland to **Plaza de la Laguna** and you will quickly realize you are in Spain: it's a delightful palm-lined square with bright, Moorish-influenced tiled benches. Here, *Passage Café* (Mon–Sat 8am–4.30pm) serves *café con leche* and tasty cakes at tables out on the square. Just south of the square is the town's handsome church, **Parroquia de las Angustias**, around which is a warren of characterful backstreets, the **shops** seeming spruce and upmarket in comparison with Vila Real.

South of the church is another square, the long palm-fringed **Plaza de la Ribeira**, adjacent to some small docks and surrounded by inexpensive cafés and **tapas bars**. Ayamonte's sleepy **turismo**, Avenida Ramón y Cajal (Mon–Sat 9am–2pm; ☎959 47 09 87), can provide a town map and information, along with details of places to stay. Buses to Huelva and Sevilla (see above) leave from the **bus station** on Avenida de Andalucía east of the centre.

CASTRO MARIM AND AROUND

The little village of **CASTRO MARIM**, tucked away 5km north of Vila Real, was once a key fortification protecting Portugal's southern coast. Castro Marim was the first headquarters for the Order of Christ, who were

THE ORDER OF CHRIST

The **Order of Christ** was a chivalric order set up in Portugal under Dom Dinis in 1320, a clever move by the king after the Order's predecessors, the Knights Templars – a Christian militia that had helped drive the Moors out of Iberia – were banned by the Pope because their power was seen as a threat to the Church and the monarchy. The new Order of Christ was allowed to exist on condition that the knights pledged allegiance to the throne.

At the time, much of Portugal was sparsely populated, the majority of its land some distance from the capital. In order to police these areas, the monarchy handed much of the land to powerful groups: noblemen, the Church and the Order of Christ, who established their southern base at Castro Marim.

As Portugal's frontiers stabilized, the knights were able to embark on overseas exploration, which were seen as a new form of crusade, a way to reach more people to convert to Christianity. In 1417, Infante Henriques (Henry the Navigator) became the Grand Master of the Order of Christ, and used much of its wealth to develop a School of Navigation at Sagres (see p.268). The techniques the school developed allowed Portugal's mariners to open up the world. One of the Order of Christ's knights, Bartolomeu Dias, became the first European to sail round the tip of southern Africa in 1488. By 1494, when Dom Manuel was Grand Master, Spain and Portugal had control of most of the world's trade routes, and the cross representing the Order of Christ became a prominent symbol in Manueline architecture (see p.216). Though the order was secularized in 1789, it was only officially dissolved with the birth of the Republic in 1910.

based at a huge **castle** (daily: April–Oct 9am–7pm; Nov–March 9am–5pm; free), built by Afonso III in the thirteenth century and rebuilt during the War of Restoration in 1640. The massive ruins are all that survived the Great Earthquake of 1755, but it's a pretty place with fine views across the mud flats of the Reserva Natural do Sapal and the impressive modern suspension bridge to Spain. A small **museum** inside the castle walls (daily: May–Oct 10am–1pm & 3–6pm; Nov–April 10am–5pm; free) displays local archaeological, ethnographical and geographical exhibits, including ceramics and carpets.

Reserva Natural do Sapal

The marshy area around Castro Marim either side of the EN122, down to Vila Real in the south and up to the Spanish border to the east, has been designated a nature reserve – the **Reserva Natural do Sapal**. The reserve office inside Castro Marim castle can give out maps with walking routes through the reserve (Mon–Fri 9am–12.30pm & 2–5.30pm; ☏281 531 141). One of the area's most unusual and elusive inhabitants is the extraordinary, ten-centimetre-long, swivel-eyed, opposing-toed, Mediterranean **chameleon** – a harmless, slow-moving creature that's severely threatened elsewhere by habitat destruction.

Practicalities

Buses to Castro Marim from Vila Real (several daily weekly and two at weekends) pull up near the tourist office on the main Rua de São Sebastião. The **turismo** is at the eastern end of the *Rua* next to a tiny square, Praça 1º de Maio (Mon–Fri 9.30am–1pm & 2–5.30pm; ☏281 531 232), just below the castle.

Rua de São Sebastião, has three or four decent **cafés**. The best positioned is *Pastelaria Europe* on Praça 1° de Maio (daily 8am–8pm), with outdoor tables spilling out onto the little square opposite the tourist office. For a full **meal**, *Eira Gaio* (daily noon–3pm & 7–10pm) on Rua 25 de Abril, down the road opposite the tourist office, has a limited but inexpensive menu with good *bacalhau* dishes.

INLAND ALONG THE RIO GUADIANA

North of Castro Marim, once clear of the fast IP1 to Spain and the new golf course, the quiet EN122 provides a little-travelled diversion to some of the least-visited parts of the Algarve. There are some good picnic spots at a couple of attractive reservoirs (*barragems*) signposted off the road at **Beliche** and **Odeleite**, but the most scenic route is along the side road signed to Foz de Odeleite and Alcoutim. Infrequent **buses** from Vila Real follow the EN122 on school days only, calling at the tiny village of Foz de Odeleite and at Alcoutim.

Foz de Odeleite is an attractive village at the mouth (*foz*) of the Rio Odeleite, a tributary of the Guadiana. Boat trips often stop off here while groups are taken round to admire the communal bread ovens and traditional flat roofs of the village, used to dry pumpkins and fruits during the summer months. There are some good marked **walks** either side of the village; the best one takes around one hour for a roundtrip to the village of Odeleite, signposted along the Rio Odeleite. Alternatively, it's around 15km from Foz de Odeleite to Alcoutim along the Guadiana, a river which Nobel Prize for Literature winner José Saramago says "was born beautiful and will end its days beautiful: such is its destiny".

From Foz de Odeleite, the road hugs the brackish banks of the wide Guadiana, its flat, fertile shores planted with citrus trees and vines. A few kilometres north, **Guerreiros do Rio** is another small, traditional village worth a brief stopover for its tiny **Museu do Rio** (Tues–Sat: May–Sept 2–5.30pm; Oct–April 9am–12.30pm & 1.30–5pm; €1), one of the region's several *Núcleos Museológicos* (see p.151). Set in one room of a former primary school, the museum consists of sketches, maps, photos and facts related to the river's wildlife and history; all the labels are in Portuguese. The village **café** (Mon & Wed–Sun 9.30am–8pm) is along the little backstreet opposite the museum.

ALCOUTIM

ALCOUTIM, 40km north of Vila Real on the banks of the Guadiana, is the only village of any size between Castro Marim and the neighbouring district of Alentejo. It has a long history as a river port, dominated in turn by Greeks, Romans and Moors who, over the centuries, fortified the heights with various structures to protect the copper that was transported down river from the nearby mines at São Domingos. Such was the town's importance in 1371, that Fernando I of Portugal and Henrique II of Castile signed a peace treaty on the river between Alcoutim and Sanlúcar de Guadiana to end one of the many wars between the two nations.

Nowadays Alcoutim survives largely on tourists who come for the river and the hilltop **castle** (daily 9am–1pm & 2–5pm; €1, free on Monday). This dates from the fourteenth century and offers fine views over the town and the Guadiana into Spain. The entrance fee includes access to a small archaeological **museum** by the main gates, which traces the history of the castle, its active service in the War of Restoration and the Liberal Wars, and the remnants of earlier structures on the site.

From the castle, cobbled backstreets lead down to the small **main square**, below which lies the appealing riverfront. In past years, you could take **boat trips** from here, but there is some doubt about this service at the time of going to press. If available, the best trip is the two-hour excursions to the old mining railhead at **Pomarão** along the verdant river alive with basking turtles and wild birds. Until the late nineteenth century, Pomarão was where copper was loaded onto boats going down to Vila Real; now the abandoned railhead is decaying atmospherically on the waterfront.

An easy boat trip is to take the **ferry** from Alcoutim over the Guadiana to the Spanish village of **Sanlúcar**, a mirror image of Alcoutim, with its own ruined castle. Although euros are now the shared currency, the clocks are still an hour apart, usually chiming slightly out of sync. The local boatmen will take you across for €1 each way; for excellent Spanish food ask directions to *Meson Julia*.

Back in Portugal, off the Mertola road on the edge of town, is the small **river beach** (*praia fluvial*). A few huts front a little bathing area on the banks of the Rio Cadavais – a popular summer spot for picnics and splashing about.

Practicalities

Buses pull in adjacent to the small main square, Praça da República, where the **turismo** (Mon–Fri: May–Oct 9.30am–1pm & 2–7pm; Nov–April 9.30am–1pm & 2–5.30pm; ⓣ281 546 179) can help with accommodation and give information about the latest **boat trips** up the river. For **internet** access, the Casa dos Condes, the town hall with a little art gallery opposite the tourist office, has a terminal (daily 9am–1pm & 2–5pm; €3/hr).

In the village itself the best **accommodation** option is the *Pensão Afonso* (ⓣ281 546 211; ❸), at Rua João Dias 10, just uphill from the main square. The small but spruce modern building offers pleasant rooms with their own

ALCOUTIM

baths, though the price does not include breakfast. Otherwise choices are just outside town: The very smart fifty-bed **youth hostel** (℡ & ℱ 281 546 004) is around 1.5km north of the village, across the Ribeira Cadavais; cross the bridge beyond Praça da República and follow the signs. It has its own canteen, bar and launderette as well as disabled access, and can help with canoe and bike rental. Double rooms from €21, en suite €23; 4-bed dorms from €9.50. Alternatively, much the smartest place, below (but on a separate road to) the youth hostel – head north out of Alcoutim and follow the signs – is the *Estalagem do Guadiana* (℡ 281 540 129, ℱ 281 546 647; Closed Jan; ❺), a very swish modern inn with its own pool, tennis court, restaurant (daily noon–3pm & 7–10pm) and Saturday night entertainment. Spacious rooms come with satellite TV, baths and fine river views.

Alcoutim has a fair choice of **cafés** and **restaurants** mainly clustered around the main Praça. *Afonso* (Tues–Sun 9am–3pm & 6.30–10pm), right on the main square, is a decent café-restaurant offering a limited menu of Portuguese staples at low prices, with a few outdoor seats. Much the nicest place for a drink or inexpensive snack is *O Soeiro* (Café Mon–Sat 9am–11pm; restaurant Mon–Fri noon–3pm), with outdoor tables on a little terrace right above the waterfront. The upstairs restaurant (lunches only) does a good range of moderately priced meals, including game and river fish such as *lampreia* (lamprey), the local specialities.

ACROSS THE SERRA DE ALCARIA

From Alcoutim, the EN122 heads north into the neighbouring district of Alentejo. Heading west from Alcoutim however, the EN124 crosses the northern reaches of the Algarve along the top of the **Serra de Alcaria** mountain range as far as Barranco Velho (see p.93). This is one of the most spectacular routes in the region and it offers the opportunity to stop off at some quirky local museums on route. These **Núcleos Museológicos** have been set up in otherwise neglected agricultural villages in an attempt to lure visitors out of their cars; a worthy concept, though none of them warrants more than a ten-minute leg stretch. Entry to each of these museums is €1, or you can buy a combined ticket for €2.50 from any of the participating museums, which also allows entry to the museums in Gueirreiros do Rio (see p.148), Alcoutim (see p.148), Pereiro, Giões, Martim Longo and Vaqueiros (see below).

The EN124 is surprisingly straight at first, lined with eucalyptus trees as it crosses a high exposed plateau. The first museum stop - though it's not much cop unless you understand Portuguese - can be made at the tiny village of **Pereiro**, where the **museum of popular culture** (Tues–Sat 10am–12.30pm & 2–6pm) displays poems, superstitions and local customs. Another 8km west, a signed road right to **Giões** takes you to a tiny agricultural hamlet with its own **artisan's museum** (Tues–Sat 10am–12.30pm & 2–6pm), a diminutive space displaying rugs, carpets, ceramics and the like. A similar museum is to be found 10km west at the otherwise dull village of **Martim Longo** (Tues–Sun 1pm–6pm). This one is a **history museum** with an eclectic collection of maps, agricultural implements, lamps, rugs and old radios.

From Martim Longo, the EN124 continues west for 13km to Cachopo (see p.153), but an even more picturesque detour south towards Vaqueiros takes in a couple of worthwhile sites. It is something of a surprise as you cross more rolling scrubland to suddenly come across the verdant slopes of a brand **new golf course**, and further touristic development sits just south of the course past the well-signed entrance to A Corvo dos Mouros.

ACROSS THE SERRA DE ALCARIA

A Corvo dos Mouros

Daily: March–May & Nov 10.30am–4.30pm; June–Oct
10.30am–6pm; €5, under-10s €4.23;
ⓦ www.minacovamouros.sitepac.pt

A Corvo dos Mouros is an innovative, German-run
theme park built on the site of an ancient gold and copper
mine. Discovered in 1865, the mines date back to around
2500 BC. Stone moulds, primitive furnaces for smelting
ore, copper axes, chisels and saws, rock tombs and two
Roman villas have all been discovered at the site.
Subsequently abandoned, the site was bought up in the
1990s and today consists of a replica furnace, reconstructed
thatched medieval houses typical of the Serra do Caldeirão,
and oddly lifelike dummies posing as Stone Age figures, all
explained by an English audio guide, and linked by a 1km
trail which passes old mine shafts and wells. There are also
donkey rides for kids (€10 extra) and a café. In summer,
you can walk down to **natural pools** where you can have a
dip in the Rio Foupana.

There are plans to get an old mining train working again
and to develop a reserve around the site for **native
wildlife**; already deer and rare griffin vultures can be spot-
ted along with tame fauna such as emus, donkeys and various species of goat and sheep.

If you like the idea of staying in rural solitude, the site
also rents out simple but very attractive **rooms** in a series of
farm buildings (❸).

Vaqueiros and west to Cachopo

A couple of kilometres south of A Corvo dos Mouros, the
village of **Vaqueiros** – its church crowned with a giant
stork's nest – contains the last of the region's Núcleo
Museológicos (see p.151; Tues–Sat 10am–12.30pm &

2–6pm), an **agricultural museum** dedicated to man's relationship with nature, and family life in a rural village; exhibits include olive presses, old measures, pots and pans.

Bear left through the village and via the tiny hamlet of Monchique and the road begins to cross a high pass with stunning views over the Serra de Alcaria. The road eventually snakes down to join the EN397. Turn left and it is 30km south to Tavira (see p.116); turn right and it is a short drive to **Cachopo**. This pretty hilltop village – with several cafés – is best known for its **natural springs** (*fontes*), where you can fill up water bottles at a pretty picnic area just out of town on the road to Barranco Velho (see p.93).

The central Algarve

T he **central Algarve** stretches some 35km from Albufeira to Portimão and embraces Portugal's most popular resorts. As you'd expect, the area is heavily developed, but with a string of superb beaches and several picturesque villages, it is easy to ignore the modern excesses. Smaller resorts such as **Alvor** and **Ferragudo** are still recognizably fishing villages, while even **Albufeira** – one of the Algarve's busiest centres – is highly enjoyable, with a sweeping town beach and an appealing historic centre. Giant beaches – backed by high-rises – can are also be found at **Armaçao de Pêra** and **Praia da Rocha**, the latter fronting **Portimão**, one of the region's more lively towns.

The area covered in this chapter is shown on map 2, at the back of the book.

If you find the coastal development too much – and all of these places are packed to the gills in summer – it is easy to escape the crowds inland, particularly if you have your own transport. Set amongst rolling countryside, the striking town of **Silves**, dominated by the walls of an imposing fortress, makes a good base – it is a relatively short drive to the coast, or you can cool off in the waters of the nearby inland reservoir, the **Barragem de Arade**. There are also some great walks in the unspoilt countryside round Silves and in the higher hill town of **Caldas de Monchique**, a nineteenth-century spa town, and neighbouring **Monchique**, a bustling market town set in the mountainous Serra de Monchique.

Albufeira and around

Albufeira is one of the region's largest resorts, but it remains relatively Portuguese in character, catering to a mixed bag of northern Europeans and local holiday makers of all ages. With your own transport, it is also possible to find relatively deserted **cove beaches**; those just west of Albufeira are some of the Algarve's prettiest.

For an alternative to a day on the beach, there are a series of **theme** and **water parks** strung along the main east–west highway – the EN125 – which winds inland past **Alcantarilha**, famed for its bizarre chapel of bones.

North of Albufeira there are fine walks round the historic castle at **Paderne**, while **São Bartolomeu de Messines** boasts an impressive church with elaborate Manueline touches. Just east of here, **Alte**, set in the foothills of the Serra de Caldeirão, is one of the Algarve's prettiest and best-kept villages.

ALBUFEIRA

Every inch a resort, **Albufeira** tops the list of package-tour destinations in the Algarve. The unusually pretty his-

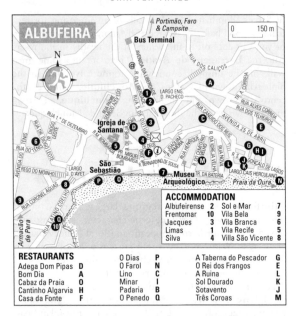

ALBUFEIRA

△ *Portimão, Faro & Campsite*

Bus Terminal

0   150 m

RUA DOS CALIÇOS

LARGO ENG.
D. PACHECO

**Igreja de
Santana**

**São
Sebastião**

**Museu
Arqueológico**

Praia d'Oura

RUA 1.° DE DEZEMBRO

LARGO
D'AYET

Armação
de Pera

ACCOMMODATION			
Albufeirense	2	Sol e Mar	7
Frentomar	10	Vila Bela	9
Jacques	3	Vila Branca	6
Limas	1	Vila Recife	5
Silva	4	Villa São Vicente	8

RESTAURANTS					
Adega Dom Pipas	D	O Dias	P	A Taberna do Pescador	G
Bom Dia	A	O Farol	N	O Rei dos Frangos	E
Cabaz da Praia	O	Lino	C	A Ruina	L
Cantinho Algarvia	H	Minar	I	Sol Dourado	K
Casa da Fonte	F	Padaria	B	Sotavento	J
		O Penedo	Q	Três Coroas	M

toric centre, with narrow, twisting lanes of whitewashed
houses criss-crossing the high red cliffs above a beautiful
spread of beaches, still feels removed from the hundreds of
new apartment buildings strung across the local hillsides. It
is the sort of place where you could start your day with a
full English breakfast, watch live cricket or soccer on TV
in a bar, and later down a Guinness or two at the Happy
Hangover. But there are plenty of things going for
Albufeira beyond hedonistic pleasures, including some fine
churches, a couple of **museums**, an art gallery and above
all a superb **beach**.

Some history

There was a settlement here in Roman times, when it was known as Baltum, though its name derives from the Moorish occupation when it was called "Al-buhera", Castle of the Sea – a reference to the inland lagoon which formed when the tides were high (the Portuguese word for lagoon remains "*albufeira*"). There's still a Moorish feel to parts of central Albufeira, as well as the more tangible remnants of a Moorish castle. This was taken by the Christians in 1189, and it was donated to the Order of Aviz, one of the Holy Orders who controlled much of the Algarve during the early days of Christian rule. The 1755 earthquake severely damaged much of the town, and most of the current historic centre was rebuilt at the end of the eighteenth century, when the town flourished as a fishing village. Tourism began to take hold in the late 1960s.

Arrival, information and orientation

Albufeira's **bus terminal** (⏍289 589 755) is on Avenida da Liberdade, at the top of town, five minutes' walk from the central Largo Engenheiro Duarte Pacheco, just to the west of which is the main street, Rua 5 de Outubro. At the end of here is the tunnel that's been blasted out of the rock to give access to the town beach. Albufeira's nearest **train station** is actually 6km north of town at Ferreiras; a bus connects it with the bus terminal every 45 minutes or so (daily 7am–8pm), or a taxi will set you back about €6, depending on the time of day. There's a large, free **car park** just back from the bus station; any closer in and you have to pay to park, though there are usually free places to the west of town – follow signs to "Albufeira Ponte".

The **turismo** (May–Sept Mon–Fri 9.30am–7pm, Sat & Sun 9.30am–5pm; Oct–April daily 9.30am–12.30pm & 2–5.30pm; ⏍289 585 279) is on Rua 5 de Outubro, close

ALBUFEIRA

to the tunnel. If you need to connect to the **internet**, *Augusto's* at Avenida da Liberdade 81 (Mon–Sat 10am–midnight; €3.50/hr; ☎ 289 515 738), just south of the bus terminal, has access.

If you're in Albufeira on a package holiday, you might well not be staying in the centre of town at all, but in one of the handful of small resort-villages on either side. The largest of these, **Montechoro** is a downmarket suburb known as "the strip" with a gaudy Eurotrashy appeal. However, like Albufeira's other satellites, Areias de São João and Praia da Oura (see p.84), Montechoro has access to its own superb beach and is within easy reach of the town centre on regular local **buses** or by **taxi**.

Accommodation

Finding a room can be difficult in high season since most of the **hotels and pensões** are block-booked by package holiday companies. Those listed below may have vacancies, otherwise the tourist office can help recommend a **private room**.

The finely appointed (and expensive) **Camping Albufeira** (☎ 289 587 629, ☎ 289 587 633; €4.50/person, €4.20/tent) – complete with swimming pools, restaurants, bars, shops and tennis courts – 2km to the north of town, off the N396, has regular connections from the bus station (any bus to Ferreiras passes it), though again space can be at a premium in high season – book ahead if possible.

Pensão Albufeirense
Rua da Liberdade 16–18
☎ 289 512 079
Comfortable and reasonably priced if drab rooms, with and without bath. It's set on a narrow pedestrianized stretch, though that means the front rooms can get noisy. ❷

Pensão Residencial Frentomar
Rua Latino Coelho
☎ 289 512005

Simple, clean rooms on a quiet side road just above the steps down to the beach. Try to get one with a terrace and a sea view, though these are usually snapped up quickly. **❸**

Jacques Accommodation,

Rua 5 de Outubro 36
T 289 588 640

The best budget option in town. Large, airy en-suite rooms, some with balconies, although front rooms can be noisy. There's a shared terrace and each floor has an area with a fridge and coffee-making facilities. Breakfast not included. April–Oct. **❹**

Residencial Limas

Rua da Liberdade 25–27
T 289 514 025

Ten spruce rooms in a pretty, yellow-faced building; avoid the front ground floor rooms or you'll feel as if you're sleeping on the street. Prices halve out of season. **❹**

Pensão Silva

Trav André Rebelo 18, off Rua 5 de Outubro
T 289 512 669, F 289 514 318

Adequate little pension on a quiet side street just off the main drag to the beach. Small, just-about comfortable rooms with shower, and a toilet down the hall. **❸**

Hotel Sol e Mar

Rua Bernardino de Sousa
T 289 580080,
E hotelsolmar@mail.telepac.pt

On the cliff above the tunnel to the beach, this characterless four-star stretches down five floors right onto the beach. The balconies have a prime spot overlooking the sands, while there's also a swimming pool. Rates drop considerably out of season. **❻**

Residencial Vila Bela

Rua Coronel Águas 32
T & F 289 512 101

To the west of the centre, this good value *residencial* offers rooms overlooking a small swimming pool; front ones have balconies with distant sea views across a busy main road. There is a pleasant patio brightened by bougainvillea. Often booked up by tour groups. April–Oct. **❹**

ALBUFEIRA

159

Residencial Vila Branca

Rua do Ténis 4

☎ 289 586 804, ⓕ 289 586 592

A mixed bag of rooms in a modern block with small, wedge-shaped balconies. There's a small bar downstairs and an appealing roof terrace with fine views. ❹

Residencial Vila Recife

Rua Miguel Bombarda 6

☎ 289 583 740, ⓕ 289 587 182

A huge, rambling old town house complete with its own garden and small pool. The rooms are smallish but comfortable with en-suite facilities, some with sea-views, and the *azulejos*-lined communal areas are spotless. May to October. ❹

Villa São Vicente Hotel

Largo Jacinto D'Ayet 4

☎ 289 583 700,

ⓔ vila.s.vicent@marciano-dias .com

A tasteful modern three-star with tiled floors and whitewashed walls. It has its own small pool and a terrace facing the beach. Rooms facing the street are less (❺) but it is worth extra for sea views. All rooms are en suite with TVs and air conditioning. ❻

The old town

The focus of historic Albufeira is the main square, **Largo Engenheiro Duarte Pacheco**, a pretty pedestrianized space with a small fountain and benches beneath palms trees. But, although the surrounding buildings are traditionally Portuguese, their contents are decidedly international, mostly pizza restaurants and bars with English names. After dark, the square becomes a focus for families and promenaders, accompanied, in high season, by live performers and buskers.

For a quieter take on the town, head up the side street off Largo Eng. Duarte Pacheco alongside Harry's Bar and walk up the steps beyond for great views back over the town's rooftops.

ALBUFEIRA

The south side of the square contains the **Galeria de arte Pintor Samora Barros** (July to mid-Sept 4.30pm–11pm; mid-Sept to end of June Mon–Sat 10.30am–5pm; free), an art gallery named after contemporary artist Samora Barros, an Algarve resident who specializes in relief paintings of Portuguese themes – Manueline windows and doors in particular – though the gallery is often taken over by temporary exhibitions.

The pedestrianized Rua 5 de Outubro leads past the post office and tourist office to the tunnel connecting the town to the beach (see below).

Head up the steps to the west of the tunnel and you reach **Praça Miguel Bombarda**, a small square close to two of the town's most important churches. On the square itself, the **Ermide de São Sebastião** has a distinctive Manueline door, though most of the building was constructed in the early eighteenth century with Baroque touches. Today the hermitage contains the **Museu Arte Sacra** (April–Sept Tues–Sun 2.30pm–8pm; Oct–March Tues–Sun 10.30am–12.30pm & 2.30–5pm; free), a picturesque if uninspiring sacred-art museum containing plaster images of saints.

Just north of the museum is the **Igreja de Santana**, a whitewashed eighteenth-century church with an attractive dome. From the patio at the front there are lovely views over the distinctive filigree chimneys of the old town to the sea.

Museu Arqueológico and around

Tues–Sun: mid-Sept to May 10am–5pm; June to mid-Sept
2.30–8.30pm; free

Albufeira's most interesting museum, the **Museu Arqueológico**, is in the former town hall on Travessa da Bateria, reached by taking the steps to the east of the tunnel. It has a rather sparse but well-laid-out collection of artefacts gathered from the area dating from Neolithic times to the present. There are fragments of mosaics from a Roman villa unearthed nearby, Visigoth rock tombs and jars, and even a Moorish silo excavated *in situ* beneath the museum. More recent remains include Manueline fragments from the old Igreja Matriz, while upstairs there are atmospheric black-and-white photos showing the town and its beach with barely a trace of tourism.

Beyond here the museum, Travessa da Bateria runs parallel to the beach past some of the town's most atmospheric **backstreets** – Rua do Cemitério Velho, Rua da Igreja Velha and Rua Nova – narrow cobbled streets lined with little cottages. At the end of Travessa da Bateria, steps wind down to the beach via the former fish market which is now a shelter for buskers and people chilling out under its shady roof.

The beach

The **beach** fronting Albufeira is a glorious sweep of soft sand flanked by strange tooth-like rock formations and backed by a sandstone cliff which cuts the beach off from the bustle of the town. Indeed the only completely visible buildings are the cafés and restaurants lined up behind the colourful fishing boats on the fisherman's beach. The western end of the beach can be reached via the tunnel or via steep steps which wind down the cliff below the *Hotel Rocamar*. This tends to be the busiest stretch of sand, where you can hire out pedaloes or be whisked out water-skiing, parasailing or on inflatable bananas.

Where this section of the beach ends, a path continues round the headland, before winding up to join Rua Latino Coelho high above a brand new yachting marina and tourist complex (due to open in 2003). En route you pass a grotto, **Gruta do Xorino**, which was used as a hideout by liberals during the Miguelite wars in 1833 (see p.306); today it's the haunt of local kids who swim in the shimmering green waters. Various stalls along the beach sell tickets for boat trips to the grotto, a pleasant-enough excursion but hardly one that warrants the cost of €14.

WALK TO OURA

An invigorating coastal walk from central Albufeira to the neighbouring beach of Praia da Oura (see p.84) takes around 45 minutes, or you can continue a further 30 minutes or so to the superb beach at Olhos de Água (see p.84), though this can only be done at low tide. Tide times are posted in major hotels and in the tourist office. Regular buses shuttle back to Albufeira if you don't fancy the return walk.

Head east down the beach – at low tide, you can walk the length of Albufeira's beach in 20–30 minutes (at other times some of the beach gets cut off by the tide). The beach ends at a low rocky cliff, where there's a makeshift wooden ramp to help you climb up onto the cliff-path above. The well-worn route follows a rocky ledge along the coast; at times the track splits, but the different strands all join together again further up the coast. The path passes a series of natural grottoes, rock bridges and blowholes carved into the rock by the sea. After another 20 to 30 minutes – at times along quite steep, narrow sections (take care when it's wet) – you will see Praia da Oura in front of you, a wide stretch of beach backed by a rash of modern apartments, villas and cafés. If you want to get the bus back to Albufeira, it is a short walk from the beach to the main road. Alternatively, you can continue along the sands and round the headland to the next resort of Olhos de Água (see p.84) in another 30 minutes. From here, regular daily buses depart back to Albufeira from the main road.

The eastern end of the beach is divided by a concrete **jetty** next to the fisherman's beach, where anglers wait for fish to bite and kids jump off the steps. When the waves get up, this is the most popular section for surfers.

At low tide you can walk on for another twenty minutes or so beyond the jetty below more low cliffs. The sand here is marginally less busy, though still backed by the odd beach café. Take care when swimming as the beach becomes gradually rockier towards the cliffs at the far end.

Eating

Albufeira has **restaurants** to suit every budget – and most tastes. As well as Portuguese restaurants, there's a whole range of places serving pizzas, Chinese and Indian food, even fish and chips. Naturally, you tend to get what you pay for (and prices in the top restaurants are ten percent higher than resorts further east), but budget places compete with each other, offering bargain deals most days; you'll often be presented with enticements in the form of drinks vouchers and the like.

Cafés

Pastelaria Lino
Trav Cândido dos Reis 2
Daily 8am–midnight. **Moderate**
Just off the main square, this is one of the few genuinely Portuguese central cafés. It's nothing special inside, but it does good pastries, and there are a few outdoor tables.

Padaria
Largo Candido dos Reis 17
Mon–Fri 7am–7pm, Sat & Sun 7am–1pm. **Inexpensive**
The local bakery sells bread, croissants and pastries and has a Gaggia machine for fresh coffee at the counter or at a couple of indoor tables.

Sol Dourado
Cais Herculano
Mon–Sat 10am–midnight.
Moderate

Relatively inexpensive (for this part of town) sandwiches, milkshakes and Portuguese

dishes served on a breezy roof terrace overlooking the fishing boats right on the beach.

Restaurants

Adega Dom Pipas
Trav dos Arcos 78
Daily 11am–3pm & 6.30pm–midnight. **Moderate**
The mock olde-worlde decor and Portuguese staples are nothing special, but it does have outdoor tables on what it claims is "the most typical street in Albufeira", an attractive narrow alley usually strung over with coloured ribbons for shade.

Bom Dia
Rua Alves Correira 37–39
Daily noon–3.30pm & 6pm–midnight. **Inexpensive**
Modest backstreet restaurant which usually has space when other places are full. Offers mostly grilled Portuguese food at cheaper-than-usual prices and less predatory waiters than many.

Cabaz da Praia
Praça Miguel Bombarda 7
Daily noon–2pm & 7–10pm.

Expensive
With a roof terrace offering fine views over the beach, this French-inspired restaurant serves excellent but expensive meals. Dishes include duck breast with quince and honey, onion soup, carpaccio of salmon and a long list of desserts.

Cantinho Algarvia
Trav São Gonçalo de Lagos 3a
Daily 10am–2am. **Moderate**
Mid-range restaurant with a varied menu where you can fill up on cuts of grilled meat and other standard Portuguese dishes.

Casa da Fonte
Rua João de Deus 7
Tues–Sun noon–3pm & 7pm–midnight. **Moderate**
This popular restaurant is set round a beautiful Moorish-style courtyard complete with *azulejos*, lemon trees and a resident parrot. The extensive

ALBUFEIRA

menu features the usual range of fish and meats, but arrive early as the courtyard tables fill up fast.

Restaurante O Dias
Praça Miguel Bombarda 3
℡ 289 515 246
Daily 12.30–2.30pm & 6.30–10.30pm. **Expensive**
On a prime spot with a back terrace overlooking the beach, this is a top-notch restaurant offering a long list of seafood, salad, barbecued fish, meat and lobster.

Restaurante O Farol
Cais Herculano
Daily 10am–11pm. **Inexpensive**
Simple beachside café-restaurant right behind the boats on the fisherman's beach. The generous portions of fresh fish and grilled meats are good value, and the atmosphere is refreshingly unpretentious – though service can get excessively laid-back.

Minar
Rua Diogo Cão, off Largo Cais Herculano
Mon–Sat noon–3pm & 6–11pm, Sun 6–11pm. **Inexpensive**
A fine Indian restaurant, with good-value tandoori dishes, the usual range of curries and breads and tasty veggie dishes. There's an outdoor terrace but it lacks a view.

O Penedo
Rua Latino Coelho 15
Mon, Tues & Thurs–Sun 6.30–11pm. **Moderate**
A little out from the centre, which means it's a little cheaper for dining on a terrace with superb views over the beach. Dishes include salads, pasta, fish and a few token vegetarian options.

A Taberna do Pescador
Trav Cais Herculano
Daily noon–3pm & 6–11pm. **Inexpensive**
A rarity in central Albufeira: an authentic Portuguese *taberna* attracting as many locals as tourists. The fish, seafood and meats are grilled to perfection on an outdoor terrace and portions are huge; wash it all down with the house sangria.

O Rei dos Frangos

Trav dos Telheiros 4, off Avda 25 de Abril

Daily noon–3.30pm & 6pm–midnight. **Inexpensive**
Common all over Portugal, but hard to pin down in resorts like Albufeira, here's a first-rate little *churrasqueira* – the chicken comes smothered in *piri-piri* and there's also grilled steak, swordfish and a speciality meat *cataplana*.

A Ruina

Praia dos Pescadores, Largo Cais Herculano

Daily 12.30–3pm & 7–11pm. **Moderate–expensive**
Rustic restaurant in the cliffs behind the beach, serving fresh fish. The lower area is the best place for those with kids, as they can play in the sand while you eat. There are also two floors inside and a roof terrace. Sardines and salad make an inexpensive lunch, but otherwise you're looking at €20 per person and up.

Sotavento

Rua São Gonçalo de Lagos 16

Daily noon–midnight. **Moderate**
Behind the fishing harbour, this small tiled bar-restaurant serves an affordable selection of Portuguese and international standards.

Restaurante Três Coroas

Rua do Correiro Velho 8.

Daily noon–3pm & 6.30–11pm. **Inexpensive**
Tranquil place with a leafy terrace with sea views and a small aviary in one corner. The short menu features decently priced fish and meat dishes, along with the house speciality of sole cooked with bananas. There's live music some nights which rather spoils the otherwise peaceful setting.

Drinking and nightlife

The natural magnet after dark is around Rua Candido dos Reis. In high season the long street becomes a writhing mass of humanity parading past handicraft and souvenir stalls or sitting at the bars and cafés which vie to play the loudest music and offer the most over-the-top cocktails.

Like the restaurants, Albufeira's **bars** and **discos** are into self-promotion. There's not much to choose between them, and you may as well frequent those offering the cheapest drinks at the time – happy hour is an extremely flexible concept here. The other main areas for carousing are along Rua São Gonçalo de Lagos, around Largo Eng. Duarte Pacheco and Rua Alves Correira. Most bars stay open until around 1am, the discos until 6am or later in summer.

7/12

Rua São Gonçalo de Lagos 5
May–Sept Tues–Sun 9pm–6am
Central Albufeira disco on a street full of late-opening bars. The entry price of €6 includes one drink; be warned there is a fairly strict dress code; beachwear and trainers are best avoided.

Bizarro Bar

Esplanada Dr. Frutuosa Silva 30
☎ 289 512 824; Mon–Sat 9am–1am
This is a laid-back bar in a traditional, blue-faced building high above the eastern end of the beach, with superb views over the sands from its front terrace.

Central Station

Largo Eng. Duarte Pacheco 44
Daily 9am–midnight
Bang on the main square, though all its tables are under cover. The downstairs is fairly tacky, serving as a café-restaurant-*gelateria* during the day. There's a big circular bar at the back and a spiral staircase leading to an upper cocktail bar with its own terrace and live music most nights.

Garden Bar

Residencial Vila Recife, Rua Miguel Bombarda 6
Daily 3.30pm–midnight
Glassed-in hotel bar with ceiling fans, a snooker table and its own garden on a strip of grass with a few palm trees. Live music – usually jazz or pop – most nights.

Harry's Bar

**Largo Eng. Duarte Pacheco
36–37**

Daily 10am–3am

Attractive blue and white building on the main square sheltering a mock pub offering English breakfasts, light meals and a long list of cocktails. The drinks – including British beers – are overpriced and it's only really worth coming for the nightly music – you name it, the guitar-playing house musician can play it.

Jardim de 1001 Noites

Beco Bernardino de Sousa

Daily 6pm–2am

An extravagant pseudo-Moorish complex with a huge courtyard by the municipal library. There's a bar, live entertainment most nights, fado on Tuesdays, an art gallery and nightly *rodizio à Algarvia* – a giant buffet barbecue.

Jo Jo's

Rua São Gonçalo de Lagos 1

Mon–Sat 10am–4pm & 6.30pm–2am, Sun noon–4pm & 6.30pm–2am

Friendly family-run pub with British soccer and other sports on satellite TV. It also serves pub-style food which always includes a vegetarian option. The owner proudly remembers the day Paul Gascoigne and his mates got hopelessly drunk here.

Kiss

Rua Vasco da Gama

May–Sept daily midnight–6am; Oct–April Sat & Sun midnight–6am

Out of town, at the southern end of Montechoro near the Forte de São João, this is regarded as the best club around town, and often hosts foreign guest DJs, but it tends to be overcrowded and very glitzy; watch for posters advertising events. You'll need to rely on a taxi to get back to central Albufeira (around €6).

Café Latino

Rua Latino Coelho 59

☏ 289 585 132; Tues–Sun 10am–2am

With spinning ceiling fans, a snooker table and a back terrace with fantastic views,

ALBUFEIRA

this is a superb spot to start off an evening. Along with the usual drinks there are exotic juice cocktails; and snacks ranging from croissants to sandwiches and pizzas.

Portas da Vila
Rua da Bateria
Daily noon–2am

This high-ceilinged, traditionally decked-out bar lies just above the old fish market next to the site of the old gates to the castle. The menu features a long list of cocktails and sangria. There are a few outdoor tables on the pedestrianized steps, too.

Listings

Banks Around Largo Eng. Duarte Pacheco.

Bike/motorbike hire Henrique Rent A Bike, Rua da Igreja Nova 17 (℡289 425 132).

Bookshop The Algarve Book Centre, Rua Igreja Nova 6 (Mon–Fri 10am–6pm, Sat 10am–2pm) stocks a large range of English language books.

Bullfights Twice weekly in the summer (€25–35) at the bullring to the east of the centre. You can buy tickets from travel agents (see below) or from the bullring.

Buses Information from the terminal (℡289 589 755).

Car rental Europcar, Rua Dr. Diogo Leote (℡289 512 444, ℻289 586 400); Hertz, Rua Manuel Teixeira Gomes Bloco 1, Areias de S. João (℡289 542 920, ℻289 589 937).

Health Centre Urbanização dos Caliços (℡289 588 770/289 587 550; open 24 hours).

Markets The lively flea market (1st & 3rd Tues of each month) takes place to the north of the centre at Caliços. The fruit and fish market (Mon–Sat) is in the Largo do

Mercado off Estrada Vale Pedra, north of the centre. There is also a clothes market (daily 8am–6pm) on the central strip of Avenida da Liberdade opposite the bus terminal.

Pharmacy Farmácia de Sousa, Rua 5 de Outubro 40.

Police ☏289 512 205.

Post office Near the tourist office on Rua 5 de Outubro.

Supermarket Supermercado S. Nicolau, Avda da Liberdade (daily 8am–8pm). Just down from the bus station.

Taxis There's a rank next to the bus station, or phone ☏289 583 230.

Trains Travel information from the station in Ferreiras (☏289 571 755).

Travel agents Rua 5 de Outubro has rows of agents offering everything from tickets to local theme parks to half-day trips to inland Algarve and full-day trips to Lisbon, Spain or Gibraltar.

BEACHES WEST OF ALBUFEIRA

The stunning red rocky headland beaches that begin a couple of kilometres to the **west of Albufeira** were largely unexploited until the 1980s, when the development of a strip of villa resorts began to change the landscape. The first of the beaches, **São Rafael**, is a lovely Blue Flag sandy cove studded with sandstone pillars and backed by low cliffs. There is a tacky beach **restaurant**, owned by the São Rafael Villa complex a little up the hill.

A few kilometres west, and reached down a steep road, **Praia do Castelo**, is a smaller sandy bay nestling below cliffs, with its own appealing beachside café-restaurant (see p.172). Development becomes more intense at **Praia de**

Galé, some 7km west of Albufeira, and where the massive sweeping swathe of sand stretches all the way west to Armação de Pêra (see p.179). Another Blue Flag beach with a cluster of hotels, cafés and restaurants, this is as good a place as any to enjoy a day on the beach.

Practicalities

There are no direct **buses** to these resorts, though the regular Albufeira–Portimão service drops passengers on the main road, a steep 2km walk.

ACCOMMODATION

Pensão Maritim/Vila Madelena
São Rafael
ⓣ 289 591 005, ⓕ 289 591 345
A smart three-star pension with its own restaurant just uphill from the lovely Praia de São Rafael. The best rooms have sea views (€15 extra). ⑤

Estalagem Vila Joya
Praia da Galé
ⓣ 289 591 795, ⓕ 289 591 201
This is one of the Algarve's most exclusive hotels, a pseudo-Moorish construction sitting right above the beach. A room here will set you back around €400. ⑨

EATING AND DRINKING

Bar Pic Nic
Praia do Castelo
Daily: May–Sept noon–midnight; Oct & March–April 10am–7pm.
Moderate
Superb beachside café-restaurant wedged into cliffs behind the sands. Great grilled meats, though as you'd expect, fresh fish is the best bet.

Restaurante Praia da Galé
Praia da Galé
Daily March–Oct 10am–midnight. Moderate
One of the best of the cluster of beach café-restaurants at

the eastern end of Praia da Galé, offering fresh fish, grills and snacks on a breezy terrace facing the waves.

Vila Madelena
São Rafael

Daily noon–2.30pm & 6–10pm.
Moderate
Below the *Pensão Maritim* (see above), this offers well-presented fish and dishes of the day in a bright room with distant sea views.

INLAND: SÃO BARTOLOMEU DE MESSINES AND AROUND

Few tourists head inland north of the main EN125 and the coastal highway, but there are several reasons to stray a little from the beaches. **Krazy World** is a theme park attracting summer visitors in droves, but a tourist-free lifestyle still takes place around **Paderne**, close to the ruins of a fine hilltop castle. A little further north, the church at **São Bartolomeu de Messines** boasts a superb example of Manueline architecture, while to the east in rolling countryside lies **Alte**, one of the Algarve's prettiest villages.

Krazy World

Thirteen kilometres northwest of Albufeira, just north of Algoz, **Krazy World** (daily: Jan–April & Oct–Dec 10am–6pm; May–Sept 10am–7.30pm; €13, under-12s €8; ⓦ www.krazy-world.com) has expanded into a sizeable zoo-cum-theme park. Buses from Albufeira to São Bartolomeu de Messines stop near the entrance. Entry allows access to a neatly landscaped park with a fairground – mostly traditional rides such as ferris wheels and round-abouts – as well as a mini zoo, children's farm, swimming pools and crazy golf course. Quad bikes and bumper cars cost extra, and in high season expect to queue for the more popular rides.

Paderne

Six kilometres east of Algoz, **Paderne** – served by hourly buses from Albufeira – is a traditional village set on a low hill. The parish church dates from 1506 and its doorway retains some fine flourishes; otherwise the village's appeal lies in strolling round the sloping streets and soaking up the relaxed atmosphere. A worthy detour is the pleasant walk to the scant remains of a Moorish castle, which lie some 2km southeast of town on the road to Boliqueime. The **castle** is signed down a dirt track, officially labelled as a 1.4km pedestrian route, though a steady stream of cars usually bumps its way up the track to avoid the steep final ascent. It's a lovely walk through olive groves, accompanied by the rhythmic screech of cicadas.

At the top of the hill lie the atmospheric remains of a twelfth-century Moorish fort which commands great views of the surrounding countryside. The fort was taken by knights from the Order of Christ (see p.145) in 1248 during the Christian reconquest of the Algarve and you can still see walls of the later brick fourteenth-century Ermida de Nossa Senhora do Castelo inside the castle's crumbly walls.

São Bartolomeu de Messines

Twelve kilometres northwest of Paderne, or reached on the fast EO1 from Albufeira, the small town of **São Bartolomeu de Messines** is an unspoilt market town which preserves an important sixteenth-century parish church, remodelled in Baroque style and incorporating Manueline interior columns decorated with twisted stone rope. The town's only other claim to fame is as the birthplace

VIA ALGARVIANA

The rolling but not too strenuous 12km (3–4hr) walk from Alte to São Bartolomeu de Messines is the first waymarked section of an east–west trans-Algarve walking route known as the **Via Algarviana**. Started by a walking club – The Algarve Walkers – combined with the Loulé-based environmental group Almargem (© almargem@mail.telepac.pt), this section will eventually form part of Euro Route E4, one of several cross-European walking routes being developed in the EU. Once complete, the route will begin at Alcoutim on the Spanish border and end at Cabo de São Vicente, 213km away, passing through some of the Algarve's wildest and more mountainous terrain. At the time of going to press, a part of the Alte–São Bartolomeu walk was closed due to construction of a new motorway. Contact Almargem for more details.

of two leading nineteenth-century Algarvian figures, the writer João de Deus (see p.307) and the rebellious Remexido (see p.306). Nowadays, the only time the town is remotely animated is on the last Monday of the month, when it hosts a livestock market just off the central Rua 1 Maio. There are regular **buses** here from Albufeira, Portimão and Silves.

Alte

From São Bartolomeu, the N124 heads west to Silves via the Barragem do Arade (see p.197). In the other direction, it's 10km east to the pretty village of **Alte**. Tacked across the hillside, a series of narrow cobbled streets make this one of the region's most picturesque villages; unfortunately coachloads of visitors are disgorged daily in summer – especially July to early September – though at other times and at the end of the day the place is given over to locals once more.

Alte holds a lively flea market on the third Thursday of every month. There's a folk festival on May 1 and the main annual fair on September 17.

Alte's only sight is the graceful sixteenth-century **Igreja Matriz**, with a Manueline doorway, though most people spend their time wandering round the cobbled backstreets and out to a couple of natural springs or *fontes* around ten minutes' walk from the centre. The first of these, **Fonte Pequena**, is marked by the restaurant of the same name set in an old mill. A further five minutes' walk up a reed-filled valley lies the larger and more appealing **Fonte Grande**, where the river passes an old weir lined with picnic tables set under shady trees. Notices by the water warn "No Fishing, Swimming or Washing", though you'd be hard pushed to attempt any in the first place.

Practicalities

Alte is poorly served by public transport, with just one bus daily from Loulé, though it is well served by summer tours and jeep safaris; ask around at the travel agents in Albufeira for details (see p.171).

The **turismo** is located on the main road just below town on the Estrada da Ponte (Mon & Sun 9am–12.30pm & 2–5.30pm, Tues–Thurs 9am–6pm, Fri–Sat 9.30am–12.30pm & 2–6pm; ☎ 289 478 666), and can give out local maps of the village and information about private **rooms** if you decide to stay. It also doubles as a small museum of limited interest showing local crafts and images of rural life.

From Alte, it is a short drive east to the delightfully unspoilt countryside round Benafim and Penina (see p.93).

TOM TEEGAN/ROBERT HARDING

Typical cove beach, central Algarve

Serra de Monchique

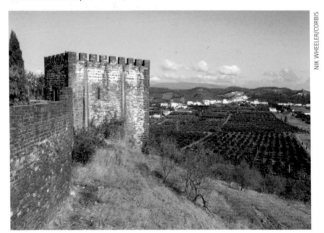

Castle walls, Silves

Streets of Monchique

Praia de Odeceixe

Ponta da Piedade, near Lagos

If you decide **to stay** and enjoy Alte when the tour crowds have gone, *Casa d'Alte* (☎289 478 426; ❷) is a bright, white town house right next to the church; its airy front rooms have stunning views over town. The village's main **café**, *Café Regional*, on Largo da Igreja 1 (daily 8am–9pm) serves pastries, snacks and drinks at outdoor tables facing the main street. For a full **meal**, *Restaurante Fonte Pequena* (Tues–Sun noon–3pm & 7–10pm) is a large grill house with wooden benches laid out on a shady terrace facing the water at the *fonte*.

GUIA, ALCANTARILHA AND AROUND

Around 23km southwest of Alte, and some 6km inland from the coast, the dull stretch of the EN125 between Albufeira and Lagoa links several tourist attractions – a **zoo**, a **water park,** the **Chapel of Bones** at Alcantarilha and the crafts centre of **Porches** – which are all well connected by regular **buses** from the main coastal resorts. Alternatively resort travel agents sell tickets combining entry and special transport to and from the theme parks.

Guia and Zoo Marine

Guia, around 6km northwest of Albufeira, is a fairly non-descript town with a couple of historic churches, the seventeenth-century Igreja Matriz and the Baroque Nossa Senhora da Guia. The latter has a particularly striking interior of sumptuous blue and white *azulejos*. A more modern attraction lies at **Zoo Marine** on the edge of town (mid-March to 22 June & 19 Sept to end Oct daily 10am–6pm; 23 June–18 Sept daily 10am–8pm; Nov to mid-March Tues–Sun 10am–5pm; adults €14, children €9, mini-Formula 1 rides extra; ☎289 560 300, ⓦwww.zoomarine .com). Part zoo and part theme park, tickets allow entry to swimming pools, an aquarium, parrot and peacock enclosures, dolphin and sea lion performances. There are also various fairground rides and a selection of cafés and restaurants; all in all it makes a pretty perfect day out for those with young kids.

Alcantarilha and The Big One

Five kilometres west of Guia, **Alcantarilha** is a surprisingly unspoilt town, considering its position on the EN125, just 3km north of Armação de Pêra. Its main sight is its eighteenth-century Igreja Matriz which contains a **Capela dos Ossos**, a chapel lined with the bones of around 1500 humans, similar to that in Faro (see p.66). These chapels were part reminder of people's mortality, and partly a practical solution to lack of cemetery space. Unfortunately the chapel is not routinely open, though when it is, entry is free. Beyond Alcantarilha just off the EN125, **The Big One** (May–Sept daily 10am–5.30pm; adults €11, children €9; ⓦwww.bigone-waterpark.com) is another giant water park set among lawns and palms, with an array of pools and slides with apt names such as "labyrinth", "crazy leap" and "kamikaze". Best of all is the "Banzai Boggan", a terrifying 23m, near vertical slide into water.

Porches

Five kilometres west of Alcantarilha along the main EN125, **Porches** is a pleasant if unexceptional village which has become famous for its hand-painted **pottery** (*majolica*). Thick, chunky, hand-painted *majolica*-ware has a good, heavy feel, and employs glazing techniques that have been used since Moorish times. Workshops – usually open daily – line the main road, although not all the goods on sale are produced in Porches; you can find everything from Barcelos pots from northern Portugal to totally impractical souvenirs such as wood-burning ovens and *azulejos*-inlaid marble-topped tables. A good place to browse is Casa Virgílio, Vale de Lousas, on the main EN125 just east of Porches (daily 9am–7pm).

Armação de Pêra and around

Around 3km south of Alcantarilha, **Armação de Pera** is one of the Algarve's most popular summer retreats for Portuguese holiday makers, a bustling high-rise resort that lies at the western end of another fantastic sweep of sand. West of here the coastline is fringed by low cliffs punctured with delightful cove beaches including **Praia da Marinha** and **Praia de Benagil**. Though not exactly undiscovered, these beaches' relative inaccessibility thins out the crowds, and they are conveniently linked by an invigorating clifftop coastal path.

ARMAÇÃO DE PÊRA

Three kilometres south of the main EN125 and around 15km west of Albufeira lies the resort of **Armação de Pêra**. Once the beach here was used by sardine fishermen from the village of Pêra, a couple of kilometres inland, to launch their *armação* (see p.120). In time, a fishermen's community grew up around the beach itself, and though the boats are still pulled up onto the beach, nowadays the town has expanded into a major resort. Locals claim theirs is the largest beach in the region (not a unique claim in these parts) and the area boasts fine caves and unusual rock formations to the west around **Praia da Senhora da Rocha**, visited by daily **boat trips** in summer departing from the stretch of sands just east of the town centre, known as the fisherman's beach.

It's not the greatest-looking of resorts by any means; indeed it can lay claim to having some of the ugliest high-rises in the Algarve. But the beach is superb, and stand with your back to the modern excesses at the terraced gardens with its children's play area and cafés, and the place becomes decidedly appealing. The remains of the town's fortified **walls** are at the eastern end of the seafront road where a terrace in front of a little white chapel provides sweeping views. Just beyond here lies the town church and a superb seafront villa surrounded by palms above the jumble of fishing boats and nets on the fishermen's beach. The most interesting backstreets are the narrow, cobbled ones winding up behind *O Serol* restaurant (see p.182).

Practicalities

Armação de Pêra's **bus terminal** (☎282 315 781) is at the eastern end of the town and there are regular services from Albufeira, Portimão and Silves. Walk up a block south to the beach and then head right for ten minutes along the seafront Avenida Marginal, which changes its name several times as it makes for the centre. The **turismo** is along here on the seafront Avenida Marginal (Mon–Fri 9.30am–1pm & 2–5.30pm; ☎282 312 145), and is good for maps and accommodation information. If you want to plug into the **internet**, the *Hotel Garbe* (see p.181; €0.50/4min) has a public terminal.

Accommodation

The majority of hotels and apartments are block-booked for package tours. For **private rooms**, ask at *O Serol* restaurant,

Rua da Praia (☏282 312 146; ❷), overlooking the beach near the fishing boats – you'll pass it on the way in from the bus station – or, alternatively at the tourist office. The most upmarket **hotel** choice is *Hotel Garbe* at Avenida Beira Mar 1 (☏282 315 187, ✉hotelgarbe@mail.telepac.pt; ❸). A few minutes' walk west of the tourist office, this modern block has a prime site facing the beach. Rooms are varied although most have balconies; sea views are an extra €30. The hotel also has a pool, TV and games room, in-house Indian restaurant and a baby-sitting service. The nearest **campsite**, the shady *Parque de Campismo Armacão de Pera* (☏282 312 260, ⓦwww.roteiro-campista.pt/faro/armpera.htm; €4.50/person, €4/tents)*, is out of the centre, 1km north along EN269-1, towards highway EN125. It's well equipped with its own pool, supermarket, restaurant and gardens. It also rents out smart **bungalows** for up to four people from €55 a night.

Eating and drinking

There are countless **bars and restaurants**, all with more or less the same menus. The following are always good bets.

Beach Bar O Gato
Avda Marginal
March–Oct Mon & Wed–Sun
10am–1am. Inexpensive
Near the tourist office, with outside tables on a series of terraces overlooking the beach. The perfect place to watch the sun go down over a Superbock or two.

Estrela do Mar
Praia dos Pescadores
Daily 11am–3pm & 6–11pm.

Inexpensive
Right on the fisherman's beach nestled among the boats, this simple beach shack offers bargain-bucket Portuguese staples; the *sardinhas assada* (grilled sardines) are superb.

A Santola
Largo da Fortaleza
Daily 11am–3pm & 6–11pm.
Expensive
One of the town's more

upmarket choices, full of bubbling tanks of lobsters and attentive waiters. Pricey fish, seafood and grills come with superb sea-facing views.

O Serol
Rua Portas do Mar 2

Mon, Tues & Thurs–Sun noon–3.30pm & 6–10.30pm.
Expensive
Just east of the church near the fisherman's beach, with a cosy interior and an outdoor terrace, this is one of the town's best fish restaurants.

PRAIA DA ALBONDEIRA AND PRAIA DA MARINHA

The 10km or so of coast between Armação de Pêra and Centianes (see p.183) is flat and scrubby, fronting a series of

PRAIA DA ALBONDEIRA AND PRAIA DA MARINHA

COASTAL WALK FROM PRAIA DA ALBONDEIRA TO BENAGIL

This 4km (90min) walk is one of the region's most alluring coastal paths – but the well-tended, easy-to-follow route is also extremely popular; don't expect a solitary experience unless you're there in winter. There is very limited public transport to these beaches, so you'll have to walk back the way you came. The path is signed just west of Praia da Albondeira, skirting sea cliffs and gullies; take care as there are a few steep drops next to blowholes. After a fenced-off villa, the track becomes cobbled as you approach the half-way point above Praia da Marinha, where there are steps leading down to the beach and a seasonal café (see p.183). Continue along the coast past the car park, and soon the way divides as it climbs a fairly steep slope; all the different branches eventually meet up at a higher clifftop. After another 10 minutes or so, the path skirts another blowhole. Stick to the clifftop route and eventually you will emerge next to a building on the main road, just above Praia de Benagil (see p.183).

delightful cove beaches that have somehow escaped any large-scale development. The first of these, **Praia da Albondeira**, marks the start of a superb coastal footpath which stretches for 4km all the way to Benagil (see opposite). Next along, **Praia da Marinha**, nestles below a craggy red sandstone cliff, with the only trace of development being a tasteful villa complex a little up the hill. The beach can also be reached by **car**, turning south off the EN125, between Porches and Lagoa, opposite the International School, 8km west of Armação. There is also one weekday **bus** here from Lagoa. To reach the beach from the neatly tended car park, descend the cobbled track that leads off to the left from the clifftop picnic tables. The beach has a simple **café-restaurant**, *Café Praia da Marinha* (March–Sept Tues–Sun noon–7pm), offering hot and cold drinks and light meals.

BENAGIL AND PRAIA DE CENTIANES

A couple of kilometres further west, the road winds round to the next bay at **Benagil**, a tiny village with a cluster of buildings above a narrow gully. The road loops down over a dried-up river valley, at the bottom of which under high cliffs is a fine beach dotted with fishing boats pulled up out of the water.

West of Benagil, the scenery changes again with coastal development crowding in around another fine beach at **Praia de Centianes**, the road lined with villas and modern apartments all the way to Carvoeiro (see p.184).

Most **accommodation** on this stretch consists of private villas, though it is worth booking ahead to bag one superb option just above Benagil. Here, *Vila Linda Mar* (☎282 342 331, ℗282 352 847; ❹, ❺ with sea views), 1km east of Benagil, is a tasteful, traditionally decorated **guesthouse** with its own lawns and a small pool. There are just a handful of rooms, all with bathrooms, TVs and fridges; the best ones with balconies offering distant sea views.

Just above Benagil beach, *Bar da Lota* (June–Sept daily 9.30am–8pm) is a kiosk-**bar** serving decent breakfast plus inexpensive snacks and drinks. For something more substantial **to eat**, book for a meal at *Vila Linda Mar* (see above; ☎282 342 331; Mon & Wed–Sun 7pm–10pm). This attractive guesthouse serves superb Algarvian dishes such as *presunto de Monchique* (smoked ham from Monchique) and *gambas com espinafres* (prawns with spinach); pricey but worth it.

Carvoeiro and around

Three kilometres west of Centianes, and 5km south of the main EN125, the former fishing village of **Carvoeiro** has developed over the last two decades into a firm favourite for package holidays. Out of season the town has more appeal, and it is within easy range of a couple of superb neighbouring sights, the rock formations at **Algar Seco** (see below) and the wonderful beach at **Centianes** (p.183), as well as the inland wine centre of **Lagoa** (see p.186).

Carvoeiro

Cut into the red cliffs, this was once a quaint fishing village, but has become a slightly tacky resort with its small cove beach having to support the prostrate bodies of hundreds of tourists. The beach is pleasant enough, though actually rockier and less impressive than many along this stretch.

Accessible by the coast road, a short drive or walk 1km east, are the impressive rock formations of **Algar Seco**, where steps lead down the cliffs to a series of dramatic overhangs past sculpted rocks, pillars and blowholes above slapping waves. There's a small **café-bar**, *Boneca* (May–Sept 9.30am–midnight) which offers drinks and snacks, including mango mousse, next to A Boneca, a rock window reached through a short tunnel, offering unusual sea views. Boats trips from Portimão (see p.202), often stop off here.

Practicalities

The **tourist office** (mid-Sept to May Mon–Fri 9.30am–1pm & 2–5.30pm; June to mid-Sept daily 9.30am–7pm; ☎282 357 728), just behind the beach, can suggest **private rooms**. In high season, most accommodation is in the form of block-booked apartments, though the following are worth a try and usually have spaces outside of July and August.

ACCOMMODATION

Hotel Carvoeiro Sol
☎ 282 357 301,
ⓔ carvoeirosol@mail.telepac.pt
Comfortable if unimaginative four-star concrete block right by the beach. Rooms come with small balconies, though you pay around €20 extra for sea views. There's also a pool, courtyard bar and a baby-sitting service. ❻, ❼ with sea views.

O Castelo
Rua da Casino 59–61
☎& ⓕ 282 357 416,
ⓔ casteloguesthouse@clix.pt
Overlooking the beach, five minutes' walk uphill from the tourist office, this is the best bet in town, but book ahead as there are just three rooms. Each is clean and

CARVOEIRO AND AROUND

modern with superb views; two have their own balconies. Price does not include breakfast. There's also a restaurant downstairs (see below). ❸

EATING AND DRINKING

O Barco
Largo da Praia
Daily 10am–midnight.
Inexpensive
Unexceptional, reasonably priced food – from snacks to Portuguese dishes and pasta – with an excellent position facing the sands.

Bote Disco Club
Largo da Praia
June–Sept 11pm–4am;
Oct–May Fri & Sat only
Loud disco sat on a prime coastal spot, with a beach-facing terrace for a breather between the contemporary sounds.

O Castelo
Rua da Casino 59–61
Tues–Sun 6.30–10.30pm.
Expensive
Below the guesthouse of the same name (see above), this is a slightly pricey place for standard Portuguese food, but it does boast a great terrace overlooking the beach.

Lagoa

Regular buses shuttle the 5km along the main EN125 between Carvoeiro and **Lagoa**, a fairly nondescript little town best known as the centre of the Algarve's wine trade. You can taste or buy the local wine from the **Adega Cooperativo de Lagoa** (Mon–Fri 9.30–11.30am & 2–5.30pm; free), on the south side of the EN125. There's not a lot else to Lagoa, though it does come alive in August when it hosts an annual **craft fair** known as Fatacil.

Silves and around

Eight kilometres north of Lagoa, **Silves** – the medieval residence and capital of the Moorish kings of the al-Gharb – is the Algarve's most enticing inland town. The red ring of the castle walls emerges as you approach through the rolling hills. Dominated by a Moorish castle, the town also boasts an imposing cathedral and a fine archaeological museum amongst quiet cobbled streets. It makes an ideal day-trip, or a good overnight base, especially if you're visiting the inland reservoir, the **Barragem do Arade**, or the mountains of Serra de Monchique (see p.222).

Some history

Silves was an important port for the **Phoenicians** and was named Silbis by the **Romans**. Under the **Moors**, Silves, then called Xelb, became capital of the al-Gharb and had a population three times the current one. Before the river silted up, it was a thriving port and a place of grandeur, described in contemporary accounts as "of shining brightness" within its three dark circuits of guarding walls. It was also famed for its artistic community and in the tenth century it was considered culturally more important than Granada, the leading Moorish city in Spain. Such glories and civilized splendours came to an end, however, in 1189, with the arrival of Sancho I, at the head of a mixed army of **Crusaders**. Sancho, desperately in need of extra fighting force, had recruited a rabble of "large and odious" northerners, who had already been expelled from the holy shrine of Santiago de Compostela for their irreligious behaviour. The army arrived at Silves toward the end of June and the town's thirty thousand Moorish residents retreated to the citadel. There they remained through the long, hot summer, sustained by huge water cisterns and granaries, until

SILVES AND AROUND

September, when, the water exhausted, they opened negotiations.

Sancho was ready to compromise, and guarantees for the inhabitants' personal safety and goods were secured but his Crusaders had been recruited on the promise of plunder, and were not prepared to forgo the pleasure of wrecking the town. The gates were opened and the Crusaders duly ransacked the town, killing some 6000 Moors in the process. Today a statue of Sancho remains guarding a wall inside the fortress, on the left-hand side as you enter.

Silves passed back into Moorish hands two years later, but by then the town had been irreparably weakened, and it finally fell to Christian forces in 1249. Under Christian rule, Silves continued to be a major port and housed the Algarve's bishopric until this moved to Faro in 1577, and with the gradual silting up of the Rio Arade, Silves lost importance. Many of its finer buildings were destroyed in the earthquake of 1755, and the town dwindled into the provincial market town it remains today.

ARRIVAL AND INFORMATION

The **train station** lies 2km south of town; there is a connecting bus, but it's a pleasant walk if you're not weighed down with luggage - as you leave the station, simply turn left and follow the EN124–1 into town. Arriving by **bus**, you'll be dropped on the main road at the foot of the town near the riverfront, next to the market.

There are two small tourist offices in Silves. The main town **turismo,** is in a small kiosk below the town hall on Largo de Município (Mon–Fri 9.30am–1pm & 2–5.30pm; ⊕ 282 442 325), and can give out details of local events. Just round the corner at Rua 25 de Abril 26–28 is a **regional tourist office** (hours as town turismo; ⊕ 282 442 255), which covers information about the whole Algarve.

SILVES

2, **3** & S. Bartolomeu de Messines

ACCOMMODATION

Colina dos Mouros	5
Dom Sancho	1
Ponte Romana	6
Quinta do Rio	2
Sousa	4
Vila Sodré	3

Cruz de Portugal

N

150 m

0

Museu da Cortiças

Fabrica Inglês

Rio Arade

Lagos & Portimão **5**

RUA CÂNDIDO DOS REIS

RUA DO CASTELO

RUA DO MIRANTE

RUA DIOGO MANUEL

RUA JOSÉ FALCÃO

RUA LATINO COELHO

Silves Station

Cisterna Grande

Fortress

LARGO DO CASTELO

A

Sé Cathedral

RUA M. ARRIAGA

RUA DR. F. VIEIRA

RUA ELIAS GARCIA

R. C. FIGUEREDO

Ponte Romana (Roman bridge) **6**

R. POLICARPO DIAS

Igreja da Misericórdia

1

LARGO JERÓNIMO OSÓRIO

RUA DA SÉ

DE LOULÉ

RUA DAS PORTAS

Museu Arqueologia

R. M. ALBUQUERQUE

RUA 5 DE OUTUBRO

Torreão das Portas da Cidade

Torreão das Portas da Cidade

LARGO DO MUNICÍPIO

B **i**

RUA BERNARDO MARQUES

RUA C. VILARINHO **C**

RUA JOSÉ ESTEVÃO

Market **D**

RUA D. AFONSO III

i

RUA 25 DE ABRIL

RUA F. PABLOS

RUA SAMORA BARROS

4

RUA ALEXANDRE HERCULANO

RUA ALEXANDRE DE DEUS

RUA JOÃO DE DEUS

RUA DO CORREIO

Monchique

RUA MIGUEL BOMBARDA

RUA CRUZ DA PALMEIRA

CAFÉS & RESTAURANTS

Inglês	A
Marisqueira Rui	C
U Monchiqueiro	D
Rosa	B

SILVES

189

ACCOMMODATION

If there are no spaces in the places listed below, the town turismo can help arrange **private rooms**. Particularly recommended are those at Rua Cândido dos Reis 36 (℡ 282 442 667; ❷), which are spotless and share the use of a kitchen and a little outdoor terrace.

Hotel Colina dos Mouros

℡ 282 440 420,
🄵 282 440 426

A modern hotel over the bridge from the fortress offering the most comfortable accommodation in town. Pleasant rooms with TVs and spotless bathrooms are complemented by an outdoor pool in the small, tranquil grounds. Large reductions out of season. ❹

Estabelicimentos Dom Sancho

Largo do Castelo
℡ 282 442 437

Superbly positioned by the entrance to the fortress, in a modern block above a commercial complex, the rooms here are large and airy with private bathrooms. Price does not include breakfast. ❸

Residencial Ponte Romana

Ponte Romana
℡ 282 443 275

Reached by the old pedestrian bridge over the river, this has simple, rather poky rooms with their own bathrooms; the best ones face the river. Price does not include breakfast. ❷

Quinta do Rio

Sitio São Estevão, Apartado 217
℡ 282 445 528, 🄵 282 445 528

Around 5km out of town, off the road to São Bartolomeu de Messines, this country inn has six delightful, rustic-style rooms with passionflower-shaded terraces facing open country. Breakfast consists of fresh fruit grown on the farm, and the Italian owners can supply evening meals on request. ❸

Residencial Sousa

Rua Samora Barros 17

ⓣ 282 442 502

Simple, faded rooms in an attractive town house a couple of blocks up from the riverfront. Communal bathrooms. ❷

Vila Sodre

ⓣ 282 443 441

Around a kilometre out of town on the busy Messines road, after the Galp service station, this spruce white villa offers small, clean rooms with a little pool out the back; there is also a popular old-world restaurant downstairs. ❸

THE TOWN

Silves has a diverse array of attractions encompassing the flat riverfront right up to the steep side streets around the castle, though you can comfortably see all of them on foot. Down on the riverfront, near the narrow thirteenth-century bridge, is the **market** (Mon–Sat 8am–1pm) with some fine outdoor grill-cafés (see p.196) where you can sit and watch life go by. The river valley opposite here is still cultivated, the fields dotted with superbly scented orange trees. From the riverfront road, a series of bustling cobbled streets lead uphill past shops and cafés to the small, leafy, central square, Praça do Município. Next to here is the town hall and the Torreão das Portas da Cidade – the remains of the Moorish town gate, from where it is a short walk to the **archaeological museum**. Above the town gates lie the oldest parts of town, dominated by the cathedral and the imposing **fortress** beyond.

During the summer, regular boat trips pass up the Rio Arade to Silves from Portimão; see p.204.

The Fortress

Daily: July–Aug 9am–8pm; Sept–June 9am–5.30pm; last entry 30 min before closing time; €1.25, under-12s free

The Moorish **fortress** remains the focal point of Silves. Restored in 1835 and again in 1940, it dominates the town centre with an impressively complete set of sandstone walls and detached towers. The interior is a bit disappointing: there's nothing much left of the old citadel, although the modern gardens are attractive enough, especially in spring when the jacaranda trees flower bluey-purple. One survivor is the wonderful vaulted thirteenth-century water cistern, the **Cisterna Grande**, that once served the town. Some 10m in height and supported by six columns, the cistern is said to be haunted by a Moorish maiden who can be seen sailing across the underground waters during a full moon. You can also clamber onto the castle **walls** and walk the complete circuit for impressive views over the town and surrounding hills.

The Sé

Mon–Fri 8.30am–6.30pm, Sun limited hours between Mass; free

Silves's cathedral, or **Sé**, sits below the fortress, an impressive thirteenth-century edifice built on the site of the Grand Mosque. Between 1242 and 1577, this was the Algarve's most important church, but then the bishopric was moved to Faro when Silves lost its role as a major port. Flanked by broad Gothic towers, it has a suitably defiant, military appearance, though the Great Earthquake and centuries of impoverished restoration have left their mark inside. The tombs lining the cathedral walls are of bishops and of Crusaders who died taking Silves back from the Moors.

Opposite the Sé, is the newer **Igreja da Misericórdia** (Mon–Fri 9.30am–1pm & 2–5.30pm; free), a sixteenth-century church with a fine Manueline doorway and hung with seven impressive religious images, painted on wood.

Museu Arqueologia

Mon–Sat 9am–6pm; €1.50

Below the Sé, in Rua das Portas de Loulé, is the town's **Museu Arqueologia**. It's engaging enough, despite a lack of English-language labelling, loosely divided into sections of Stone Age, Iron Age, Roman, Moorish and early Portuguese remains from Silves and the surrounding area. There are Stone Age pillars, Roman pots and coins and beautiful Moorish and later Portuguese ceramics. Upstairs, the temporary exhibition hall offers a great vantage point for looking down into the ten-metre-deep Moorish well, left *in situ* in the basement. You can also go out onto parts of the old **town walls** offering fine views over the town.

Fabrica Inglês

Daily 9am–midnight; free except during special events when hours and charges vary

On the riverfront some five minutes' walk east of the road bridge lies the **Fabrica Inglês**, an exhibition centre-cum-theme park embracing a small cork museum. The site is set in a former cork factory, opened in 1894 by a three-man team from Catalonia, Silves and England (hence the name). A series of cafés and bars are clustered round a large central courtyard filled with outdoor tables below scented orange trees. It is a lovely space, most animated when it hosts the annual summer **Silves Beer Festival**, usually in July, and on Friday nights when there are special events.

SILVES: THE TOWN

A RIVERSIDE WALK FROM SILVES TO ESTÔMBAR

This 10km (2.5hr) mostly level walk takes you along the south side of Rio Arade until it joins the Ribeira Odelouca and swings southwards. The walk offers the chance of sightings of birds galore including storks, egrets and herons – many of them in the tranquil setting of the Parque Nacional around Sítio dos Fontes do Estômbar, where you can swim in spring water and picnic. The walk ends at the town of Estômbar from where you can catch a train back to Silves.

In Silves, begin the walk by crossing the Ponte do Romano, leaving the restaurant of that name on your left. Follow the sign for Quinta dos Mata Mouros on your right, just short of the main road to Lagoa. Turn right at the sign to the Quinta following the river.

After 30 minutes, you'll reach the Quinta dos Mata Mouros, a politician's private residence enclosed by a high white wall. Stay with this track until 15 minutes after the tarmac turns to gravel, you'll come to a house with palms by the Rio Arade. Continue straight on as the track narrows and broadens again and follow the sign for "Fontes de Estômbar". When you reach a junction shortly after two houses, take the right turn. The path starts to climb, passing under high-tension wires, then descends to a farmhouse on the right (70min; 4km). The track widens, passes a raised irrigation canal and climbs quite steeply to an orange grove where you pass between two concrete posts, keeping a wire fence to your left. Head for the

Museu da Cortiças

Mon–Sun 9.30am–12.45pm & 2–6.15pm; €1.25

The Fabrica's permanent **Museu da Cortiças** (Cork Museum) is in the northwest corner of the complex, and concrete post on the hillbrow ahead and when you get there take a breather to absorb the wonderful views that unfold of the Rio Arade beyond.

Cross over the track and you'll find another path heading westwards where you can follow the green ventilation tubes of an underground water pipe, heading towards a white water tower in the distance. Descend steeply between boundary posts marked "ABA", to an old farmhouse-cum-store (95min; 6km). Pass to its northern side to continue southwest uphill to an imposing blue-and-white gateway to a house, called Monte dos Lusitanos (after 110min; 6.5km). Continuing straight on takes you to Fontes de Estômbar. By the "Entrada" sign, there's a picnic area with an open-air theatre and mill-house; just a little further up there's an inviting swimming area where you can take a dip. (120min; 7km).

Leave the Fontes by the track you came in on and continue onto the Silves–Estômbar road beneath the new motorway and turn right (southwest), past piles of rocks quarried for the new road; take the first wide, walled track leading westwards. Descend until you find an underpass to the EN125 on your left. Go through the underpass and bear left for Estômbar (140min; 9km), ending with a short climb to the church ahead. Estômbar's railway station is 15 minutes southeast through appealing streets. The train ride back to Silves (roughly hourly until 3pm, then every 2hr) gives magnificent views.

won the European Industrial Museum Award in 2001. But, unless you have a keen interest in the cork industry, its displays are unlikely to set your pulse racing. There are a few evocative black-and-white photos of local cork cutters, but otherwise the dull line of old cork-punching machines are about as exciting as a dentist's waiting room.

EATING AND DRINKING

Silves has a decent selection of places where you can eat and drink at any time of the day. After dark it's delightfully tranquil, a good antidote to the bustling nightlife of the coastal resorts.

Café Inglês
Escadas do Castelo
Mon 9.30am–6pm, Tues–Fri 9.30am–10pm, Sat 6pm–10pm.
Moderate
Touristy but very appealing town house decorated with period furnishings; tables spill onto the cobbles outside and there's also a roof terrace. Choose from moderately priced breakfasts, snacks, or full meals from Portuguese fare to pizzas. Friday and Saturday night often sees live Latin American or jazz music.

Restaurante Marisqueira Rui
Rua Comendador Vilarinho
☎ 282 442 682
Mon & Wed–Sun noon–3pm & 7–10pm. **Expensive**
This famous seafood restaurant continues to attract locals and tourists from all over the Algarve. You should definitely try to squeeze in and sample the restaurant's speciality shellfish.

U Monchiqueiro
Mon, Tues & Thurs–Sun noon–3pm & 7–11pm.
Inexpensive
The best of a handful of grill-cafés opposite the market. Sit outside and tuck into inexpensive *piri-piri* chicken, fries, salad and wine, or huddle under the awnings for live soccer on TV.

Pastelaria Rosa
Largo do Município
Daily 8am–10pm. **Inexpensive**
Superb old *pastelaria* with cool interior stone walls covered in *azulejos* and a

counter groaning with cakes and goodies. Outdoor tables spill onto the pretty main square next to the fountain.

BARRAGEM DO ARADE

Around 8km northeast of Silves, signed off the road to São Bartolomeu de Messines (see p.174), the **Barragem do Arade** is a good spot to visit for a swim, walk or for some more exerting water sports. There are various *barragems*, or reservoirs, dotted round the Algarve, many of them built during Salazar's dictatorship, and this is one of the area's main sources of water set amongst rolling, tree-lined hills. It's a bucolic spot popular with migrating birds, though when the water level falls in summer its scarred sides spoil the picturesque effect.

Just as the dam itself comes into view, take the left-hand fork in the road to *Café Coutada* (daily 10am–10pm), a café offering decent if slightly pricey drinks and meals on an outdoor terrace. The café can also organize **boat trips** to a scraggy, tree-lined offshore islet known as **Paradise Island**; the fee (€6.50 per person or €5 per adult with child; children free) covers the return boat trip together with use of canoes, sun loungers, and swimming in cordoned off areas of the reservoir (as the reservoir is a water supply, swimming elsewhere is discouraged). You can also hire jet skis.

Portimão and around

Some 16km southwest of Silves, 8km west of Lagoa on the EN125, **Portimão** is one of the largest towns in the Algarve, with a population of more than 30,000. Sitting on the estuary of the Rio Arade, it has made its living from fishing since pre-Roman times and remains a sprawling port today, a major sardine-canning centre and a base for the construction industries spawned by the tourist boom. Most visitors are just here for a day's shopping, or on their way to the town's nearest beach at the lively resort of **Praia da Rocha**, 3km south. Nevertheless, Portimão's bustling riverfront, with its boat trips and fish restaurants, is a good place to spend at least a couple of hours.

Just across the estuary to the east of Portimão – signed off the main EN125 – is the low-key and prettier town of **Ferragudo**, yet to be totally swamped by development and within reach of some fine cove beaches. For alternatives to the beach head inland to **Estômbar**, an unspoilt village with a fine church, and a nearby **water park**. Heading west from Portimão, coastal development intensifies around the superb swathes of beach at **Vau** and **Praia de Alvor**, the beach fronting the lively and picturesque estuary town of **Alvor**.

PORTIMÃO

Though not the most handsome town in the Algarve, **PORTIMÃO**'s largely pedestrianized central streets make it one of the area's better venues for shoppers. It's also the best place to catch a boat trip up the coast. Away from the riverfront, however, its cafés and restaurants cater largely to the local population, which means good food at decent prices.

Some history

Known as Portus Magnus in Roman times, Portimão became a major departure point for Portuguese **explorers**: Bartolomeu Dias set off from here in 1487 to become the first European to round the southern tip of Africa. Forts

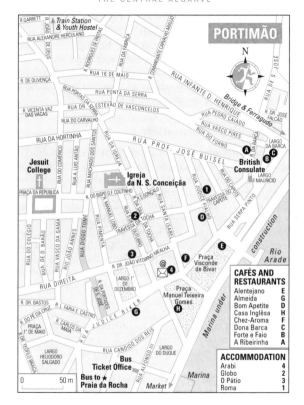

PORTIMÃO

N

Train Station & Youth Hostel

R GARRETT
RUA ALEXANDRE HERCULANO
RUA DA FABRICA
RUA RODRIGUES DE FREITAS
R DE OLIVENÇA
RUA 16 DE MAIO
RUA PONTA DA SERRA
RUA PORTAS DA SERRA
RUA DR ESTEVÃO DE VASCONCELOS
R. VICENTA VAZ DAS VACAS
RUA DR DA SERRA
RUA DO CARVALHO
RUA DA HORTINHA

RUA COMANDANTE CARVALHO ARAÚJO
RUA INFANTE D. HENRIQUE
Bridge & Ferragudo
RUA DE S JOSÉ
R. DR. JOSÉ FALCÃO
RUA PEDRO CAIADO
RUA VASCO PIRES
RUA DO FORNO
LARGO DA BARCA

RUA PROF. JOSÉ BUISEL

R DA BARCA

British Consulate

LARGO F. MAURICIO

Jesuit College

RUA DO COMÉRCIO
RUA A. LUIS ANTÃO
RUA MACHADO DOS SANTOS
RUA DA IGREJA
Igreja da N. S. Conceição
R. DO BISPO D.F. COUTINHO
R. S GONÇALO
RUA SANTA ISABEL
RUA DO CAPOTE
TRAVESSA DO CAPOTE
RUA SERRA PINTO
RUA DO CAPOTE

PRAÇA DA REPÚBLICA

RUA DR MANUEL LOBO
RUA DA ROCHA
TRAVESSA DO OUTEIRO

construction

Rio Arade

RUA DO COLÉGIO
RUA D DE D GAMA
RUA D DE D BARÃO
RUA DIOGO TOMÉ
RUA PIMENTA
RIO JOÃO ANNES
RUA DR JOÃO VITORNO MEALHA

Praça Visconde de Bivar

RUA DIREITA
LARGO 1º DE DEZEMBRO
@

Praça Manuel Teixeira Gomes

Marina under

CAFÉS AND RESTAURANTS	
Alentejano	E
Almeida	G
Bom Apetite	D
Casa Inglêsa	H
Chez-Aroma	F
Dona Barca	C
Forte e Faio	B
A Ribeirinha	A

R. DR. BASTOS
R. L. FARIA E. CASTRO
R. DO PÉ DA CRUZ
R. DA PORTUGUES DE S JOSÉ
RUA JUDICE BIKER
RUA CARLOS DA MAIA
PRAÇA 1º DE MAIO
R. DR. TEÓFILO BRAGA
RUA CANDIDO DOS REIS
RUA ALFONSO III

LARGO HELIODORO SALGADO

LARGO DO DUQUE

ACCOMMODATION	
Arabi	4
Globo	2
O Pátio	3
Roma	1

0 ___ 50 m

Bus Ticket Office
Bus to ★ Praia da Rocha

Marina

Market ▶

were built at either side of the Rio Arade in the sixteenth and seventeenth centuries to protect the town from pirate attacks, but protection was futile in 1755 when most of the town was destroyed in the Great Earthquake. It then fell into relative obscurity until 1924, when Portimão was given city status by President Manuel Teixeira Gomes, who was born here. Later in the twentieth century, under the authoritarian regime of Salazar, it developed into the Algarve's second most important **fishing centre**, but a reduction in subsidies after the dictatorship saw a steep decline in fishing and the fish canning industry. **Tourism** and construction are now the two main components of its economy.

Arrival and information

The **train station** is inconveniently located at the northern tip of town on Largo Ferra Prado. From here a bus runs every 45 minutes (Mon–Fri) into the centre; a taxi costs about €3–4, or it's a fifteen-minute walk. **Buses** (including those to and from Praia da Rocha) pull up much more centrally, in the streets around the Largo do Duque, close to the river. From here it's a five-minute walk past the riverside gardens to the quayside, which stretches as far as the bridge over to Ferragudo. The **turismo** recently closed in Portimão; the nearest one is in Praia da Rocha (see p.205).

Accommodation

There are not many places to stay in Portimão, though as most visitors simply drop in for an hour or two, you can usually find a space.

Pensão Arabi
Praça Manuel Teixeira Gomes 13
☏ 282 460 250, ℻ 282 460 269
Bright, airy and friendly *pensão*; front rooms face the noisy riverfront, while back ones are quieter but lack views. ❸

Hotel Globo
Rua 5 de Outubro Apartado 151
☏ 282 416 350, ℻ 282 483 142
Good-value modern high-rise close to the Igreja Matriz. The decor is dull but it has its own restaurant and top rooms overlook the harbour. ❸

Residencial O Pátio

Rua Dr. João Vitorino Mealha 3
ⓣ 282 424 288, ⓕ 282 424 281
Characterful guesthouse just
off Largo 1 de Dezembro,
with simple rooms and a
groovy little downstairs bar-
breakfast room complete with
fur-lined seats – and there's
an outside patio, of course.
Price does not include
breakfast. ❸

Residencial Roma

Rua Júdice Fialho 34
ⓣ & ⓕ 282 423 821
Cheap and cheerful place on
a lively cobbled street, some
rooms have little wrought-
iron balconies; shared
bathrooms. ❷

Youth Hostel

Lugar do Coca, Maravilhas
ⓣ & ⓕ 282 491 804
Well-equipped, large,
modern hostel with its own
small swimming pool, bar,
canteen, and sports facilities
that include snooker and
tennis courts. There are
plenty of dorm rooms
(sleeping four; €9) and a
handful of double rooms
(€20).

The Town

Modern **Portimão** is fairly undistinguished – most of the
older buildings were destroyed in the 1755 earthquake –
and these days pedestrianized shopping streets and graceless
concrete high-rises dominate. The most historic building is
the **Igreja da Nossa Senhora da Conceição** – five minutes' walk northwest of the riverfront Praça Manuel
Teixeira Gomes along Rua 5 de Outubro – rebuilt after the
earthquake but retaining a Manueline door from the original fourteenth-century structure; the interior is more
impressive, with three aisles and a vaulted ceiling. The walls
are covered in seventeenth-century decorative *azulejos*.

The encircling streets are pleasant enough, filled with
shops catering to the day-trippers – selling lace, shoes, jew-
ellery, ceramics and wicker goods; the main shopping streets

PORTIMÃO

are around the pedestrianized **Rua Diogo Tomé** and **Rua da Portades de S. José**. Just off the latter lies Largo 1 de Dezembro, an atmospheric square with benches inlaid with *azulejos* depicting Portuguese historical scenes, including Pedro Álvares Cabral's landing in Brazil in 1500.

The riverfront

The best part of town is undoubtedly the riverfront gardens, a series of squares – **Largo do Duque**, **Praça Manuel Teixeira Gomes**, and **Praça Visconde de Bivar** – with bustling cafés beneath shady trees right by the fishing **harbour**. Along here, you'll be approached by people offering **boat trips** along the coast to see weird and wonderful grottoes, including trips to Carvoeiro, Lagos and even up the Rio Arade to Silves; see p.204.

Heading north towards the bridge, a series of open-air restaurants have traditionally served inexpensive grilled sardine lunches, but these are all due to be removed to the other side of the river by late 2002 to make way for Portimão's expanding **marina**. This will join up with the existing marina at the mouth of the Rio Arade, a mass of flash yachts and a growing number of international restaurants.

The streets just back from the old bridge over the Rio Arade – off Largo da Barca – are Portimão's oldest: narrow, cobbled and with more than a hint of their fishing-quarter past. **Largo da Barca**, itself is a lovely little hidden square, lined with tables from various upmarket fish restaurants (see p.203).

Eating and drinking

Bar Alentejano

Praça Visconde de Bivar

Daily 10am–10pm. **Inexpensive**
Kiosk café-bar on the leafy square; take a seat under the trees for anything from a beer to an ice cream, pizza or a plate of snails.

Bom Apetite
Rua Júdice Fialho 21
Daily 10.30am–11pm.
Inexpensive
Bargain meat, fish, omelettes and jugs of house wine and sangria on a lively street full of bars and restaurants. The tourist menu is good value at around €9.

Casa Inglêsa
Praça Manuel Teixeira Gomes
Daily 8am–10.30pm.
Inexpensive
Large, cavernous café on the riverfront square, offering a good range of fresh juices and snacks; its sunny terrace is a popular meeting spot for the local ex-pat population.

Chez-Aroma
Rua Santa Isabel 14
May–Oct Mon–Fri noon–2pm & 6–10pm. Inexpensive
Dutch-owned restaurant serving very good value pan-Asian food including spring rolls, *sate ajam* (chicken kebab with peanut sauce), curries and set specials, with all you can eat for €15.

Dockside
Marina do Portimão ⓣ 282 417 208
Daily 10am–11pm. **Expensive**
One of a growing number of flash modern restaurants overlooking the marina; this *cervejaria* and *marisqueira* serves pricey but top quality seafood, fish and grills.

Dona Barca
Largo da Barca
Daily noon–3pm & 6–10pm.
Expensive
Very highly rated fish restaurant – it has frequently represented the Algarve at Lisbon's gastronomy fair – with a stone interior and outdoor tables on this pretty square. Serves typical Algarve cuisine including *feijoada de Buzinas* (shellfish with beans) and regional desserts such as *tarte de amendoa* (almond tart).

Forte e Faio
Largo da Barca
Daily noon–3.30pm & 7–11pm.
Moderate
Another highly regarded fish restaurant; not quite as pricey as *Dona Barca* but less well-positioned on the square.

PORTIMÃO

Pastelaria Almeida
Largo 1 de Dezembro 4
Thurs–Tues 8am–7pm
Simple *pastelaria* facing one of the town's nicer squares, famed for its traditional Algarvian sweets and pastries.

A Ribeirinha
Rua da Barca 15
Mon–Sat 10am–3pm & 6pm–midnight. **Inexpensive**
The decent prices and reliable meat and seafood attract a largely local clientele; it's on a side street near Largo da Barca.

Listings

Banks There are several round the central Praça da República and ATMs can be found on all the main shopping streets.

British consulate The Algarve's only consulate is in Portimão near the old bridge at Largo Francisco A. Mauricio 7–1° (☎282 417 800).

Boat trips Most operators work March–Oct: *The Santa Bernarda,* Rua Vasco da Gama 43, Ferragudo (☎282 461 097), is a 75ft, two-masted sailing caravelle which does 3hr return trips to Carvoeiro and Lagos for €25. *Algarve's Big Game Fishing Centre*, Rua António Dias Cordeiro 1 (☎282 425 866, Ⓦwww.cepemar.pt), offers daily fishing trips and dolphin-watching trips (from €47). *Agualta Lda*, Rua António Dias Cordeiro 3 (☎282 426 882, Ⓕ282 423 023), offers daily 3hr coastal trips (€20) and 4.5hr barbecue trips (€30). Many of the boat operators also offer 3hr return cruises up the Rio Arade to Silves, for around €18.

Bus information Portimão ☎282 418 120.

Hospital Sítio do Poço Secos, on the Monchique road (☎282 450 300). *Hospital Particular do Algarve*, Estrada do Alvor (☎282 420 400, Ⓕ282 420 404), is a privately run hospital on the Alvor road, with English-speaking staff and 24-hour emergency service.

Internet There's a terminal in the post office (see below).

Pharmacy *Dias*, Rua Direita, Portimão (Mon–Fri 9am–8pm, Sat & Sun 9am–2pm & 4pm–8pm).

Police Avda Miguel Bombarda 16 (℡ 282 417 510).

Post office Praça Manuel Teixeira Gomes.

Taxis There's a rank by Largo do Duque.

Train information ℡ 282 423 056.

PRAIA DA ROCHA

Praia da Rocha, five minutes south of Portimão by bus, was one of the first Algarve tourist developments and it's easy to see why. The magnificent **beach** is one of the most beautiful on the entire coast: a wide expanse of sand framed by jagged sea cliff and strange rock formations stretching east to the harbour walls at the mouth of the Rio Arade. Sadly the beach is backed by rather characterless high-rise hotels, discos and a casino, though here and there among the hotel blocks *fin-de-siècle* villas testify to the resort's more upmarket past. Most of the modern development is channelled into a strip just two-blocks wide north of the main street, Avenida Tomás Cabreira; from the *avenida* steep steps lead down to the sands.

The eastern end of Avenida Tomás Cabreira runs up to the walls of an old fort, the **Fortaleza da Santa Caterina**, built in 1691 to protect the mouth of the River Arade. The fort offers splendid views at sunset – beach and ocean on one side, Ferragudo, the marina and river on the other; there's also a small garden below the fort with great views back over the beach. Down the steep steps to the beach

PRAIA DA ROCHA

N

ACCOMMODATION

Algarve	5
Bela Vista	4
Jupiter	1
Oriental	6
Rocha	2
Solar Penguin	3
Vila Lido	7

RESTAURANTS

Estrela do Mar	D
La Cabassa	E
La Dolce Vita	C
A Portuguesa	A
Safari	B

0   150 m

below the castle, you can walk out along the harbour walls for more great views back to the fort. The opposite end of the beach, to the west, is marked by a **miradouro** with further views up the coast, though this end of Avenida Tomás Cabreira is tackier than the less-commercialized eastern end.

Practicalities

Bus connections from Portimão are regular, with services every fifteen to thirty minutes leaving from the stop just south of Largo do Duque (daily 7.30am–8.30pm); in Praia da Rocha they stop in front of the *Hotel da Rocha* on Avenida Tomás Cabreira. The return bus to Portimão leaves from the other side of the road (every 15–30min until 11.30pm; €1.50 single), or from the stop on Rua Engenheiro José de Bivar, at the back of the *Hotel da Rocha*. If you plan to do much to-ing and fro-ing between Rocha and Portimão, buy a block of ten tickets from a kiosk in Portimão, and you'll save around fifty percent on the fare.

The **turismo** (May to mid-September 9.30am–7pm; mid-September to April 9.30am–12.30pm & 1–5pm; ☎282

419 132) is in the hut next to the return bus stop. If you want to go on the **internet**, *windcafe.com* at Avenida Comunidade Lusiada, Edifício Girassol Loja 8 (☎282 417 290, ⓔind@windpoet.net), on the main Portimão road a few blocks north of the seafront is a one-stop tourist shop with 12 computers, internet (€4/hr) plus faxes, public phones, bike rental, postcards and souvenirs.

Accommodation

Finding accommodation is rarely a problem; ask at the turismo for an array of **private rooms**, or try one of the following **pensões** or **hotels**; the latter are expensive in high season but reduce their rates dramatically in winter.

Hotel Algarve

Avda Tomás Cabreira
☎282 415 001,
ⓦwww.solverde.pt
On a prime spot facing the beach, this modern high-rise has its own clifftop gardens; five-star facilities include two pools, a restaurant, bar and tennis courts, not to mention an attached casino. Disabled access. ❾

Hotel Bela Vista

Avda Tomás Cabreira
☎282 450 480,
ⓔinf.reservas@hotelbelavista.nt
The most stylish place to stay on the seafront, this pseudo-Moorish mansion was built in 1903; the interior is an exquisite mixture of carved woods, stained glass, and yellow, white and blue *azulejos*. Rooms are large and airy and there's a great downstairs beach-facing terrace. ❻

Hotel Jupiter

Avda Tomás Cabreira
☎282 415 041,
ⓔhoteljupiter@mail.telepac.pt
A modern hulk on the wrong (land) side of the *avenida*; comfortable enough, with disabled access, but you pay €20 more for a balcony ❻, up to ❼ for sea views.

Hotel Oriental

Avda Tomás Cabreira

PRAIA DA ROCHA

ⓣ 282 413 000,
ⓕ 282 413 413
A Moorish-influenced extravaganza of arches, domes and gardens on a clifftop right next to the beach, with all the comforts of a modern hotel. ➑

Hotel da Rocha
Avda Tomás Cabreira
ⓣ 282 424 081/2/3, ⓕ 282 415 988
This three-star is more affordable than many along this road and though it's on the land side of the *avenida*, it faces the ramp down to the beach so boasts sea views across the road; it also has its own restaurant and bar. ➏

Solar Penguin
Rua António Feu
ⓣ 282 424 308
Just off the main avenue on the cliffs above the beach this delightful, old *pensão* has a few comfortable rooms overlooking the sea; slightly fading at the edges, it is highly charismatic and it also has a restaurant. Closed mid-Nov to mid-Jan. ➌

Residencial Vila Lido
Avda Tomás Cabreira
ⓣ 282 424 127, ⓕ 282 424 246
This beautiful blue-shuttered building sits in the less tacky east end of the *avenida* in its own small grounds facing the fort; front rooms have superb views over the beach. ➎

Eating
Restaurants are plentiful in Portimão, and the half a dozen down on the beach mean that you don't have to leave the sands during the day.

La Cabassa
Avda Tomás Cabreira
Daily noon–2.30pm & 6–10.30pm. **Inexpensive**
Good value Italian fare and pleasant surroundings can be had at this Swedish-run place,

in a modern building set back off the main road towards the fort.

La Dolce Vita
Avda Tomás Cabreira, Edifício Mar Azul

Daily 11am–3pm &
6.30–10.30pm. **Inexpensive**
Out towards the fort on the
avenida, this is a lively place
with rustic decor. It is
owned and run by Italians,
so the home-made pasta,
pizzas, salads and ice creams
are reliably tasty; set lunches
start at €6.

Estrela do Mar
Areal da Praia da Rocha
Daily 9am–7pm. **Moderate**
Right on the beach with a
terrace facing the sands, this
simple place offers good value
fish, salads, meat dishes and
ice creams.

A Portuguesa
Avda Tomás Cabreira
Mon–Sat 3pm–2am. **Moderate**
At the far western end of the
avenida, this specializes in
solid Portuguese grills backed
by gentle jazzy sounds.

Safari
Rua António Feu
Daily noon–10pm. **Moderate**
Next to the *Solar Penguin*, this
decent restaurant overlooks
the beach and serves mainly
Portuguese dishes, a few with
an Angolan influence.
Various set menus start from
€13.

Drinking and nightlife

Praia da Rocha has a pulsating nightlife, with bars filling up
towards sunset, revving up at around midnight and going
full throttle into the small hours. The western end of the
main Avenida Tomás Cabreira is virtually one long strip of
bars and clubs; below are some of the better ones.

Babylone
Avda Tomás Cabreira
June–Sept daily 11pm–6am;
Oct–May Thurs–Sat 11pm–6am
Set just north of the *avenida*
in a basement, so no views to
distract punters from the

serious stuff of dancing to
thumping music til dawn.

Hotel Bela Vista
Avda Tomás Cabreira
Daily 8.30pm–midnight
For a civilized drink, the bar

of the hotel *Bela Vista* is open to the public in the evenings and offers lovely views over the beach, though as you'd expect, drinks aren't cheap.

Katedral
Avda Tomás Cabreira
June–Sept daily midnight–6am;
Oct–May Thurs–Sat
midnight–6am

Housed in a futuristic building next to the *Penguin*, this is the largest and highest-profile disco in town, with a lightshow and sounds from techno to house and garage.

On the Rocks
Avda Tomás Cabreira, Lojas B & C
Daily 10am–4am

A modern disco bar with a sunny terrace to catch the sunset before loud music

takes hold inside. Live soccer sometimes vies for attention in the bar; there's also a dance floor and live music on Fridays.

Pé de Vento
Avda Tomás Cabreira
Daily 3pm–4am

Another good-time disco bar over two floors. The upstairs bar has a beach-facing terrace next to a large dance floor which features live music on Wednesdays and Thursdays.

Tropicool
Avda Tomás Cabreira, Loja C
Daily midnight–4am

Small, intimate bar, popular with local travel reps, that gets louder and more libidinous as the night progresses.

FERRAGUDO

FERRAGUDO, facing Portimão across the estuary, is a resort with a very different feel. Although many of the old fishermen's cottages have been snapped up by wealthy Lisboans and ex-pats, few concessions have been made to international tourism and the village retains its traditional character. The town spreads round a strip of palm-fringed gardens running alongside a narrow riverlet up to the cobbled main square, Praça Rainha Dona Leonor, a wide space dotted with cafés. Just west of here, the riverlet ends at the Rio Arade estuary, where there is a small fishing harbour and a few fish restaurants. South of here, a warren of atmospheric cobbled backstreets straggle up the side of a hill, to the town's **church**, which dates back to the fourteenth century; there are great views over the estuary to Portimão from the church terrace. Running along the foot of the hill below the church – accessible from the fishing harbour or by taking the road that skirts the old town – lies the town **beach** – Angrinha – a thin stretch of sand which gets progressively more appealing as it approaches the **Castelo de São João do Arade**. The sixteenth-century fort, one of a pair to defend the Rio Arade (the other is opposite in Praia da Rocha, see p.205), is a tremendous site right on the sands. Remodelled in the early twentieth century by the poet Coelho Carvalho, it is currently in private hands and there are plans to turn it into a *pousada*.

Practicalities

Ferragudo is connected to Portimão by a regular bus service (daily hourly 7.30am–7.30pm).

ACCOMMODATION

Quinta da Horta
☏ 282 461 395, @ art-ferragudo@clix.pt
Around 2km out of town, this charming place is run by a British artist; a series of tasteful spartan studios and rooms are set round a tropical garden with a small pond. There's a little plunge pool, a sauna, TV room and a rundown tennis court. A superb organic breakfast is included in the price; evening meals on request. ❸

FERRAGUDO

Vila Castelo

Angrinha, Apartado 33

ⓣ 282 461 993, UK bookings
on ⓣ 01604 584888,

ⓦ www.vilacastelo.com

Modern, British-run upmarket
apartment complex on the
hillside opposite the castle, a
five-minute walk from the old
town church. Apartments are
well equipped with smart
kitchens and satellite TV; the
best ones have balconies or
terraces with superb views
over the castle. There's also a
communal pool. ❽

EATING AND
DRINKING

O Barril

Trav do Caldeirão

Mon–Sat noon–2pm & 7–11pm.
Expensive

Tucked under the arches in
an alley just off the main
square, this bar-restaurant
serves unexceptional and
pricey seafood and fish, but it
does offer live fado sessions
on Mon–Wed from 8pm.

Beira Mar

Praça Rainha D. Leonor

Daily 8am–10pm. Inexpensive

This smoky local café is more
appealing outside than in; its
tables on the square make a
good spot for a beer or
coffee.

Café Carramba

Rua Vasco da Gama 33

Daily 8pm–2am. Inexpensive

One of Ferragudo's livelier
bars, with pub-like decor;
down by the harbour.

Gelataria A Pérola

Praça Rainha D. Leonor

Daily 8am–9am, June–Sept until
midnight. Inexpensive

Filled with families at
weekends, this is the best spot
for ice cream and pastries;
sunny seats spill out onto the
square.

Portarade

Praça Rainha D. Leonor.

Daily 10am–1.30pm &
5.30–10pm.

Inexpensive–moderate

Large place with outdoor
tables right on the main
square. British-run and with
friendly service, though the
decor is cheesy. The
international menu features a

good range of kids' meals as well as bargain salad buffets and set lunches from €2.

O Velho Novo

Rua Manuel Teixeira Gomes 2
Daily 6pm–1am. **Inexpensive**

Five minutes' walk from the main square – cross the riverlet along the road signed to Belavista and it's on the left – this good value option offers fish and meats grilled on an outside barbecue; tables inside or sit out on wooden benches.

FERRAGUDO'S BEACHES

Though the town beach is pleasant enough, there is more space around the headland at **Praia Grande**, a wide sandy expanse lying within Portimão's harbour walls. The western end is dotted with restaurants, though the eastern end is quieter. You can walk here within twenty minutes from the town beach at low tide, or drive here along the coast road.

Better still is to walk a further twenty minutes along the coast east or drive the 2km to **Praia Pintadinho**, the next bay round with its own **café-restaurant**. Lying outside the harbour walls, the water is cleaner here, and the sandy cove has rock caves at either end to shelter from the sun. Scramble up the rocks to the east of the bay and there are some fine clifftop walks along the coast; within five minutes you reach a small lighthouse, with views to Ponta da Piedade to the west and on clear days as far as the Sagres peninsular (see p.268).

Continuing east from Praia Pintadinho along the coast path for twenty minutes or so – or a further five minutes' drive – takes you to the next beach, **Praia da Caneiros**, perhaps the best of the lot, an idyllic cove below cliffs with soft sand and another café-restaurant. Just off the beach, a rock stack known as Leixão das Gaivotas juts into view, usually flecked with basking cormorants.

FERRAGUDO'S BEACHES

ACCOMMODATION

Casabela Hotel
Praia Grande
ⓣ 282 461 580, ⓕ 282 461 581.
Set in a low modern building with fantastic grounds above Praia Grande and a short walk from Praia Pintadinho, this is a place well worth a splurge. Most rooms have wonderful views, and there's a pool, bar, tennis courts and disabled access. ❽

Parque Campismo de Ferragudo
ⓣ 282 461 121
The local campsite, 3km east of Ferragudo between Praia Pintadinho and Praia da Caneiros, is only open to those with an International Camping Carnet (see p.35). It's very well equipped with a pool, kids' play area, large supermarket and a restaurant. There's usually plenty of space for tents beneath the trees. Tents cost from €2.60, plus €4.20 per person.

EATING AND DRINKING

Escondidinho
Praia Grande
Oct–May daily 11am–5pm; June–Sept daily 10am–midnight. **Moderate**
The "little hidden one" is to the right of the steps down to the beach. Little more than a shack with an outdoor terrace, it offers a change with an international medley of dishes such as mushrooms in batter, lasagne and moussaka.

Restaurante Bar Pintadinho
Praia Pintadinho
March–Oct daily 10.30am–6.30pm.
Moderate–expensive
This simple beachside café-restaurant sits right on the sands; snacks and drinks are well priced but seafood and fish, though tasty, are expensive. The wonderful sea views, however, make it all worthwhile.

Restaurante Praia Grande

Praia Grande

Daily 11am–10pm (closed Wed from Oct–March). Moderate

Well-cooked Portuguese staples at slightly above-average prices, but it's in a great position on a raised terrace overlooking the beach. The tourist menu is better value at €11.

Restaurante Rei das Praias

Praia da Caneiros

March–Oct daily 9am–midnight.

Moderate

On stilts above the beach, this is a superb place for a meal, either on the terrace or in the wood-panelled interior. Grilled meat, fish and seafood are surprisingly reasonable, as are the bar snacks such as *bifanas*, toasts and sandwiches.

ESTÔMBAR

A few kilometres north east of Ferragudo is **ESTÔMBAR** (a stop for slow trains on the Algarve line), an unremarkable little town that was once an important Moorish town thriving on salt production and the birthplace of the eleventh-century Moorish poet Ibn Ammâr. Today the town straggles down a steep hill in a confusion of narrow lanes – nothing very special, though free from tourist trappings. The most interesting sight is the church, the **Igreja de Sant'Iago**, which looks like a diminutive version of the superb abbey church at Alcobaça north of Lisbon. The interior has superb eighteenth-century *azulejos* and two Manueline sculpted columns carved with exotic plants and vines.

For details of a superb walk from Silves to Estômbar, see p.194.

For slides, pools and aquatic fun, visit the **Slide & Splash** theme park (☎282 341 685; daily May–Oct

MANUELINE ARCHITECTURE

The Manueline period refers to the reign of Manuel I (1495–1521), one of the wealthiest most dynamic eras in the country's history. This period witnessed the peak of Portugal's maritime explorations as well as the country's wealth, which was sufficient to fund the building of numerous grand churches and mansions. Navigators returned home with exotic treasures and even more fabulous tales; these stories heavily influenced the elaborate decoration of the Late Gothic buildings. Windows, doors and supporting columns were decorated with swirling ropes, anchors, shells, mast-like pillars and exotic plant and animal life. The eclectic style often included Moorish touches, armillary spheres – Dom Manuel's emblem – or a cross representing the Order of Christ, who financed so many of the voyages.

Many of the Algarve's early Manueline buildings were destroyed in the earthquake of 1755 or, have subsequently been altered, but Manueline touches do survive in many churches in the region. Particularly noteworthy are the church of Santa Maria in Lagos (see p.242), the Ermide de São Sebastião in Albufeira (see p.161), and the churches in Alvor, Alte, Monchique, Luz de Tavira, São Bartolomeu de Messines and Estômbar.

10am–5pm; €10, children €7.50), around 3km outside Estômbar, signposted off the EN125 at Vale de Deus.

WEST OF PORTIMÃO

The coast west of Portimão between Praia da Rocha and Alvor is little more than a line of apartments, hotels and restaurants running either side of the coastal highway. But, as always it's easy to turn a blind eye to the unsightly sprawl, and enjoy the fine beaches of **Praia do Vau**, and **Praia de**

Três Irmãos, which merges with the best one at **Praia de Alvor**. The latter peters out at the estuary of the Rio de Alvor, from where it is a short walk to the town of **Alvor**, an erstwhile fishing village with a characterful riverfront harbour close to the **Quinta da Rocha** seabird refuge.

Vau, Praia de Três Irmãos and Praia de Alvor

Around 3km west of Praia da Rocha, **VAU** is an undistinguished resort facing a lovely, typically Algarvian beach backed by rock pillars and cliffs. The town's apartments make up a fairly undistinguished settlement, but there are plenty of clifftop restaurants if you fancy stopping for a meal.

Separated by a rocky headland – which you can walk round in twenty minutes or so – lies a far more extensive stretch of sands, **PRAIA TRÊS IRMÃOS** which becomes **PRAIA DE ALVOR**. Both beaches are backed by villas and hotels especially at the eastern end, but there's usually enough space to lay your towel with a little privacy, even in high season. Regular daily **buses** run from Portimão to Alvor along the coastal stretch, calling at all the beaches en route.

ACCOMMODATION

Carlton Alvor Hotel
Praia do Alvor
☎ 282 400 900,
✉ pestana.hotels@mail
.telepac.pt
One of three hotels from the Pestana chain along this stretch and the plushest of the lot: set in its own grounds right on the beach. Five-star comforts include satellite TV, three restaurants, seven tennis courts, a bar and kids' playground. ➒

Dom João II
Praia do Alvor

⊤ 282 400 700,
ⓔ pestana.hotels@mail
.telepac.pt
Around 1km from Alvor,
facing the beach, this high-
rise four-star has a large pool,
kids' club and restaurant: it's
very comfortable but soulless.
Guests have discounts at the
nearby Tennis Country Club
and the Pinta and Gramacha
Golf Courses. In low season,
prices are reduced by up to
fifty percent. Disabled access.
❽

Residencial do Vau
Apartado 158, Vau
⊤ 282 401 312, ⓕ 282 401 756
Set just off the main coast
road in delightful gardens,
this atmospheric old
guesthouse has 21
comfortable en-suite double
rooms. It's about five
minutes' walk from Vau
beach. ❸

EATING AND DRINKING

Restaurante Cinco Quintas
Praia de Alvor
Daily 10am–10pm. **Inexpensive**
This small beach shack
decorated with soccer scarves,
around ten minutes' walk
south of Alvor's fishing
harbour, attracts a young,
lively clientele and offers the
usual array of snacks, toasted
sandwiches and grilled meat
and fish.

Restaurante Rosamar
Praia de Alvor
May–Oct daily 9am–9.30pm;
Nov–April daily 10am–5pm;
closed Dec. **Moderate**
The nearest beach restaurant
to Alvor. Service can be surly
but it does serve some tasty
and unusual dishes such as
sardines with rice and beans.

ALVOR

Founded as a fishing village by the Moors, **ALVOR**, 6km
west of Praia da Rocha and less than 1km north of Praia de
Alvor, briefly achieved fame when King João II died here

in 1495. Although much of the town was razed in the 1755 earthquake, it still boasts a sixteenth-century **Igreja Matriz** with superb Manueline doors, arches and pillars carved into fishing ropes and exotic plants. It remained a sleepy fishing village until the 1960s, when tourism began to take hold, and today the old town has been outgrown by a rash of modern – though largely low-rise – buildings. The old core around the church and the central Praça da República is the most enjoyable and atmospheric part of town, and the harbour itself is a delight, lined with colourful fishing boats and aromatic fish restaurants.

The town's **turismo** is in the centre of town at Rua Dr. Alfonso Costa 51 (daily: July–Sept 9.30am–7pm; Oct–Jun 9.30am–1pm & 2–5.30pm; ☎282 457 540). From here it's a short walk uphill to the vestiges of Alvor's thirteenth-century **castle**, now a leafy ruin with a children's playground. Opposite the castle lies the small covered **market**, which is usually animated from the early hours. From here, Rua Padre David Neto leads onto the main drag, Rua Dr. Frederico Romas Mendes, lined with bars and restaurants leading down to a pedestrianized square, Largo da Ribeiro, right on the **riverside**. The square is marked by a quirky modern statue of a fish; appropriately, marking the old fish market (now deserted) and faced by half a dozen excellent fish restaurants. The views here are wonderful, overlooking the picturesque estuary of the **Rio Alvor**, swooped by seagulls and lined with beached fishing boats. Head right as you face the river and a walkway leads up the estuary for an attractive *passeio*; head left and ten minutes' walk past the fishermen's huts you reach the extensive sands of Praia de Alvor (see p.217).

Practicalities

Regular **buses** (roughly hourly) run to Alvor from Portimão. The **turismo** is in the centre of town at Rua Dr.

ALVOR

●

Alfonso Costa 51 (daily: July–Sept 9.30am–7pm; Oct–Jun 9.30am–1pm & 2–5.30pm; ⓣ282 457 540). **Accommodation** is in short supply in Alvor but the tourist office should be able to help with details of private rooms, or try *Hospedaria Buganvilia*, Rua Padre Mendes Rossio de 5 Pedro, Lote 2 (ⓣ282 459 412; ❹), just down the hill from the tourist office. The rooms are spotless, most have balconies, and there's also a roof terrace. Alternatively, Alvor has a **campsite**, *Campismo Dourado* (ⓣ282 459 178, ⓕ282 458 002; €3/person, from €2.50/tent), around 1km north of town on the EN125, a pleasant enough leafy site with basic facilities. Alvor is well catered for when it comes to **restaurants** and **bars**; there are at least a dozen Irish bars alone.

Café Alicança
Praça da República
Daily 9am–2am. Inexpensive
Opposite the turismo and next to the small Igreja Miseracordia church, this is the locals' favourite for snacks and drinks, with outside seats on a small square.

Casa da Maré
Largo da Ribeira
Tues–Sun 10am–10pm.
Moderate
One of a row of decently priced fish restaurants on the harbourfront; this one benefits from its prime position with tables spilling

out onto the square.

Pastelaria Perini
Rua Dr António José D'Almeida
Daily 8am–midnight.
Inexpensive
Just downhill from the tourist office, this traditional *pastelaria* has a counter full of speciality cakes; it also offers a good range of croissants and snacks such as crepes and pizzas.

Tasca do Margadinho
Largo da Ribeirinho 9
Daily 10am–midnight.
Inexpensive
Atmospheric *tasca* opposite the old fish market with a

local feel and superbly grilled fresh fish; tables outside on the square too.

Tasca Morais
Rua Dr António José D'Almeida 14

Daily (closed Wed) 6pm–9.30pm. Moderate

Less pricey than some of the harbourside restaurants, with good grills and seafood dishes such as *arroz de marisco* and *cataplana e choco com ameijoas*.

QUINTA DA ROCHA NATURE AREA

The **Quinta da Rocha nature area** lies on a peninsula between the mouths of the rivers Alvor and Odiáxere, northwest of Alvor's huge beach. It is an extensive area which, in the parts not given over to citrus and almond groves, protects copses, salt marshes, sandy spits and estuarine mud flats, all offering a wide range of habitats for different plants and animals – including twenty-two species of **wading bird**. Flanked by the Penina Golf Club to the northeast and the Palmares Golf Club to the west (see p.44), the area remains vulnerable as protected status has not been secured, despite attempts by environmentalists; for the time being, however, development is being kept at bay. With a car, the best approach to the reserve is along the small turning off the EN125 opposite Mexilheira Grande, signed Benavides/Quinta da Rocha – by public transport, take a bus or train from Portimão to Mexilheira Grande, which is around 2km north of the area. There are plenty of narrow roads and tracks to wander around the estuary and see wading birds and clam fishermen.

Serra de Monchique

Ten weekday buses – five at weekends – leave Portimão for the 24km journey north to the market town of **Monchique** via the historic spa of **Caldas de Monchique**. Once clear of Portimão's suburbs, the main road crosses the coastal plain, flanked by verdant orchards of apples, pears, figs, almonds, pomegranates and citrus fruits. At Porto de Lagos the road divides, east to Silves (see p.187) and north into the foothills of the **Serra de Monchique**, a green and wooded mountain range of cork, chestnut and eucalyptus trees that acts as the natural northern boundary for the Algarve. It is ideal **hiking country**, embracing two of the region's highest peaks, Picota and Fóia, or – with a bike or car – a superb route to take if you want to cut across afterwards to the wilder reaches of the western Algarve coast.

CALDAS DE MONCHIQUE

Caldas de Monchique, set in a steep valley and surrounded by thick woods, has been a spa since Roman times. It is particularly spectacular in autumn when the deciduous trees – a relative rarity in Portugal – display fantastic colours. In the nineteenth century the town became a favourite resort for the Spanish bourgeoisie. The waters are still said to have healing powers for skin and chest complaints, and the thermal spa is therapeutic as well as a leisure facility. A couple of years ago the Monchique Termas company bought virtually the entire village and began turning the rundown buildings into hotels and guesthouses, revitalizing the cafés and shops and modernizing the spa itself. They have transformed a somewhat ramshackle village into a tourist resort; old buildings have been sympathetically restored and the gardens improved.

The centre of Caldas de Monchique is reached by a looping, one-way road which branches off the main Portimão–Monchique road. Halfway down the hill on the left you'll see the cobbled, tree-shaded **main square**, fronted by the pseudo-Moorish windows of the former casino – now a *pensão* – and flanked by lovely, nineteenth-century buildings. The setting is as beautiful as any in the country, and though its attractions lure in day-trippers during high season, at other times – and by the end of the day – it can be delightfully tranquil.

Heading downhill from the main square, you pass the **Bouvet** – a little stone building where you can drink the waters straight from the ground. This was the original spa building, now earmarked to become a museum. The modern **thermal spa** (☎ 282 910 910, ✉ spa@monchiquetermas .com) sits below the main square on the edge of a ravine, flaunting its well-kept gardens and embracing a pool, sauna, jacuzzi, Turkish bath and various specialist water treatments on the ground floor of a modern hotel. Sessions range from 40-minute "healthy leg" treatment (€36) to weekend residential pampering with full board (€172 per person).

Up from the spa, above the main square, follow the stream out of the village to a tranquil picnic spot shaded by giant eucalyptus trees. Take along some of the local drink, *medronho*, a kind of schnapps made from the Arbutus or Strawberry Tree that grows on the surrounding hills and which is sold in virtually all the shops and bars in the region.

Practicalities

Regular **buses** from Portimão pass the turning to Caldas on their way to and from Monchique. Some of these call into the centre of Caldas, though most stop instead on the main road five minutes out of town.

CALDAS DE MONCHIQUE

A ROUND WALK FROM CALDAS DE MONCHIQUE

This circular 5.5km (2hr) walk is a good way to appreciate the beautiful scenery around Caldas de Monchique, passing through delightful deciduous woodland. Head southwest out of the main square, past the spa and bottling plant. After about 1km, turn right on to a steeply descending stony track to the south of the plant – you'll see a gullied stream on your right. Follow the path for another 10 minutes or so until you reach a solid bridge of railways sleepers (take care in wet weather as they can be slippery). Cross over and climb steeply up to the track on the right (30 min; 1.5km). Continue as the path zig-zags uphill. Five minutes further and you'll reach the top of the hill (after 45min; 2.5km), from where you'll see the dramatic summit of Foia, marked by antennae (see p.227). Start to descend westwards to arrive at a Y-junction after 300 metres. Turn left here and the track doubles backwards and forwards until turning eastwards.

Below, to your left lies the factory where Monchique paving stones (*calçados*) are manufactured from local granite (Monchiquite). After an hour (3km) the path descends steeply to the left, with the small hamlet of Ribeira de Banho in the valley below.

Head along this track northeast until you reach a footpath skirting the hill to your left, with a sheep fence on your right. Take this path towards a stream and you arrive at a bridge by a house (70min; 3.75km). Continue northwards, climbing gradually back up to the timber bridge across the stream and you've completed the circle (85min; 4.25km). At the bottling plant (100min; 4.8km), you can return to the main square on a different route by keeping to the right of the building, then turning left past offices to walk alongside a high granite wall. At the wall's end, there are steps up through colourful gardens that take you back to the main square.

Accommodation

Apart from the *Albergaria do Lageado* (see below), the accommodation reviewed below is all owned by the Monchique Termas company (☏ 282 910 910, ✉ fpguerreiro@monchiquetermas.com). They also hire out **apartments** overlooking the main square, with small living rooms and kitchenettes, sleeping up to four people from €90 a night.

Pensão Central

Very comfortable three-star pension partly set in the former casino building; modern comforts include fridges, satellite TV and air conditioning. ❺

Estalagem Dom João 11

Facing the main square, opposite the *Pensão Central*, this four-star inn in a converted nineteenth-century building has similar services but marginally larger rooms than the *Central*. ❺

Albergaria do Lageado

Open May–Oct; ☏ 282 912 616, ⒡ 82 911 310

Just above the main square, this lovely four-star hotel has twenty smart rooms, with TVs and en-suite bathrooms. There's a pool in the garden and an excellent restaurant. Closed Jan–April. ❺

Eating and drinking

Bar Caldas

Daily 9am–8pm. **Inexpensive**

On the far side of the main square, below the path to the picnic area, this darkened bar is housed in the oldest building in the village, in sixteenth-century stables. Specialities include bread rolls with sausage meat baked in a traditional oven outside.

Restaurante Dom João II (1692)

Daily 10am–8pm.

Moderate–expensive

High-profile restaurant in a building dating from 1692,

CALDAS DE MONCHIQUE

with lovely outdoor tables under the trees of the main square. The menu includes interesting starters such as *morcelo* (spicy sausage), followed by conventional grilled fish and meat dishes.

O Rouxinol

Tues–Sun noon–10pm.

Expensive

Highly rated restaurant set in a former hunting lodge on the main road just above town. With a giant fireplace – said to be large enough to roast a whole pig – the inside is very cosy but there's also an outdoor terrace facing wooded slopes. The Swedish owners serve up Portuguese and international dishes, salads and great desserts.

MONCHIQUE AND AROUND

Monchique, 6km to the north of Caldas de Monchique, and 300m higher up the range, is a small town whose large **market** on the second Friday of each month is famous for smoked hams and locally made furniture – especially distinctive x-shaped wooden chairs. There's also a Monday to Saturday fruit and vegetable covered market downhill north of the Igreja Matriz. There's not a great deal else to see, but it's a busy town and makes a nice excursion. The older buildings have recently been spruced up and the centre is dotted with Meccano-like metal sculptures of local characters made by the contemporary Lisbon artist, Doutor Vanancio. The most impressive building is the parish church, the **Igreja Matriz** (Mon–Sat 10am–5.30pm), up a steep cobbled street from the main square, with an imposing Manueline porch and, inside, a little chapel covered with *azulejos*.

The most evocative of the town's sights though, is the ruined Franciscan monastery of **Nossa Senhora do Desterro**, which you can walk to in fifteen minutes or so up a wooded track – brown signs point you up here from Rua do Porto Fundo leading uphill from the bus station. Only a roofless shell of this seventeenth-century foundation survives but it's in a great position overlooking the town and there's a beautiful blend of classical Renaissance facade with Moorish-influenced vaulting.

South of Monchique, the EN267 snakes through wooded mountain scenery to Aljezur (see p.285) on the Algarve's west coast. You'll need your own transport or there are two daily buses from Monchique which go as far as Marmelete, 14km west, from where you can pick up a half-day walk to Aljezur (see p.288).

Fóia

On Mondays and Thursdays, two buses (11am and 3.30pm) run from Monchique to the top of the 900m peak of **Fóia**, 8km to the west. It's a lovely journey – by car or bus, or an energetic walk (see box p.228) – up to the highest peak in the Serra, winding through wooded slopes dotted with upmarket inns (see p.231) and *miradouros* offering superb views over the south coast. Bristling with antennae and radio masts and capped by an ungainly modern complex of a café-restaurant, shop and hotel, the summit itself can be an anticlimax, especially if clouds obscure the views or you have to share the experience with multitudes in midsummer. Get here early if you can. On a clear day, the panoramic view of the Algarve takes in Portimão, Lagos, the foothills stretching to the Barragem da Bravura, and across west to Cabo de São Vicente. The poet Robert Southey claimed to have caught a glimpse of the hills of Sintra, beyond Lisbon, but that must have been poetic licence – or maybe the air's not as clear now as it was in 1801.

MONCHIQUE AND AROUND

A WALK FROM MONCHIQUE TO FÓIA

This 10.5km (3hr) walk takes you from the centre of Monchique up to the peak of Fóia, via the northern slopes of the mountain. The path avoids steep ascents and affords fantastic views over the western Algarve coast.

From Monchique bus station, follow the brown signs for the Convento, which you pick up from Rua Porto Fundo. At the top end of town, take the steep right fork (made of *calçados*). The wide road narrows into a rough stony track is you pass a shrine on your left. As you continue climbing, the path curves left. Before reaching the convent, turn right (northwards, then curve northwest) around the back up a bank covered with oak trees, using any of the numerous paths (they all end in the same place). At the top you'll find a distinct, rocky pathway (15min; 0.5km).

Follow the track under power lines until it curves left through a gap in a metal road barrier, and you're out on a wide tarmac road. Take note of this point as it's a marker on your return route. Turn left uphill on to the road and within 50m, take the steep track on your right (25min; 1km). Five minutes later the route narrows to a single pathway then, as it levels, begins to widen again, giving you good views northwards. The path meets a grey, gravelled road where you turn left, heading uphill towards a white house (40min; 1.75km). Ignore the first track to the left, taking instead the second grassy path to the left; continue uphill leaving the white farmhouse below your right. Within 100m you'll pass a *cisterna* on your left. Continue climbing as the track bends sharply left and reaches a junction, next to a small cairn. As you turn right here, look northwards for fine views over the rolling hills of the Alentejo.

After 70m or so, cut through the copse on your left (south) to pick up a track, where you turn left (southeast) and within 100m a stone wall begins on your right. Just past the end of this wall, take the indistinct path to your right and drop down onto a lower, well-used track and again turn right (60min; 2km). Climbing now (west), you leave an old building below you on your left and breathtaking coastal views appear beyond. Before you reach the tall eucalypti at the top of the hill ahead of you, turn right onto the path marked by a large rock painted red, and climb still farther uphill until you come to a bend on a tarmac road. Take a second to clamber up the rocky knoll (822m) on your right and drink in the splendid views (70min; 3km). Back on the tarmac road, continue for another 30 minutes all the way up to the Foía peak (100min; 5km). The terrain here is coarse, rock-strewn grassland above the treeline, with views down to abandoned crofts below and the Alentejo beyond.

From the peak, start your return (eastwards) by using the worn concrete track that passes between the cluster of red and white antennae and a concrete building marked NAV; keep the wire fence on your right until the concrete turns into a stony path. Your descent provides a panorama southwards and it is helpful to use the distant fire watchtower on Picota as a guideline. This shepherds' path descends southeast until it joins a track where you should turn left (east).

Shortly, you'll find a terrace of abandoned cottages next to a fine spreading chestnut tree (130min; 7km). Five minutes past the settlement is a tarmac road where you should turn right to descend between the welcome shade of some eucalyptus trees. The tarmac will take you all the way down, with beguiling glimpses of Monchique and its convent, to a large rounded rock on your left, where the tarmac meets a wider road which you turn left onto (155min; 8.8km). After a short distance, you'll recognize the metal road barrier, now on your right, which you passed through on your outward journey. From here follow the route down through the oak trees to the convent using the path by which you left Monchique (180min; 10.5km).

A WALK FROM MONCHIQUE TO FÓIA

Picota

Reaching 770m, **Picota** comes second in altitude to Fóia, though it's much more interesting in terms of its botany, and easier to reach without your own transport – you can drive the 5km here, or it's a one-and-a-half-hour walk to the peak from Monchique through attractive cork plantations, fruit orchards and eucalyptus trees, with wild goats scurrying around on the higher reaches. To reach Picota, take the EN266 Caldas de Monchique road, and turn left onto the EN267, signposted Alferce. Picota is the second turning, signed around 800m along this road off to the right. At the top there's nothing save a rickety watchtower occupied by a solitary guardian with a pair of binoculars. The coastline stretches out below all the way west to Sagres, and behind, is the magnificent Monchique mountain range.

Practicalities

Buses from Portimão arrive at the terminal in the main square, Largo 5 de Outubro. Opposite here, Monchique's helpful **turismo** (Mon–Fri 9.30am–1pm & 2–5.30pm; ☎ 282 911 189) sits on a pretty pedestrianized part of the square next to a modern fountain and a small children's play area. You can get on the **internet** at the Clube de Video de Monchique, Rua Serpa Pinto 46 next door to the tourist office (Mon–Fri 5pm–9pm, Sat & Sun 3pm–9pm).

Accommodation

There are a couple of simple **accommodation** choices in Monchique, though if you want something a bit more upmarket, it is best to head out onto the Fóia road where there are some superb *estalagems* (inns).

Bela Vista

Largo 5 de Outubro

ⓣ 282 912 252

Right next to the Monchique bus station above a decent café, with basic comforts and a communal bathroom. The front rooms have balconies facing the square, but these can be noisy. Price does not include breakfast. ❷

Estalagem Abrigo da Montanha

Estrada da Fóia

ⓣ 282 912 131,

ⓔ abrigodamontanha@hotmail .com

Just out of Monchique on the Fóia road, this modern granite and wood chalet-style inn has comfortable rooms, some with great views over the valley. There's also a pool, a downstairs restaurant, and a roaring fire when the air turns chilly. ❺

Estalagem de Santo António

Alto da Fóia

ⓣ 282 912 158, ⓕ 282 912 878

Large, modern rooms with TV and baths right on the summit of Fóia – and offering the superb views you'd expect. Price includes breakfast. ❹

Estrela de Monchique

Rua do Poço Fundo 46

ⓣ 282 913 111

Just to the east of the bus terminal, this is much the best budget option in town, with bright modern en-suite rooms; top floor rooms have balconies. Price does not include breakfast. ❷

Quinta de São Bento

Estrada da Fóia

ⓣ & ⓕ 282 912 143

4.5km out of Monchique, around 1km below the Fóia summit, this wonderful old stone *quinta* is set on a peaceful slope amongst chestnut woods. It has five comfortable rooms and one apartment and is also famed for its cuisine (see p.232). ❹

MONCHIQUE AND AROUND

Eating and drinking

Restaurante Central
Rua da Igreja 5
Daily 11am–7.30pm.
Inexpensive

A tiny place smothered with notes and postcards detailing past visitors' comments – mainly complimentary. The menu is limited to two or three average Portuguese dishes, but the place scores high on character.

Restaurante A Charrete
Rua Dr Samora Gil 30–34
Daily 12.30–10pm. **Expensive**

This smart restaurant on the road up to the convent is the best place to eat in Monchique, specializing in award-winning but not too pricey "mountain food" – cooked with beans, pasta and rice – along with more conventional Algarve fare.

A Nova
Largo dos Chorões
Daily 9am–9pm. **Inexpensive**

Bustling café-bar next to the tourist office, offering good-value snacks and light meals with tables spilling out onto the attractive main square.

Restaurante Quinta de São Bento
Estrada da Fóia, ☎ 282 912 143
Tues–Sun noon–3pm & 7–10pm. **Reservations advised.**
Expensive

It's worth booking ahead for a meal at this superb *quinta* just below Fóia (see above). The award-winning cuisine features regional specialities, prepared with local produce such as Monchique ham, goat's cheese, *chouriço*, almonds and figs.

The western Algarve

From the low-key former fishing villages of Burgau and Salema to the wild beaches near Aljezur and Odeceixe, the **western Algarve** offers a glimpse of how the region was before tourism made its mark. Its main centre, **Lagos**, the Algarve's most enjoyable town, is the former regional capital and a historic port that has grown into a large and bustling but relatively unspoiled resort within a short walk of some superb beaches.

The area covered in this chapter is shown on map 1, at the back of the book.

Head a little west from Lagos and the countryside becomes wilder and less built up, and the lush Mediterranean-type vegetation gives way to coarser Atlantic scrub and grassland. It's a highly scenic area with a gently rolling landscape embracing agricultural villages, clifftop walks and remote cove beaches. Much of the coastline here is part of the Parque Natural do Sudoeste Alentejano e Costa Vicentina and new development south and west of the main coastal highways is restricted, leaving small, family-orientated resorts such as **Luz**, **Burgau** and **Salema**. Only **Sagres**, site of Henry the Navigator's fortress, attracts more of a crowd lured by a good selection of beaches and a lively summer nightlife. The scenery becomes even wilder and less verdant as you head west, culminating in the wind-swept peninsula of **Cabo de São Vicente**, once considered the end of the world.

North of here, the Algarve's **west coast** faces the full brunt of the Atlantic, whose crashing breakers and cooler waters have deterred developers. The rocky coastline is punctuated by fantastic broad beaches accessible from the minor villages of **Vila do Bispo** and **Carrapateira**, or the prettier and livelier **Aljezur** and **Odeceixe**. These bases attract a rather more youthful and alternative crowd than resorts on the south coast, with nude sunbathing and surfing the norm.

A few kilometres inland, wild lynx still survive in the gently rolling, wooded hills of the Serra do Espinhaço de Cão, where there is a great half-day walk around **Marmelete** and some gentler strolls at the scenic reservoir, **Barragem de Bravura**.

Lagos is the most western terminus of the main Algarve **railway** line, but regular **buses** run between all the main villages and resorts throughout the year. However, if you want to get to the remoter beaches and up into the hills, it is best to arrange your own transport.

Lagos and around

At the mouth of the Rio Bensafrim, its historic centre enclosed in largely fourteenth-century town walls, **LAGOS** is one of the Algarve's most attractive and interesting towns.

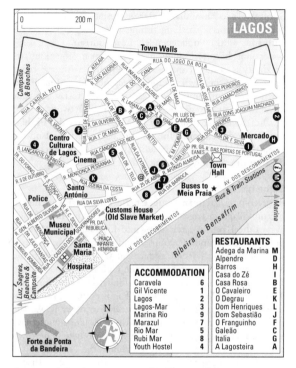

LAGOS

0   200 m

Town Walls

Campsite & Beaches

RUA CARDEAL NETO

RUA DA ATALAIA

RUA DAS ALEGRIAS

RUA INFANTE DE SAGRES

RUA DO JOGO DA BOLA

TRAV. 1 DE MAIO

RUA DOS PEIXEIROS

RUA DA. JOSÉ ALMEIDA

RUA DR. JOSÉ ALMEIDA

RUA CONS JOAQUIM MACHADO

RUA DE GIL VICENTE

RUA LUIS DE AZEVEDO

RUA DA OLIVEIRA

RUA DA FERRADURA

R. LARANJEIRA

RUA 1º DE MAIO

RUA DO. PERREIRAS NETTO

RUA DA VIANA

PR. LUIS DE CAMÕES

RUA DOS FERREIROS

R. DR. F. SILVA

RUA CAMACHINHOS

Mercado

Centro Cultural de Lagos

Cinema

RUA LANÇAROTE DE FREITAS

RUA CÂNDIDO DOS REIS

RUA DA EXTREMA

R. M. LEITÃO

PR. GIL R. EANES

DAS PORTAS DE PORTUGAL

R. 5 DE OUTUBRO

R. DO TORNO

R. G. GONÇALO

RUA MENDONÇA PESSANHA

RUA DR. J. TELO

RUA 25 DE ABRIL

R. AFONSO ALMEIDA

Santo António

RUA SOEIRO DA COSTA

@

Police

RUA DA SILVA LOPES

Town Hall

AV. DOS DESCOBRIMENTOS

★ Buses to Meia Praia

Bus & Train Stations

Marina

R. DR. DIAS SANCHEZ

R. DR. A. G. JASPRÓGER

R. SÃO ALBERTO SILVEIRA

R. CONS. J. MACHADO

R. DA GOVERNADOR

Customs House (Old Slave Market)

PR. DA REPÚBLICA

Ribeira de Bensafrim

AV. DOS DESCOBRIMENTOS

R. DR. DIANTAS

R. CASTELO DOS GOVERNADORES

Museu Municipal

Santa Maria

PRAÇA INFANTE HENRIQUE

Hospital

Luz, Sagres, Beaches & Campsite

R. MIGUEL BOMBARDA

R. MENDONÇA

N

Forte da Ponta da Bandeira

ACCOMMODATION	
Caravela	6
Gil Vicente	1
Lagos	2
Lagos-Mar	3
Marina Rio	9
Marazul	7
Rio Mar	5
Rubi Mar	8
Youth Hostel	4

RESTAURANTS	
Adega da Marina	M
Alpendre	D
Barros	H
Casa do Zé	I
Casa Rosa	B
O Cavaleiro	E
O Degrau	K
Dom Henriques	L
Dom Sebastião	J
O Franguinho	F
Galeão	C
Italia	G
A Lagosteira	A

As a port it has been connected with several key moments in world history – it was from here that many of Portugal's great explorers set off for the New World, and during the fifteenth century Europe's first slave market was established here by Henry the Navigator. Over the last few decades, it has developed into a major resort, complete with a new marina, and attracts the whole gamut of visitors – from backpackers to second-home owners; during the summer the 20,000 population swells to more than 200,000. Despite the influx, how-ever, it remains a working fishing port and market centre with a life of its own independent from tourism.

For all its historical significance, Lagos' main attraction is its proximity to some of the best beaches on the Algarve coast. To the east of the town is a long sweep of sand – **Meia Praia** – where even in summer you can find space to lay out your towel, while to the west lies an extraordinary network of cove beaches, including **Praia de Dona Ana**, **Praia do Pinhão** and **Praia do Camilo**. In contrast, a short drive inland lies one of the Algarve's most beautiful reservoirs, the **Barragem de Bravura**, a lovely destination for a picnic or walk.

Some history

Archaeological remnants suggest the Phoenicians formed a fishing village in Lagos' superb natural harbour in 350 BC. When the Romans later swept into Iberia around 210 BC, the town was named Lacobriga, and vestiges of the Roman town wall are still visible today. But it was only when the Moors built a harbour here in the eighth century that the town took off as a major centre for trade and commerce. Taken by the Christians in 1241, Lagos continued to be an important port and during the fifteenth century it was the main departure point for many of the great Portuguese nav-igators, including Gil Eanes, who was born here. The town was also a favoured residence of Henry the Navigator (see p.300), who used the port as a base for the new African trade, which led to the establishment of Europe's first slave market in 1444 (see p.243).

In 1577, Lagos became the administrative capital of the Algarve, a position it maintained during the sixty years of Spanish occupation from 1581. Its prominence meant Lagos became a target for Sir Francis Drake, who attacked the har-bour in 1587 during Britain's battle for maritime supremacy with Spain. British attacks besides, Lagos continued to thrive until much of the town was destroyed in the 1755 earthquake. As a result, Faro took over as capital in 1776 and from then on Lagos declined to become a relatively minor harbour. It was not until the 1960s that tourism revived the town, and development looks set to continue with the new extension of the main east–west Algarve motorway.

ARRIVAL, INFORMATION AND GETTING AROUND

Lagos is the western terminal of the Algarve rail line and its **train station** is on the eastern side of the river, fifteen minutes' walk from the town centre via the swing bridge at the marina. Turn left after the bridge and head down the riverside Avenida da Descobrimentos, and the town walls are on your right; taxis are usually available if you can't face the walk. The **bus station** (☎282 762 944) is a bit closer in, a block back from Avenida dos Descobrimentos, and almost opposite the bridge to the marina. If you're **driving**, aim for Avenida dos Descobrimentos, where there is free parking around the bridge to the marina, though you need to pay to park in the other spaces around the old town.

The **turismo** (June to mid-Sept Mon 9.30am–12.30pm & 2–7pm, Tues 9.30am–1.30pm & 3–7pm, Wed & Sun 9.30am–12.30pm & 2–5.30pm, Thurs–Sat 9.30am–7pm; mid-Sept to May Wed–Sat 9.30am–12.30pm & 2–5.30pm; ☎282 763 031) will help in finding accommodation, as well as dishing out maps, leaflets and timetables. It is inconveniently positioned at Sítio de São João, which is the first roundabout as you come into the town from the east. From the centre, it's a twenty-minute walk; just follow the signs; a taxi will cost about €3 each way.

Most of Lagos can be explored comfortably on foot, but the best way to see the outlying sights in the heat of summer is on the **Toy Train** (May–Sept 10am–6pm; €3), which trundles hourly from the marina along Avenida dos

Descobrimentos and out via the beaches of Praia Dona Ana and Porto de Moz to the headland at Ponta da Piedade. The trip takes around 25 minutes one way.

ACCOMMODATION

Most of the town's **hotels** and **pensões** are fully booked throughout the summer and, turning up on spec, really your only chance of a bed will be a **room** in a private house. In season, arriving early in the day you'll probably be met by touts at the bus or train station, and it's a good idea to take whatever is going (as long as it's central), and look round later at your leisure. Out of season, you should have no problem finding room at one of the *pensões* or hotels, many of which drop their rates dramatically in winter.

IN TOWN

Pensão Caravela
Rua 25 de Abril 16
ⓣ 282 763 361
In a great position right on the old town's main pedestrianized street, the rooms here are clean but pretty basic. Doubles come with or without bath. ❷

Gay Guest House/Residencial Gil Vicente
Rua Gil Vicente 26, Lagos
ⓣ 282 081 150,
ⓔ ggh@netvisao.pt
Nine neat rooms, some with cable TV, but only one with private bathroom; there's also a downstairs bar. Breakfast costs extra. The owner organizes gay events in the area and runs *Bar 7imo* at Rua da Capelinha 7. ❸

Hotel de Lagos
Rua Nova da Aldeia
ⓣ 282 769 967, ⓔ hotel-lagos@mail.telepac.pt
Lagos's most upmarket central hotel is built "village-style" with paths linking rooms, restaurants and sports facilities. There's a courtesy bus to its

own beach club at Meia Praia and hefty low-season price reductions, but the rooms aren't huge and some overlook a busy street. Service can be on the surly side. **7**

Pensão Lagos-Mar
Rua Dr. Faria e Silva 13
ⓣ 282 763 523, ⓕ 282 767 324
Upmarket *pensão*, with spotless rooms mostly facing a quiet side street. All rooms have TVs and private bathrooms while some also have small balconies. Off-season rates are virtually half those of high season. **4**

Residencial Marazul
Rua 25 de Abril 13
ⓣ 282 769 143, ⓕ 282 769 960
Beautifully decorated *residencial,* with bright rooms and communal areas tiled in *azulejos.* En-suite bedrooms vary in size, but all come with TVs and some have terraces with sea views. April–Nov. **3**

Albergaria Marina Rio
Avda dos Descobrimentos 388
ⓣ 282 769 859,
ⓔ marinario@ip.pt

This large modern inn offers decent rooms plus satellite TV, a games room and a rooftop pool. Front rooms face the harbour across the busy *avenida* (back rooms face the bus station). **5**

Hotel Rio Mar
Rua Cândido dos Reis 83
ⓣ 282 770 130, ⓕ 282 763 927
Smart, medium-sized hotel, tucked into a central street. Most rooms have a balcony – the best overlook the sea at the back of the hotel, others overlook a fairly quiet main street. **4**

Pensão Rubi Mar
Rua da Barroca 70–1°
ⓣ 282 763 165,
ⓔ rubimar01@hotmail.com
Wonderful old *pensão* with nine spacious rooms. Book ahead as this is a real treat: the best rooms have harbour views and breakfast in your room is included. **3**

Pousada de Juventude de Lagos
Rua de Lançarote de Freitas 50
ⓣ 282 761 970, ⓔ lagos @movijovem.pt

LAGOS: ACCOMMODATION

239

Modern, well-designed youth hostel, just up from the Centro Cultural de Lagos, with several dorms (€15) plus a few en-suite doubles (€30); be sure to book in advance. There's a nice central courtyard plus internet access and currency exchange.

AT THE BEACHES

Pensão Dona Ana
Praia de Dona Ana
ⓣ 282 762 322
This small, white *pensão* on the cliffs above Praia de Dona Ana has twenty simple, clean rooms, although the views are largely blocked by the neighbouring *Sol e Praia*. ❷

Hotel Golfinho
Praia de Dona Ana
ⓣ 282 769 900, ⓕ 282 769 999
One hundred metres back from the beach, this unattractive high-rise hotel offers superb views from the balconies of its rooms. The comfortable ensuites are spacious and come with all mod cons. There's also a courtesy bus into town.

Disabled access. ❹

Apartamentos Marvela
Rua Dr José Formosinho, Praia do Pinhão
ⓣ & ⓕ 282 760 600
On the road above Praia do Pinhão, the cheapest doubles here are decent but lack views, though there is a communal roof terrace. If you can, splash out on an apartment with a kitchenette and balcony; they sleep three people but cost an extra €30. ❸

Hotel Meia Praia
Meia Praia
ⓣ 282 762 001, ⓕ 282 762 008
Around 10 minutes' drive out of Lagos, just back from one of the best stretches of beach, this tasteful three-star is set in attractive grounds; the best rooms have sea-facing balconies (€10 extra). There are tennis courts, a pool, and guests are entitled to discounts at the Palmares Golf Course (see p.44). ❺

Sol e Praia
Praia de Dona Ana
ⓣ 282 762 026, ⓕ 282 760 247

Newest and best option on this stretch of coast – close to the steps down to the beach and with facilities including a pool, gym and games room. The rooms aren't huge but are comfortable and many have sea-facing balconies. ❺

CAMPSITE

Parque de Campismo da Trindade
Rossio da Trindade

ⓣ 282 763 893, ⓕ 282 762 885
A basic, cramped campsite with a small shop, on the way to Praia de Dona Ana. Pitches are €3 per person per night, plus from €3.50 per tent per night; book ahead. In season, a bus marked "D. Ana/Porto de Mós" runs to the site from the bus station. On foot, it's about ten to fifteen minutes from the Forte Ponta da Bandeira. A taxi from the centre costs around €5.

THE TOWN AND THE BEACHES

It is easy to ignore the substantial ring of new development round the centre of town, as most of Lagos's sites of interest are within the old town walls – including its churches, museums and the bulk of the accommodation and restaurants – or along the waterfront Avenida dos Descobrimentos, where you'll find the market, marina and the departure points for various boat trips. The western stretch of the Avenida dos Descobrimentos offers the best vantage points for the remains of Lagos's fortifications, which include the squat seventeenth-century **Forte da Ponta da Bandeira** (Tues–Sun 9.30am–12.30pm & 2–5pm; €1.80), guarding the entrance to the harbour. The fort itself is rather uninteresting, its interior consisting of a small temporary exhibition space, though you can enjoy fine views over the water from inside.

Just off Avenida dos Descobrimentos and next to the old town walls, the main square by the waterfront, the leafy **Praça da República**, contains Europe's first **slave market** (*mercado de escravos*), a sad, diminutive space under the arcades of the old Customs House, which nowadays serves as an art gallery, showing local art of dubious quality.

On the opposite side of the square is the church of **Santa Maria**, through whose whimsical Manueline windows the young king of Portugal, Dom Sebastião, is said to have roused his troops before the ill-fated Moroccan expedition of 1578 (see p.303).

One rare and beautiful church that survived the 1755 earthquake is the **Igreja de Santo António** just off Praça da República on Rua Henrique Correira Silva. Unless you sneak in during Mass, its ornate interior is best viewed as part of a visit to the Museu Municipal.

For a more modern take on Lagos, check out the exhibitions, at the **Centro Cultural de Lagos**, a cultural centre five minutes' walk north of Praça da República, on Rua Lançarote de Frietas. There's also a decent café in the courtyard at the back.

From Praça da República, the narrow streets of the old town straggle east to two other attractive mosaic-paved and pedestrianized squares, **Praça Luis de Camões** and **Praça Gil Eanes**, around which you'll find Lagos's best cafés, restaurants and guesthouses. The latter square is fronted by Lagos's grand-looking Neoclassical town hall, but its most prominent feature is an adolescent **statue of Dom Sebastião**. Some have compared the figure to a flowerpot man, though the Nobel Prize-winning writer José Saramago is more generous, saying that its form is "almost enough to make the traveller forgive all the disasters the half-witted, powerless and authoritarian Sebastião de Avis visited upon Portugal".

SLAVERY

Lagos has the unenviable position as the site of Europe's first slave market, set up in 1444. Exploitation of local labour was nothing new; the Algarve estates had been worked by slaves from North Africa for centuries, but as Portugal's empire expanded overseas in the fifteenth century so did the exploitation. The indigenous Berber population of the Canary Islands was enslaved as soon as the islands were colonized by the Portuguese (they later ceded the islands to Spain), while black African slaves were forced to work on cotton and sugar plantations in Cape Verde and São Tomé. Many of the slaves were also uprooted and forced into domestic and agricultural labour in the Algarve and Portugal's new colonies such as Brazil and Madeira.

By the end of the fifteenth century, the demand for slave labour was so high that Angolan chiefs were forced to pay part of their feudal dues to the Portuguese in slaves. During the sixteenth century, 10,000 slaves were shipped out of Africa a year by the Portuguese alone, a trade which helped finance a third of Portugal's overseas explorations. This figure increased to half a million slaves a year by the following century, when black Africans – mostly Angolans – were forced into slavery during military raids. The demand for human labour swelled further when gold was discovered in Brazil in the 1690s, with British and French companies competing with the Portuguese to keep up the supply.

Slavery was finally abolished within Portugal after the Great Earthquake of 1755 by the Marquês de Pombal. His motive, however, was to stop Portuguese families from importing slaves as servants from Brazil because he was worried Brazilian estates would suffer as a result, rather than anything more humanitarian. It was not until 1869 that Portugal's Prime Minister Sá da Bandeira succeeded in prohibiting the slave trade from within Portugal's colonies as well.

LAGOS: SLAVERY

Just beyond the town hall, where the Avenida dos Descobrimentos meets Rua das Portas de Portugal, you'll see the entrance to the town's **market** (Mon–Sat mornings), a bustling cavern of activity, surrounded by some of Lagos's liveliest cafés and bars. Downstairs is lined with fresh fish of all shapes and sizes; head upstairs for fruit, vegetables and dried flowers.

For details of boat trips from Lagos, see p.254.

Museu Municipal

Tues–Sun 9.30am–12.30pm & 2–5pm; €1.70

The **Museu Municipal** (municipal museum) shoehorns in just about every possible historical and quirky object relating to Lagos and the Algarve, and the random nature of the displays is all part of the appeal. Labelling is equally haphazard, with some items explained in detail while others are left to speak for themselves.

The most important items are visible on either side as you enter, including **Roman remains** from the dig at Boca do Rio (see p.263), featuring an amphora encrusted with coral and busts of Roman emperor Galiano, as well as an impressive wall-mounted decorative mosaic. Beyond the Roman remains, the rest of the collection appears in no particular order. There are Neolithic axeheads, Visigothic stone coffins, jars containing misshapen animal foetuses, a display of models of Algarvian chimneys, stuffed goats, straw hats and basketry, model fishing boats, travelogues and the 1504 town charter. Beyond the main space lie three loosely themed rooms, with **coins**, **medals** and **notes** in the first – including municipal notes from the early twentieth century – and **weaponry** in the next, sitting alongside some frightening early surgical instruments. Generally poor quality **paintings** and **sacred art** – the most important of which is a sixteenth-century diptych showing the Annunciation and the Presentation – complete the collection. You exit the museum through the interior of the neighbouring **Igreja de Santo António**. Decorated around 1715, every inch of the gilt and Baroque decor is exuberantly carved, right up to and including the barrel-vaulted ceiling – representing the life of Santo António.

The beaches

The coast around Lagos offers a variety of stunning beaches. Over the river to the east, **Meia Praia** is a giant swathe of sand curving round the bay, while to the west there are a series of cove beaches backed by cliffs, pierced by tunnels and grottoes, and studded by weird and extravagantly weathered outcrops of purple-tinted rock. Of these bays, **Praia de Dona Ana** is one of the most picturesque – certainly out of season when the crowds have gone – while the other smaller coves of **Praia do Pinhão** and **Praia do Camilo** are almost as appealing.

Meia Praia

Beginning to the **east** of Lagos and stretching almost as far as the eye can see, **Meia Praia** is a stunning tract of soft sand that extends for 4km to the delta of the rivers Odiáxere and Arão. Flanked by the railway line and well set back from the road, the wide beach gets progressively quieter further away from town towards the greenery of the Palmares Golf Club. The beach is particularly popular with backpackers and there are plenty of beachside cafés and restaurants at intervals up the beach. A regular **bus service** leaves from the Avenida dos Descobrimentos and travels the length of the beach; alternatively, there's a seasonal **ferry** from Avenida dos Descobrimentos across the river, from where the beach is a short walk away. You can also **walk** to the beach over the footbridge via the marina, though it's a good thirty-minute hike from the centre of town to the best sands.

Beaches south and west of Lagos

The promontory **south** of Lagos is fringed by eroded cliff faces that shelter a series of tiny **cove beaches**. All are within easy walking distance of the old town, though the concentration of nearby resort hotels means that you may find the least crowded strand is the **town beach** itself, just beyond the Forte Ponta da Bandeira. This is a surprisingly alluring stretch of sand, reached through a natural rock tunnel.

In late August, the town beach is the venue for the *Banho* festival, an annual beach party marking the end of summer, with evening barbecues, live music and a traditional midnight swim.

The easiest access on foot to the cove beaches to the south and west is to follow the Avenida dos Descobrimentos up the hill (toward Sagres) and turn left just opposite the fire station, where you'll see signs to the tiny **Praia do Pinhão**, some fifteen minutes' walk away. This is the first of the coves, a lovely sheltered sandy bay beneath steep cliffs. If you're driving, continue along this road and the other beaches are well signposted. Alternatively, follow the clifftop path from Praia do Pinhão to the next beach, **Praia de Dona Ana**, about five minutes away. These sands can also be reached from Lagos on the seasonal toy train (see p.237). This is one of the most photogenic of all the Algarve's beaches, a wide expanse of sand framed by cliffs, weirdly-sculpted rock pillars and caves. However, the cliffs above it are now lined with cafés, hotels and apartments, and in high season the sands are heaving; out of season it remains a delight.

Beyond here, despite the jostling hotels, you can follow a path around the cliffs to another fine beach backed by similar natural rock art, **Praia do Camilo** – which is usually a bit less crowded – and right on to the **Ponta da Piedade**, a craggy headland, where a palm-bedecked lighthouse makes a great vantage point for the sunset. It has a similar, if less desolate air, to Cabo de São Vicente with sweeping views down the coast and a handy café. This is also the final port of call for the toy train from Lagos (see p.237).

The **coastal path** from Ponta da Piedade continues as far as Luz (see p.257), another hour and forty-five minutes' walk away. After forty-five minutes you come to **Porto do Mós**. The beach here is pleasant enough, but this stretch of coast is uninspiring, the surrounding area overwhelmed by modern apartments and characterless restaurants. You'd do better to press on for an hour along a splendid stretch of coastal path, high above the ocean, until the obelisk above Luz comes into sight, from where you scramble down the hillside into town.

EATING

The centre of Lagos is packed with **restaurants**, most found along *ruas* Afonso d'Almeida and 25 de Abril. Menus are of a similar moderate standard and price almost everywhere, though there are a couple of places where you can sample more upmarket Portuguese fare.

If you want to get a picnic together head to **Padaria Central** at Rua 1 de Maio 29 (Mon–Fri 7.30am-8pm, Sat 7.30am–1pm), a superb old-fashioned baker's which offers piping hot fresh bread, pastries and cakes.

LAGOS: EATING

IN TOWN

Adega da Marina
Avda dos Descobrimentos 35
Daily noon–2am. **Moderate**
Set in a former warehouse, this great barn of a place serves excellent food at tables lined up as if for a wedding party. Stonking portions of charcoal-grilled meat and fish plus great house wines.

Alpendre
Rua António Barbosa Viana 17,
℗ **282 762 705**
Daily noon–3pm & 6–11pm.
Expensive
One of the oldest – and more formal – restaurants in the Algarve, serving memorable smoked swordfish and decent *arroz de marisco,* plus some international dishes. The dessert crepes – flambéed at your table – are the best reason to come.

Barros
Rua Portas de Portugal 83
Mon & Wed–Sun noon–3pm & 6–10.30pm. **Moderate**
Right by the town market, *Barros* is packed with locals

here for the decent grilled fish and meat in a room decorated with *azulejos* and golf clubs.

Casa do Zé
Avda dos Descobrimentos
Daily 24 hours. **Inexpensive**
On the corner with the market, this bustling bar-restaurant with outside seats facing the harbour stays open all day and night. Filling dishes – mostly fish but some meat – are chalked up on the board.

Casa Rosa
Rua do Ferrador 22
Tues–Sun noon–3pm & 7–11pm. **Inexpensive**
Bar-restaurant that bills itself as a "backpacker's paradise". Set meals start at €3.50 and other dishes – ranging from stir fries and chocolate muffins to Portuguese staples – are good value too. Drinking begins in earnest with a 10–11pm happy hour.

O Cavaleiro
Rua Garret 23
Daily 6am–5am. **Inexpensive**
Just off the Praça Luís Camões, this bar/restaurant

offers snacks and full meals at reasonable prices. With outdoor tables on the square, it makes a welcome late-night refuelling stop.

O Degrau

Rua Soeira da Costa 46, ☎282 764 716

Tues–Sun noon–3pm & 6–midnight. **Moderate**

This welcoming establishment is decorated with pages from the comment book praising the international dishes such as excellent Thai curry, stir fries and pasta; some Algarvian dishes and a vegetarian option too. Book in advance to avoid queuing.

Dom Henriques

Rua 25 de Abril 75, ☎282 763 563

Daily noon–3pm & 6–11pm.

Expensive

Very popular haunt for Portuguese and international dishes such as beef stroganoff. Its dark wood interior usually bustles with spruce waiters serving a predominantly middle-aged clientele; reservations advised.

Dom Sebastião

Rua 25 de Abril 20–22, ☎282 762 795

Daily noon–3pm & 6–11pm.

Expensive

Arguably the town's finest restaurant, with outdoor seating and a traditional cobbled interior. Serves good seafood and a fabulous selection of appetizers and reasonable vegetarian dishes, though meat dishes can be disappointing. A full meal runs to about €20; with careful selection you could get away with less.

O Franguinho

Rua Luís de Azevedo 25

Tues–Sun 11am–2.30pm & 5.30–10.30pm. **Inexpensive**

Bustling, good value *churrasqueira* with a tiny, first-floor dining room. This is the place to go for fine (if greasy) chicken or *febras de porco* (grilled pork steaks). There are daily changing specials.

Galeão

Rua de Laranjeira 1

Mon–Sat 12.30–2.30pm & 6.45–8.30pm. **Moderate**

Slightly formal place, a little

hidden away, but usually packed because of its slightly old-fashioned menu featuring dishes such as beef stroganoff and melon with port. It also does a few Algarvian classics such as swordfish and superb steaks.

Italia
Rua Garrett 26–28, off Praça Luís Camões
Daily noon–3pm & 6.30–11.30pm. Moderate
Bright, cheery restaurant run by Italians offering pasta, pizzas cooked in a wood-burning oven, Italian wine, and a full menu besides. There are a few tables outside on the busy square.

A Lagosteira
Rua Iº de Maio 20, ☎ 282 762 486
Daily noon–3pm & 6–11pm. Expensive
Upmarket, blue-tiled restaurant specializing in *camarão flambé* (flambéed prawns), *peixe na cataplana* (fish cooked in a circular pan) and, of course, *lagosta* – lobster. Daily specials too. Reservation advised.

AT THE BEACHES

Restaurante Gaivota Branca
Meia Praia. Daily 10am–midnight. Moderate
The perfect beachside café, set just over the railway lines on an idyllic stretch of beach opposite the *Dom Pedro Hotel*. The 'white seagull' serves the usual range of snacks and seafood as well as drinks.

Restaurante Maharaja de Lagos
Rua Dr José Formosinho, Praia do Pinhão
Daily noon–3pm & 6pm–midnight. Inexpensive
A surprisingly good Indian restaurant right above Pinhão beach, offering decently priced curries, with a range of vegetarian options.

Cervejaria Mirante
Praia de Dona Ana
Daily 9am–midnight. Moderate
Right on the cliff overlooking the sands, this is a great place to enjoy the house specialities such as *espetada de tamboril* (monkfish

kebab) and *norvilho na brasa* (chargrilled steaks). Also does

pizzas, snacks and a range of drinks.

DRINKING AND NIGHTLIFE

Lagos has some great **cafés**, and to be a true local, it is essential to refuel regularly on coffee, pastries and cakes, from breakfast time pretty much through to bedtime. There is also no shortage of **bars** and **disco bars** around town, many of them owned by expatriates – in particular Irish and British. Most bars stay open until at least 2am, with the disco bars pumping out the music even later if the party is in full flow.

CAFÉS

Snack Bar Abrigo
Rua Marquês de Pombal 2
Mon–Sat 8.30am–9.30pm.
Inexpensive
With outdoor tables in a little square under scented orange trees, this aromatic café makes a great breakfast stop, with fluffy fresh croissants; also serves beer, cocktails, snacks and meals all day.

Esplanade Rosa
Praça Infante D. Henrique
Daily 9am–2am. Inexpensive
This kiosk opposite the Igreja Santa Maria has outdoor tables sprawling across the

leafy square adjacent to Praça da República. Serves inexpensive pastries, pizzas, coffees and beer.

Pastelaria Rubi
Rua Candido dos Reis 30
Daily 8am–midnight.
Inexpensive
A good breakfast stop, with fresh croissants and coffee; also does cakes, snacks and a range of drinks with tables outside on a pedestrianized street.

DRINKING AND NIGHTLIFE

Eddie's Bar
Rua 25 de Abril 99

Daily 4pm–2am

Small, friendly bar with a happy hour from 5 to 9pm, a good selection of sounds and attracts a surf-dude kind of crowd.

Cervejaria Ferradura
Rua de Ferradura 26A
Mon–Sat 10am–2am

Atmospheric *cervejaria* that is very much a locals' place, with walls covered in soccer posters and stacks of inexpensive *petiscos* on the bar.

Hideaway
Trav 1º de Maio 9, off Praça Luís de Camões
Daily 6pm–2am

Cosy bar with cheap beer, more than fifty cocktails, laid-back sounds and bar food till late. Attracts a mixed thirty-something clientele.

The Irish Rover
Rua de Ferradura 9
Thurs–Sat 9pm–2am

No surprises but all the comforts of an archetypal Irish bar, with Murphys, Guinness, bar snacks, a games room with a pool table,

satellite TV showing sports events, plus internet access.

Joe's Garage
Rua Iº de Maio 78
Daily 7pm–2am

Disco bar that's thronging with Antipodeans drinking heavily and dancing on the tables. A filling plate of food costs €4 and you know it's closing time when they set fire to the bar.

Lords Tavern
Rua António Crisogono Santos 56
Daily 12–3pm & 6pm–2am

Near the bus station, this British-style pub offers dismal crooners most nights and sports channel TV for the big games. There's also reasonably priced, if very average, bar food.

Mullens
Rua Cândido dos Reis 86
Daily 8pm–2am

This atmospheric, cavernous *adega*, is the most appealing late-night choice in town. Inexpensive drinks including Guinness, sangria and *vinho verde* on tap, are served alongside excellent and moderately priced meals to a jazz and soul soundtrack.

Naufragio Bar
Avda dos Descobrimentos
Daily 10am–2am

Pleasant beach bar with a youthful clientele, jazzy sounds and moderately priced bar snacks. Out the back there's a great terrace facing the town beach and the Forte da Ponta da Bandeira.

Roskos
Rua Cândido dos Reis 79
Daily 8pm–4am

Down the road from *Mullens*, this lively Irish bar has loud music, an 8–10pm happy hour and fifty serious cocktails which keep happy

punters fuelled until the small hours.

Bar Vivante
Rua 25 Abril 105
Daily 10pm–4am

Just north of the slave market, this late-night disco bar has gaudy marble pillars and a superb "tropical" roof terrace; a good place to hit when the other bars have closed.

Whyte Bar
Rua de Ferrador 7A
Fri–Sun 8.30pm–2am

Weekend retreat that positively thrives on drunken behaviour, as photos outside illustrate. Offers a dodgy combination of darts, cocktails and lethal measures of spirits.

LISTINGS

Banks Banks are grouped around Praça Gil Eanes.

Bike and motorbike rental *Eddie's Bar*, Rua 25 de Abril 99 (℡282 768 329, Ⓔfree_tours@hotmail.com), organizes mountain bike excursions. For motorbikes try Motor Ride, Rua José Afonso 23 (℡282 761 720), in the new town towards Ponta da Piedade, which hires out bikes from €60 a day.

Boat trips It's worth shopping around for the best deal, but most cost around €10 per person for a 2hr trip. Fishing boats gather around the Forte Ponta da Bandeira or there are many stalls along Avenida dos Descobrimentos up towards the marina. Bom Dia (℗282 764 670, ⓔbomdia-cruises@ip.pt) offers sailing trips to the nearby grottoes, half-day trips to Sagres and dolphin "seafaris".

Bullfights Saturdays in summer (€30) at the Praça de Touros de Lagos, on the Portimão road. Mbtours offer tickets and return buses; ℗282 426 045.

Buses Travel information from the bus terminal (℗282 762 944).

Car rental Auto Jardim, Rua Vítor da Costa Silva 18 (℗282 769 486; three-day minimum); LuzCar-Sociedade, Largo das Portas de Portugal 10 (℗282 761 016).

Doctor For an English-speaking doctor, call MediLagos ℗282 760 181.

Hospital Rua do Castelo dos Governadores, adjacent to the church of Santa Maria (℗282 763 034).

Internet *Eddie's Bar*, Rua 25 de Abril 99 (daily 4pm–2am; €4/hr).

Police Rua General Alberto Silveira (℗282 762 930).

Post office Next to the town hall, off Avenida dos Descobrimentos.

Taxis There are ranks in front of the post office or call Lagos Central Taxi (℗282 762 469 or 282 763 587).

Telephones It's easiest to make long-distance calls at the Telecom office, next to the post office (June to mid-Sept Mon–Fri 8.30am–10pm, Sat 9am–1pm & 5pm–midnight, Sun 6–10pm; Mid-Sept to May Mon–Sat 8am–6pm).

Travel agency Clubalgarve, Rua Marreiros Netto 25
(☎282 762 337); Tourlagos, Rua Infante de Sagres 31
(☎282 767 967).

AROUND LAGOS

There are a couple of sights inland from Lagos which warrant a break from the beach. The **Barragem de Bravura** is one of the region's main reservoirs, while nearby lies a private zoo, which makes a good day out for kids. There is no public transport to either site, but with your own transport, the journey itself is a delight.

Barragem de Bravura

BARRAGEM DE BRAVURA, one of the most picturesque of the Algarve's several *barragens* (dams), lies around 15km north of Lagos. Head either along the IC4 up the Ribeira da Bensafrim valley towards Aljezur – from where the *barragem* is signed off to the right – or along the coast road towards Portimão, from where the *barragem* can be reached by taking the EN125-9 from Odeáxere. Both roads pass through bucolic countryside, delightfully flower-filled in spring and early summer.

When the reservoir comes into view, a car park on the left is the spot to pull over and admire the views over the glittering waters and densely wooded hills. A few hundred metres from the car park lies a seasonal **café**, *A Recanto da Barragem* (April–Oct Tues–Sun 10am–6pm), which serves drinks and decent snacks inside or on an outdoor terrace next to a small children's playground. Another 400m beyond the café, the road stops at the top of the dam over the river Bravura; to the south, the deep valley is little more than an overgrown stream fed by a waterfall from the dam, while behind the dam lie the deep, still green waters of the reservoir, stirred by basking carp. It's an idyllic spot, and you can walk right over the top of the dam and round the edges of the reservoir on the other side along a dirt trail. Swimming, fishing and water sports, however, are prohibited.

Lagos Zoo

May–Sept daily 10am–7pm; Oct–April daily 10am–5pm; €6, children €3.5

Around 8km north of Lagos just off the main E120 to Aljezur and close to the village of Barão de São João, **LAGOS ZOO** makes an enjoyable diversion. Set in 30 square kilometres of land, the well-tended zoo is keen to publicize its environmental awareness, and the various birds including flamingos, toucans, ibis, parrots and emus, as well as a few mammals such as wallabies and monkeys, certainly seem as happy as can be expected. There are also farm animals in a special children's enclosure that children can pet and help feed. There's a shop, a decent restaurant, and an exhibition centre giving information about the animals' natural habitats.

The southwest coast

The 40km stretch of wild coastline between Lagos and Sagres offers a very different face of the Algarve. Even the coastal E125 highway is relatively quiet, most of the traffic filtering off up the IC4 from Lagos towards Lisbon. The coast contains just three resorts, of which **Luz** is the most upmarket, filled with villas and apartments spilling down towards a superb beach backed by a high cliff. Further west, **Burgau** marks the eastern boundary of the Parque Natural do Sudoeste Alentejano e Costa Vicentina, a natural park set up to protect the coast from further development. Both Burgau and **Salema**, a few kilometres to the west, retain vestiges of their former status as fishing villages, though tourism has taken over as the main source of income. Away from these resorts, you can still find quiet isolated beaches largely devoid of tourists at **Figueira**, **Praia de Ingrina** and **Praia da Zavial**.

LUZ

With a wide crescent of sandy beach towered over by high cliffs, **LUZ** is one of the most picturesque of the resorts west of Lagos, 5km away. White chalets and villas pile up behind the beach, but the development is generally low-key and low-rise. Outside summer the beach is quiet, with just a few ex-pats walking their dogs, and most of its beachside restaurants close down. Between May and September, however, its proximity to Lagos means the beach gets packed, especially at weekends. For **swimming**, it is best to stay at the western end of the sands; the other end, below the dramatic cliffs, becomes more rocky. After the beach, most people take an early evening stroll to the western end of the promenade, which passes above a rocky foreshore to the town's unobtrusive church and an old fort, now a **restaurant** (see p.259).

There are some excellent local **coast walks** within easy reach of the town. The easiest of these is to the triangulation point **obelisk** (*atalaia*) on the clifftop to the east of Luz, a forty-minute round trip which offers great views down the coast. To get there, follow the road that runs parallel to the beach eastwards. At the edge of town you'll see a cobbled track in front of you. Take this, turning left away from the shore at a fork. The cobbles turn to dirt as you head up a very steep hillside towards the obelisk, clearly visible ahead of you. The coast path continues more gently along the clifftops from here all the way to Porto de Mós (1hr) and Lagos (a further 45min), an exhilarating and

LUZ

breezy clifftop walk with striking views towards Ponta da Piedade, though it becomes increasingly built up from Porto de Mós on (see p.247).

A shorter but equally bracing walk from Luz is to head west along the **coast path to Burgau** (1hr). From the beachside promenade pass the fort and take the first left, continuing straight on until the road turns into a track. You'll pick up the coast path on the left after around ten minutes. The track runs parallel to the coast until you reach Burgau offering more superb views over the sea and back towards town.

Luz is a popular base for **sports** enthusiasts, with good facilities at the plush *Luz Bay Club*, just south of the main road from Lagos. Among the facilities on offer are a sauna and pool plus tennis, squash and wall tennis. Day membership is €11.

Practicalities

Buses from Lagos drop you at the edge of the old village, from where it's a short walk downhill to the attractive palm-lined beachside promenade, lined with cafés, restaurants and souvenir stalls. Below here lies the alluring beach, one of the largest between Lagos and Sagres.

Accommodation

Most of the **accommodation** in Luz consists of holiday apartments and villas, often block-booked in high season, though at other times of the year it is possible to pick up an apartment for reasonable rates, often with sea views.

Hotel Belavista da Luz
℡ 282 788 655, ℻ 282 788 656
Around 1km uphill on the road towards Sagres, this pink, modern, four-star is the best option for comfort, complete with all mod cons including a restaurant and pool. Character, however, is in short supply. Disabled access. ❻

Luz Bay Club
Rua do Jardim
Ⓣ 282 789 640; Ⓕ 282 789 641
Sports club which also rents out various high-standard apartments round the town. All come with kitchenettes, TVs and balconies, some of which have views of the sea. Studios for two people ❹; two-bed apartments sleeping up to four people. ❼

Ocean Club
Rua Direita 20
Ⓣ 282 789 472,
Ⓔ ocean.club.luz@mail.telepac
A complex of upmarket villas and apartments, the best ones with their own beach-facing terraces and small plunge pools. Others are set back from the sea but close to one of the pools. There's also a bar and restaurant with barbecue evenings. ❼

Camping Valverde
Ⓣ 282 789 211; advanced bookings Ⓣ 218 117 070,
Ⓦ www.orbitur.pt
An attractive leafy campsite 1.5km from Luz close to the highway, with the full range of tourist facilities including a kids' playground, restaurant, supermarket and bar.

Eating and drinking

Luz doesn't win any culinary prizes but though nowhere is particularly cheap, you can eat well. Nightlife is also muted, with just a handful of bars.

The Bull
Rua da Calheta 2
Daily 11am–2am. **Inexpensive**
Just up from the fort, this English-style pub has a range of drinks and inexpensive pub grub firmly geared to British tastes. There's an outdoor terrace, but it's liveliest when everyone crams inside to catch the latest soccer game on TV.

Fortaleza da Luz
Rua da Igreja 3
Daily noon–3pm & 7–9.30pm.
Expensive
The town castle is the most upmarket choice in Luz, with pricey top-notch pasta dishes,

LUZ

259

omelettes and Algarvian dishes, such as pork Monchique-style and delicious *Bolo de Amendôa* (almond cake). There are tables on the grassy terrace and its ornate dining room also offers superb sea views.

Kiwi Pastelaria
Avda dos Pescadores

Daily 9am–10pm. **Inexpensive**
Right on the beachside promenade, the outdoor tables offer an ideal breakfast stop, with fresh croissants, fruit juices and coffee. Also serves a good range of ice creams, salads and sandwiches.

O Poço
Avda dos Pescadores

Daily 12.30–3pm & 7–10pm.
Moderate

"The well" boasts a prime spot overlooking the sands and the beachside promenade. Service is snappy and reasonably priced seafood and meat dishes include an excellent *espadarte de tamboril* (monkfish kebab).

Praia á Vista
Avda dos Pescadores

May–Sept daily 10am–10pm; Oct–Apr 10am–7pm.
Inexpensive
Simple beachside café with seats on a wooden terrace facing the sands. A good spot for a drink, a croissant or a sandwich.

BURGAU

Despite a cluster of new development around it, **BURGAU**, 5km west of Luz, remains a picturesque resort whose steep, cobbled streets tumble down to a lovely sandy beach backed by cliffs. Colourful boats line the lower roads, which double up as slipways, while the upper roads weave around the coastline to a clifftop *miradouro* offering fine views over the sands. Out of season, it's truly attractive, the beach deserted and the shutters down in most of the shops and restaurants, leaving the streets and side alleys to echo to your footsteps. In summer, however, there's no mistaking that Burgau is a full-blown resort and its narrow streets and beach are packed day and night.

Practicalities

Not all the **buses** from Lagos/Sagres call into Burgau itself, though all will stop, if requested, at the turn-off on the highway, from where it's a 2km walk to the village along a road through arid farming country. This road into Burgau passes the *Burgau Sports Club* (☎282 697 350), a well-equipped **sports centre** with a gym, tennis, squash, basketball, swimming pool and a kids' playground; there's also a bar and restaurant.

In Burgau, **accommodation** is limited largely to apartments and quickly gets booked up in high season, though you can usually find a **private room** if you shop around; look for the signs advertising *quartos* around the village. Alternatively, the best option is *Casa Grande* (☎282 697 416, Ⓔcasagrande@mail.telepac.pt; ❸), at the northeastern point of town on the road towards Luz. Set in its own grounds and fronted by a spiky dragon tree, this beautiful manor house has giant rooms with soaring ceilings, each decorated with a motley assortment of period furniture. Upstairs rooms are largest with their own balconies (❺). Book ahead in high season as there are only a handful of rooms.

Eating and drinking

Considering its small size, Burgau is generously endowed with an array of bars and restaurants and the competition means prices are relatively modest.

Adega Casa Grande
March–Oct daily 7–11pm.
Moderate

Attached to the *Casa Grande* guesthouse (see above), this bar-restaurant is set in a former wine cellar (*adega*) and offers great Portuguese grills. There are also vegetarian options.

A Barraca
Largo dos Pescadores 2
Daily noon–3pm & 7–10pm.
Moderate
This clifftop restaurant is a top spot for meat dishes and seafood. It's best in summer as, at other times, plastic sheets over the terrace put paid to the wind but also the views.

Beach Bar Burgau
Praia de Burgau
Restaurant Tues–Sun noon–3pm & 7–10pm; bar Mon 10am–6pm, Tues–Sun 10am–midnight.

Moderate–expensive
Restaurant-bar with a splendid terrace on the beach; at high tide the waves crash round the restaurant. Chicken is the best bet; the seafood is overpriced and the grilled meats are unexceptional. Better still just enjoy a beer or five at its late opening bar.

Bar Brizze
Rua 25 Abril
Daily 7am–midnight
Small bar with a series of outdoor terraces stacked up on Burgau's steepest beachside approach. It's a great stop for a morning coffee and croissant or an evening beer.

WEST TO SALEMA

The rolling, unspoilt coastline west of Burgau marks the beginning of the Parque Natural do Sudoeste Alentejano e Costa Vicentina, a natural park stretching along the coastline west to Cabo de São Vicente and all the way north to Odeceixe. From Burgau, a small back road runs parallel to the coast past a couple of bays. The first of these is **Cabanas Velhas**, a pretty if stony cove reached from the tiny village of Barrancão. Wedged between two low cliffs

WEST TO SALEMA

and backed by a few palm trees to shade the parked cars, the bay is an attractive spot to escape the crowds. From Barrancão, the rough road descends steeply past a ruined seventeenth-century fortress to a broad, flat river valley and on to **Boca do Rio**, the "mouth of the river", a bay strewn with giant boulders. Once this was an important Roman settlement, and many of the remains at Lagos's Museu Municipal were found at this spot. Hardly the most pleasant spot for a swim, the rocky bay nevertheless makes an atmospheric spot for a picnic, or a drink at the seasonal **café** (May–Sept 10am–8pm).

The walk to Salema from Burgau takes 1hr 30min along the clifftop coastal path, which begins west of Burgau and passes the bays of Cabanas Velhas and Boca do Rio before winding down to Salema.

From Boca do Rio, the road heads north to join the main EN125 towards Salema. The EN125 here marks the southern boundary of the Parque Natural. Just north of the turning to Salema by Budens you'll see the extensive grounds of the **Parque da Floresta**, a huge sports centre and holiday village complex set round the western Algarve's main golf course (see p.45).

Salema

From the EN125, a side road snakes down a delightful, cultivated valley, to the small fishing village of **SALEMA** with a long stretch of beach. Regular buses from Lagos stop just above the fishing harbour, where the slipway is cluttered with brightly coloured boats. The atmospheric old centre spreads east from the bus stop parallel to the beach. The western edge of the **beach** – a wide, sheltered bay – is magnificent: in winter, the sea comes crashing right up to

WEST TO SALEMA

the edge of the village, while in summer the gentle breakers are ideal for swimming. Of course, there has been apartment and villa construction in Salema, but for the most part it spreads back up the valley from the village in a fairly homogenous white splodge.

Like Luz and Burgau, a fair proportion of Salema's **accommodation** is in apartments, usually block-booked in high season. However, there are also a handful of reasonably priced hotels, which make Salema a good base for independent travellers. There is usually plenty of alternative accommodation in private **rooms** around the old village – ask at the bars and the post office, or just stroll along the street and look for signs: you should be able to secure something with a terrace and kitchen.

ACCOMMODATION

Estalagem Infante do Mar

Ⓣ 282 690 100, Ⓕ 282 609 109
Around 1km steeply uphill on the road to Figueira, this smart four-star inn has comfortable rooms with panoramic views. There are all mod cons including a restaurant, bar and pool. ❺

A Mare

Ⓣ 282 695 165,
Ⓔ johnmare@mail.telepac.pt
On the hill above the main road into town, this good value and attractively renovated house has a lovely sea-facing terrace and an airy breakfast room. Rooms are tiny but spotless. ❸

Parque da Floresta

Vale do Poço, Budens
Ⓣ 282 690 007,
Ⓦ www.vigiasa.com
This holiday/sports complex, 4km north of Salema, rents luxury apartments for a 7-day minimum. The myriad facilities include a giant pool, golf course (see p.45), beauty spa, tennis, archery, restaurants, bars, kids' entertainment and theme nights. ❻

Camping Quinta dos Carriços

ⓣ 282 695 201,
ⓕ 282 695 122

Excellent campsite with landscaped grounds 1.5km from Salema up towards the main highway – the bus passes on the way into the village. Beautifully positioned and well equipped with a mini market, restaurant, bar, launderette and even a car wash. Prices are €3.50 per person plus tents from €3.50 per night.

Hotel Residencial Salema

Rua 28 de Janeiro
ⓣ 282 665 328,
ⓕ 282 685 329

Plonked rather unceremoniously by the cobbled square just back from the beach, this modern block offers decent accommodation in small rooms, some with their own balconies with skewed sea views. There's also a bar and TV room. Open March–Oct. ❹

EATING AND DRINKING

- - - - - - - - - - - - - - - - - - -

Restaurante Atlântico

Praia da Salema
Daily noon–10am. **Moderate**
In a prime location right on the beach with a wooden terrace, this bustling place is usually packed thanks to reasonably priced *cataplana*, chicken *piri piri* and whatever fresh fish is on display.

Bar Aventura

Rua das Pescadores 85
Daily 11am–11pm.
Attractive bar on the road into the old village with the usual range of drinks and the chance to surf the net for €4.50/hr.

Boia Bar Restaurante

Rua das Pescadores 101
Daily 10.30am–2am.
Inexpensive
On the edge of the old centre, this bar-restaurant serves breakfasts through to full meals; the superb *caldeirada* (fish stew) for four is the speciality. There's also a children's menu.

WEST TO SALEMA

WEST TO RAPOSEIRA

The area between Salema and the inland village of Raposeira offers one of the best reminders of what the Algarve must have been like before tourism made inroads: a delightful stretch of rolling hills, small farms and villages spreading inland from a few isolated and undeveloped coves.

Just off the main EN125, and also reached by the rough back road from Salema past the *Estalagem Infante do Mar* (see p.264), lies the village of **FIGUEIRA**, 3km to the northwest of Salema, a small agricultural village whose surrounding fields are still tilled by donkeys. There's not a lot to the place, though it's worth stopping at the welcoming *Bar Celeiro*, by the bus stop at Rua Direita 44a, a barn-like place which specializes in local cider. Opposite here, an unlikely-looking unsigned farm track is the main approach to the local beach, **Praia da Figueira**, a fine bay that is often deserted except for a few naturists. It's a bumpy drive down the track through lush fields down a river valley, to within 400m or so of the beach. From here you have to walk, crossing a stream at the end. If you're walking down the track all the way from Figueira, it takes around half an hour.

Between Figueira and Raposeira, a sign points off the main EN125 to the chapel of **Nossa Senhora de Guadalupe**, a squat, dark-stoned chapel some 4km from Figueira, reached down the old road which runs parallel to the highway. Built in the thirteenth century by the Knights Templar and said to have been frequented by Henry the Navigator, the chapel stands in rural solitude. It is usually kept locked, but it's a pleasant place to stroll around or have a picnic.

Henry the Navigator is believed to have lived for a while in the small rural village of **RAPOSEIRA**, 5km further west. It's an attractive enough place with a dignified-looking church, but, sliced through by the speeding highway, there's not much reason to come here except to turn off the road to a couple of fine beaches. The road is signed left at the traffic lights on the highway: about 1km along, take the left fork that passes through **Hortas do Tabual**, an agricultural village set in rolling countryside. After another 2km or so the road splits; take the left-hand fork and you'll reach **Praia do Zavial**, a small, rock and sand bay below low cliffs, a popular spot with surfers thanks to its large breakers. For better swimming in a more sheltered spot, continue down the road another kilometre round the bay to **Praia da Ingrina**, a small sandy cove, good for beachcombing amid the rock pools.

Practicalities

There are no **public transport** connections from the main road to either beach, though plenty of buses head along the main road itself via Raposeira and Figueira to Sagres. **Accommodation** options are limited along this stretch of the Algarve. In summer, **private rooms** are advertised in Hortas do Tabual, some way from the coast. The best bet is the **campsite**, *Camping Ingrina* (T & F 282 639 242; €18/person, from €35/tent), around 1km inland from Praia da Ingrina, a basic campsite in a lovely rural setting. Facilities include a small shop and an attractive bar-restaurant. You can **eat and drink** well at *Café Rodrigues*, on Largo da Igreja 9 in Raposeira (daily 7am–midnight), a simple bar and restaurant with an outdoor grill opposite Raposeira's church. At Praia do Zavial, *Restaurante Zavial* (Tues–Sun noon–11pm) is set in a modern stone building with a beach-facing terrace, and serves a decent range of moderately priced and tasty grilled meat and fish. There's also a special kids' menu. Down on Praia da Ingrina, *Casa de Pasto Sebastião* (Mon & Wed–Sun 11am–10pm) is an inexpensive, basic beachside café where you can tuck into filling grills or enjoy drinks on a wooden terrace facing the waves.

Sagres and around

The 12km drive from Raposeira to Sagres crosses an exposed flat plateau, and it is something of a surprise when the expansive white apartments of **Sagres** come into view after such an empty landscape. Spreading along a clifftop above a working fishing harbour, Sagres is great place to stay, especially in winter, when the wind blows hard and there's a bleak, desolate appeal to the scenery, with hardly a tourist in sight. Throughout the summer, by contrast, the sprawling village draws a lively mixed crowd: young beach-goers flock here, well catered for by rooms for rent, restaurants and bars, while the area is also popular with families in villas and guests from the *pousada*. Visitor numbers are swelled further by day-trippers who come to see Henry the Navigator's imposing **fortress**, which lies just to the north of town. There are also plans to open a new Oceanography centre – with an aquarium and museum of the sea – in the next few years.

Sagres's main appeal, however, is its proximity to superb **beaches**, two of which are below the town itself. Further fine sandy stretches can be found just east and west, the latter ones on the bleak promontory leading to **Cabo de São Vicente**, a dramatic lighthouse-capped headland.

Some history

It was at the headlands of **Sagres** and **Cabo de São Vicente**, in the fifteenth century, that Prince Henry the

Navigator set up a school of navigation, gathering together the greatest astronomers, cartographers and adventurers of his age. Fernão de Magalhães (Magellan), Pedro Álvares Cabral and Vasco da Gama all studied at Sagres, and from the beach at Belixe – midway between the capes of Sagres and São Vicente – the first long caravels were launched, thus revolutionizing shipping with their wide hulls, small adaptable sails, and ability to sail close to the wind. Each year new expeditions were dispatched to penetrate a little further unto the unknown, and to resolve the great navigational enigma presented by the west coast of Africa, thereby laying the foundations of the country's overseas empire.

After Henry's death here in 1460, the centre of maritime studies was moved to Lisbon and the town began to lose its importance. In 1587 Drake's navy damaged the small Fortaleza de Baleeira while attacking the occupying Spanish forces, and in 1755, the Great Earthquake laid both the Fortaleza de Baleeira and Henry's fortress school to ruins. Sagres village was rebuilt in the nineteenth century, but slipped back into the obscurity from which Henry had raised it. For over 200 years it remained little more than an isolated fishing village.

In the early 1980s, the one-street village began to attract a growing number of young backpackers and windsurfers, drawn by the string of magnificent, isolated local beaches. In recent years, the improved road from Lagos has put Sagres within easy reach of the rest of the region and the inevitable trail of villas and apartments has quickly followed.

ARRIVAL AND INFORMATION

Buses from Lagos stop by Sagres's main Praça da República and continue down to the harbour. On the square, you'll find a privately run **tourist office**, *Turinfo* (daily 9.30am–1pm & 2-5.30pm; ☎ 282 620 003, ⊕ 282 620 004),

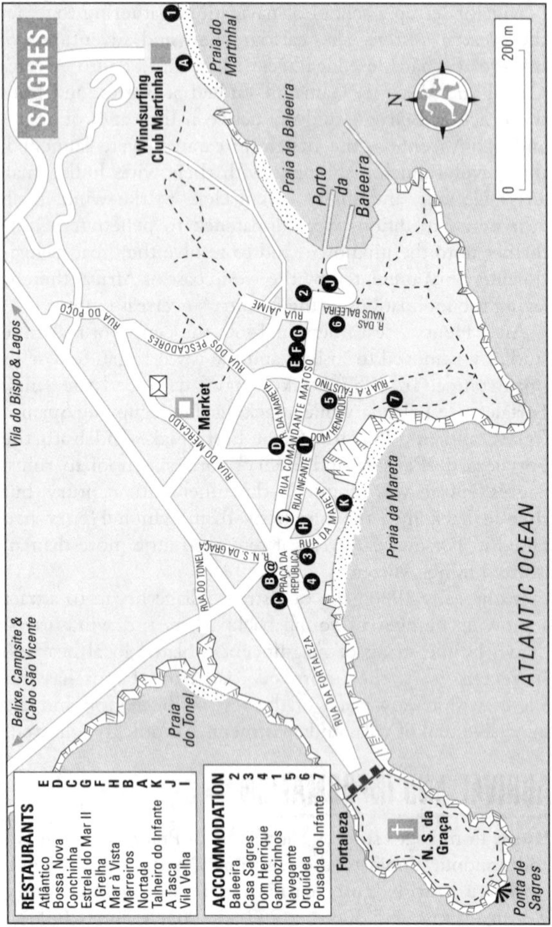
SAGRES
RESTAURANTS
Atlântico E
Bossa Nova D
Conchinha C
Estrela do Mar II G
A Grelha F
Mar à Vista H
Marreiros B
Nortada A
Talheiro do Infante K
A Tasca J
Vila Velha I
ACCOMMODATION
Baleeira 2
Casa Sagres 3
Dom Henrique 4
Gambozinhos 1
Navegante 5
Orquídea 6
Pousada do Infante 7
Belixe, Campsite & Cabo São Vicente
Vila do Bispo & Lagos
Windsurfing Club Martinhal
Praia do Martinhal
Praia da Baleeira
Porto da Baleeira
Praia da Mareta
Praia do Tonel
ATLANTIC OCEAN
Fortaleza
N. S. da Graça
Ponta de Sagres
Market
RUA DO POÇO
RUA DOS PESCADORES
RUA JAIME
R. DAS NAUS BALEEIRA
RUA COMANDANTE MATOSO
RUA P. A. FAUSTINO
R. DA MARETA
DOM HENRIQUE
RUA INFANTE
RUA DA MARETA
RUA DO MERCADO
R. N. S. DA GRAÇA
PRAÇA DA REPÚBLICA
RUA DO TONEL
RUA DA FORTALEZA
N
0
200 m

which can arrange room rental, book you on a local jeep or boat tour, rent out **mountain bikes** and offer **internet access** (€3/30min). The main **turismo** (Tues–Sat 9.30am–1pm & 2–5.30pm; ℡ 282 763 031) is a lonely hut a couple of minutes' walk along the village road from the square towards the fishing harbour and can hand out free town maps and bus timetables. Past the tourist office, Rua Infante Dom Henrique and the parallel Rua Comandante Matoso hold Sagres's **shops** and **banks**. The **post office** is out on Rua do Mercado, a couple of hundred yards north of the tourist office near the covered town **market**. On the first Friday of each month, this area forms the venue for a lively regional flea market.

ACCOMMODATION

There are plenty of **guesthouses**, **apartments** and **hotels** so there is usually no problem finding a place to stay except in high season, when places can get booked up. However, you'll be approached by people offering **rooms** in private houses (from around €30) and, if you want it, access to a kitchen too. The nearest **campsite**, *Belixe* (℡ 282 624 351, ℻ 282 624 445; €4/person, from €34/tent), is 2km north-west of the village, along (and off) the main road; it is convenient for Praia de Belixe (see p.275).

Hotel da Baleeira

Porto da Baleeira
℡ 282 624 212,
✉ hotel.baleeira@mail.telepac
.pt
This modern hotel has sweeping harbour views, a large pool and tennis courts. Rooms are spacious and comfortable with TVs and en-suite facilities. **6**

Casa Sagres

Praça da República
℡ 282 624 358
Behind the main square on the road down to Praia da Mareta, this is primarily a

restaurant (see p.277) that also lets out decent en-suite rooms. The best ones have sea-facing balconies (€10 extra). ⑤

Residencial Dom Henrique
Praça da República
ⓣ 282 620 000, ⓕ 282 620 001
In a perfect position on the main square and with a terrace offering wonderful sea views, this is a good first port of call. There's an airy bar and rooms have bath and satellite TV; rooms with sea-facing balconies ⑤, otherwise ④

Fortaleza do Belixe
Belixe
ⓣ 282 624 124, ⓔ guest @pousadas.pt
Set in the small Fortaleza do Belixe, perched high on the cliff edge, 2km out of town at Belixe, this four-room hotel is an upmarket annexe of the *Pousada do Infante*. There's a highly regarded restaurant downstairs. ⑤

Motel Gambozinhos
Praia do Martinhal

ⓣ 282 620 160, ⓕ 282 620 169
Very attractive, simple motel with a line of rooms and apartments set in peaceful gardens just back from the sands of Praia do Martinhal. Rooms with a sea view cost an extra €10, while self-catering apartments cost a further €10. ④

Navegante
Rua Infante Dom Henriques
ⓣ 282 624 354, ⓦ www .hotel-navigator.com
Behind the *Pousada do Infante* in a modern block, this hotel offers double rooms with satellite TV along with self-catering apartments. What it lacks in character it makes up for with facilities, including two pools and a squash court. ⑤

Aparthotel Orquídea
Sítio da Baleeira
ⓣ 282 624 257, ⓕ 282 624 340
An ungainly concrete lump that's superbly positioned above the harbour with great sea views. Facilities, which include a pool, make the simple one-bedroom apartments good value. ④

Pousada do Infante

☎ 282 624 222, ✉ guest
@pousadas.pt
One of two *pousadas* in the
Algarve, this attractive clifftop
mansion is decorated with

Moorish flourishes. The en-
suite rooms are spacious and
there are splendid views from
the terrace, plus a swimming
pool, tennis courts and a
games room. ❼

THE TOWN

Praça da República is the main focus of the town, an
attractive cobbled space lined with squat palms and white-
washed cafés. From here, it's a short walk southeast to
Sagres's best **beach**, Praia da Mareta, while Rua da
Fortaleza heads southwest to Henry the Navigator's
Fortaleza; it's quicker to walk this way than follow the signs
by road, which lead you to a giant car park. The rest of the
town is little more than a main road, Rua Comandante
Matoso, connecting the fishing harbour and Praia da
Baleeira at the eastern end with the main square, Praça da
República, to the west.

Sagres's lively saint's day, **Nossa Senhora da Graça**, is on
15 August, when the town celebrates with music, dancing
and fireworks.

Fortaleza

Daily: May–Sept 10am–8.30pm; Oct–April 10am–6.30pm; €3,
students €1.20

The walls of Henry the Navigator's **Fortaleza** (fortress)
dominate the clifftops north of the village. It is believed that
Henry developed thirteenth-century fortifications to form a
secure base for his seafaring academy, and Henry spent the

last three years of his life working in the fort from his home in Sagres. An immense circuit of walls once surrounded this vast, shelf-like promontory, high above the Atlantic. But what you see today was largely rebuilt in 1793: only the north side survives intact, the rest destroyed in the 1755 earthquake.

The entrance is through a formidable rock tunnel, before which is spread a huge pebble wind compass known as the **Rosa dos Ventos** (wind rose) unearthed beneath a church in 1921. Wind compasses are used to measure the direction of the wind, but most are divided into 30 segments. This is unusual in that its 43-metre diameter is divided into 40 segments. No one is sure whether the compass dates back to Henry's time, though the simple, much-restored chapel of **Nossa Senhora da Graça** besides the compass is accepted as dating from the fifteenth century.

Over the last few years there has been an attempt to beef up the contents of the fortress with new buildings within the walls – a **shop, café** and **exhibition space** showing maps of Portugal and other nautical memorabilia – but, gracelessly constructed with concrete, they have done little to enhance the beauty of the site. Elsewhere, it's a pleasant enough place to wander around the walls or out to **Ponta de Sagres**, a headland with a small lighthouse beacon offering fine views up and down the coast.

THE BEACHES

Despite the fame of the fortress, your days in Sagres are likely to be spent on one of the excellent beaches, most of which are within easy walking distance of the village. The nearest, best and therefore most crowded beach, **Praia da Mareta**, is a lovely stretch of soft sand lapped by warm water just five to ten minutes' walk downhill southeast from Praça da República. Sagres's other beaches tend to be slightly less crowded, lying at the far end of Rua Comandante Matoso, around the harbour, **Porto da Baleeira**, 1km to the east. This is very much a working harbour, lined with fishing boats and boat-building yards. You can squeeze past the slipways and boatyard debris onto the small **Praia da Baleeira**, another fine, if diminutive, sandy beach. For space, however, you're better off continuing east for five to ten minutes along the clifftop above the harbour to **Praia do Martinhal**, a wide sandy crescent that is generally quieter than the other beaches, backed by a marshy lagoon and complete with a **windsurfing school** (☎282 624 333) – which can also organize kayaking and snorkelling – and a beachside café.

Another couple of beaches, Praia de Tonel and Praia de Belixe, lie a little further away with correspondingly fewer crowds, though swimming must be approached with caution – there are some very strong currents so it is best not to go out of your depth. From Sagres, the road to São Vicente heads northwest parallel to the coast past **Praia de Tonel**, a slightly rocky beach around 1km from the village. Continuing northwest a further 1km you pass **Praia de Belixe**, from where Henry the Navigator's caravels first set off to explore the New World; little can have changed here since, and you are usually guaranteed plenty of sand to yourself.

Cabo de São Vicente

Four kilometres beyond Praia de Belixe lies the exposed **Cabo de São Vicente**, the most southwesterly point of the Iberian peninsular. Promontorium Sacrum was sacred to the Romans, who believed the sun sank hissing into the water beyond here every night. The chapel built to house the remains of St Vincent became a Christian shrine in the eighth century.

ST VICENT

St Vicent was born in Zaragoza in Spain in the fourth century AD and became the town's deacon during the early days of Christianity in Iberia. He was later imprisoned in Valencia and sentenced to death in 304 during the days of Christian persecution. It is said that while he was being burned alive, the room filled with flowers, light and the voices of angels, and he was proclaimed a martyr and then a saint. In the eighth century, his remains – which had somehow survived the fire – were miraculously washed up in an unmanned boat piloted by ravens at what is now Cabo de São Vicente. Perhaps more credible is the theory that Christians took whatever was left of Vincent with them to flee invading Moors, arriving at the safe outpost of the Cape where they later built a chapel to house his remains. In 1173, Afonso Henriques, Portugal's first Christian monarch, had the saint's remains moved to Lisbon. Legend has it that the faithful ravens followed to the capital, and guarded over him in the cloisters of Lisbon's Sé (cathedral), until the last one died in 1978. Today São Vicente remains Lisbon's patron saint.

Today the only buildings to be seen are the ruins of a sixteenth-century Capuchin monastery and a nineteenth-century **lighthouse**, which has the most powerful beam in Europe. If the lighthouse keeper is not too busy, he may let you look around. There is nothing left of any of the other houses that once surrounded the monastery; those that survived the attacks of the piratical Sir Francis Drake in 1587, came crashing to the ground in the Great Earthquake of 1755, the monks staying on alone until the Liberal suppression of the monasteries in 1834.

The cape is a dramatic and exhilarating six-kilometre walk from Sagres, with a cliff path skirting the vertiginous drop for much of the way. Walking on the road is easier if slightly less scenic – it'll take less than an hour and a half, with glorious views all the way. Try to be at the cape for sunset, which is invariably gorgeous, though frequently very windy too. En route you pass the seventeenth-century Fortaleza do Belixe, which has now been turned into a hotel and restaurant (see p.272). Today the sea off this wild set of cliffs shelters the highest concentration of marine life in Portugal, and it is also rich in **birdlife**: at the right time of year you should be able to spot blue rock thrushes and peregrine falcons nesting on the cliffs along with rare birds such as Bonelli's eagles, white storks, rock doves, kites and white herons.

EATING

Sagres's main street, Rua Comandante Matoso, is lined with **restaurants** and bars, catering for a range of tastes and budgets, while the various places offering sea views above the harbour or round the main square generally offer more expensive fish and seafood.

Atlântico
Rua Comandante Matoso
Daily 9am–2am. **Moderate**
This busy place with an outside terrace is one of the more reasonably priced fish restaurants along the Rua, though quality can be hit or miss. Specialities include *caldeirada* and *bife na frigadeira* (pan-fried beef).

Bossa Nova
Rua da Mareta
Tues–Sun noon–11pm.
Moderate
Quietly trendy place noted for its eclectic mix of dishes; choose from the excellent pizzas, curries, pasta, salads and imaginative vegetarian meals. There are a few tables in the inner courtyard.

Casa Sagres
Praça da República
Daily noon–3pm & 6.30–9.30pm. **Expensive**

SAGRES: EATING

On the road towards Praia da Mareta, this upmarket restaurant has a superbly positioned terrace overlooking the sea. Pricey but well-cooked specialities include *cataplana* and *arroz de marisco*.

Café Conchinha
Praça da República 8
Daily 8am–8pm. Inexpensive
Very popular tourist spot, thanks to the attractive outside tables on the main square, offering a good range of snacks – croissants, *tostas* and sandwiches – along with hot and cold drinks.

Estrela do Mar II
Rua Comandante Matoso
Daily 8am–2am. Moderate
Reasonably priced fish and meat dishes served in this cheap and cheerful restaurant near the harbour. Decorated with bright fish murals, the mixed clientele tend to be locals and backpackers.

A Grelha
Rua Comandante Matoso
Daily noon–3pm & 6–10pm.
Inexpensive
Simple, family-run grill house with a more local feel than many of the restaurants along this stretch.

Mar à Vista
Sítio da Mareta
Mon, Tues & Thurs–Sun 10am–midnight. Moderate
On a scrubby patch of ground just off the road to Praia da Mareta, this shack-like eatery serves a long list of good value fish, omelettes and salads.

Pastelaria Marreiros
Praça da República 12
Daily 8am–midnight.
Inexpensive
More Portuguese clientele than the *Conchina* next door, though with a similar range of snacks and drinks.

Nortada
Praia da Martinhal
Daily: May–Oct 10am–midnight; Sept–April daily 11am–5pm.
Moderate
Jazzy beach bar and restaurant set in a modern wood hut with a terrace right on the sands. Serves a good range of international dishes along

SAGRES: EATING

with the usual Portuguese fare and baguettes. Also does fine milkshakes and fresh juices.

Talheiro do Infante
Praia da Mareta
Mon & Wed–Sun 9am–11pm.
Expensive
Set on a raised bluff with a superb terrace facing the beach, this is a lovely place for a splurge, with top quality fish and seafood such as *arroz de lagosta* (lobster rice) and *cataplana de tamboril e marisco* (seafood and monkfish stew).

A Tasca
Porto da Baleeira
Daily: May–Sept 8am–midnight;
Oct–April Sun–Fri 8am–mid-night. **Inexpensive**
The best of Sagres's fish restaurants, with bargain fish

straight from the harbour – as well as a few meat dishes. Tables outside face the harbour, though it's just as fun in the barn-like interior, its walls encrusted with pebbles and old bottles.

Vila Velha
Rua Patrão A. Faustino, ☎ 282 624 788
Daily: May–Sept 6.30–10pm;
Oct–April Tues–Sun 6.30–10pm.
Expensive
In a pretty white house, this upmarket restaurant serves superior dishes that blend new and traditional Portuguese cuisine, including *tagliatelle com camarão e tamboril* (pasta with shrimp and monkfish) and *delícia tropical*, a dish with chicken, shrimps, bananas and cashews. Reservations advised.

DRINKING AND NIGHTLIFE

Sagres has a pretty lively **nightlife**, and in high season the place thrums all the way from the main square to the harbour. At other times, most of the action takes place in and around Praça da República.

Batedor
Rua das Naus Baleeira
Daily 8am–2am

A modern café-bar in a superb spot right above the harbour, with an extensive list of drinks – try the lethal *caipirinhas* – as well as ice creams, snacks and pizzas.

Dromedário
Rua Comandante Matoso
Daily noon–10pm

Energetic bistro that also serves a mean range of cocktails and juices, along with inexpensive pizzas and baguettes.

Last Chance Sallon
Sítio da Mareta
Tues–Sun 6pm–midnight

In a wooden shack overlooking the beach, this is a laid-back place to down an early evening beer or two.

Polvo Dreams
Rua Nossa Senhora da Graça
Daily 8pm–2am

Just past the main square on the road to Belixe, the "octopus dreams" is the liveliest late-night place in Sagres, with a giant TV screen and a snooker room to aid and abet the drinking.

Rosa dos Ventos
Praça da República
Tues–Sun noon–midnight

Atmospheric bar which also does simple food. Gets packed most evenings with a young, drunken crowd.

The West Coast

Unlike the southern stretches of the Algarve, the **west coast**, stretching north from Sagres to Odeceixe, is relatively undeveloped. There are several reasons for this: the coast is exposed to strong Atlantic winds; the sea can be several degrees cooler; and swimming can be dangerous. The designation in 1995 of the stretch of coast from Burgau to Cabo de São Vicente and up through the

Alentejo as a nature reserve – the Parque Natural Sudoeste Alentejano e Costa Vincentina – should go even further to protect this dramatic and rugged scenery from harmful development.

With its wild scenery and stunning – if wind-buffeted – beaches, this coast makes an ideal destination, with most of the accommodation found at low-key villages a few kilometres inland such as **Vila do Bispo** and **Carrapateira**. The pretty villages of **Aljezur** and **Odeceixe** are the most popular bases, with summer crowds of campervanners hanging out at the nudist beaches nearby.

VILA DO BISPO AND PRAIA DO CASTELEJO

VILA DO BISPO, at the junction of the west and south coast roads, is a fairly traditional if rundown Algarve village with a core of old white houses. It is centred on a lovely seventeenth-century parish **church** (Mon–Sat 10am–1pm & 2–6pm), every interior surface of which has been painted, tiled or gilded. If you drop enough in the plate in the sacristy, the old custodian will show you round the collection of assorted carvings, chalices and ecclesiastical vestments. The town has no other sights, but it makes a pleasant spot for a coffee or a meal in one of the bars and restaurants by the town garden, or to look out over the hills from the terrace outside the church.

If you have your own transport, the town could make a reasonable accommodation base, ideally suited for day-trips to the surrounding beaches. The nearest stretch of sand, **Praia do Castelejo**, is reached via the bottom of town – from the main square, take the road downhill past the post office and bear right – along a narrow road leading 5km west. It crosses a stretch of bleak moors and hills, the final approach down a winding and precipitous descent. But it is worth the effort: the beach is a huge swathe of sand lashed by heavy waves below dark grey cliffs. Like Cabo de São Vicente, the beach has an edge-of-the-world feel, though the beachside café adds a slight touch of civilization.

Practicalities

Vila do Bispo is served by several **buses** daily from both Sagres and Lagos, which drop you right at the bottom of the village, five minutes' walk from the church. **Accommodation** is limited to just one basic **guesthouse**, the *Pensão Mira Sagres* at Rua do Hospital 3 (☎ 282 639 160), opposite the church. It has simple rooms facing the square or green rolling countryside to the back and there's a downstairs bar where time seems to have stopped. You can also try asking around in any of the cafés or restaurants for **private rooms**.

Eating and Drinking

There are a surprising number of **places to eat and drink** in Vila do Bispo, most of them off to the left of the main square as you face it from the church. The beach also has a seasonal café-restaurant.

Restaurante Central
Rua Comandante Matoso 20
Daily 10am–2am. **Moderate**
One of the smartest restaurants in town, just off the main square, though it lacks character. Reasonable dishes include *arroz de marisco* and fresh fish.

Convivio Bistro
Praça da República
Daily 8am–2am. **Inexpensive**
With tables outside on the central square by the church, this is an enjoyable place to have a pizza or light meal. Its lethal range of cocktails also makes it the liveliest place in town for a drink.

Restaurante Correia
Rua 1° de Maio
Mon–Fri & Sun 1–3pm &
7–10pm. **Inexpensive**
Just down from the church,
this is an attractive, roomy
restaurant with *azulejos* on
the walls and a reasonably
priced menu of grilled meats
and fish; the best-value place
in the village.

Restaurante Praia do Castelejo
Praia do Castelejo
May–September Tues–Sun
12–8pm. **Moderate**
Welcoming café-restaurant
supplying drinks, snacks and
the usual Portuguese grilled
fare on a terrace facing the
sands.

CARRAPATEIRA AND ITS BEACHES

Fifteen kilometres north of Vila do Bispo, past spinning
wind turbines, the scenery becomes more lush, the road
tree-lined with aromatic pine and eucalyptus. A daily weekday bus runs this stretch to **CARRAPATEIRA**, a fairly
nondescript village that's little more than a cluster of houses
round a hilltop church, though it is at least closer to its
beaches than Vila do Bispo and has a slightly better range of
accommodation.

The closest beach, **Praia da Bordeira**, lies some 3km
northwest. After the craggy, cliff-backed beaches further
south, it is something of a surprise to come across such a
spectacular deep stretch of sands spilling inland to merge
with dunes and the wide river valley behind. The road west
from Carrapateira passes a small car park next to the river,
from where you cross a narrow stretch of the water onto
the back of the beach. Alternatively, carry on up the hill
where another car park sits just above the sands. It's a beautiful spot, popular with families; the sandbanks also provide
shelter from the wind for an unofficial campsite, which
seems to be tolerated by the local police.

Horse treks are on offer to experienced riders at the Herdade do Beiçudo (℡ 96709 5937), a riding centre 4km east of Praia da Bordeira. One-hour treks start at €25, up to €100 for all-day treks with a picnic.

Four kilometres south of Praia da Bordeira, along the coast road, lies **Praia do Amado**, which is also signed off the main road just south of Carrapateira. This fantastic, broad sandy bay backed by low hills with a couple of seasonal cafés is particularly popular with surfers. There's a **surf school** here (℡ & 🖷 282 624 560) which offers equipment hire and surf courses from €60.

Practicalities

In high summer, **accommodation** can be in short supply, but try asking in *Bar Barroca* (see below) for details of **private rooms**. At other times, or with advanced bookings, the best budget place is *Pensão das Dunas*, Rua da Padaria 9 (℡ & 🖷 282 973 118; ❶), a very pretty building on the beach-side of the village which has a number of simple rooms overlooking a flower-filled courtyard; there is also one apartment (❷). *Residencial Casa Fajara* (℡ 282 973 184/96709 5937, 🖷 282 973 186; ❸), a couple of kilometres north of Carrapateira, is the most upmarket choice: a spruce modern villa with neat gardens and its own pool beautifully positioned overlooking a wide, green valley. Smart rooms have their own terraces; there is a communal kitchen and breakfast can be supplied on request.

For a **meal** or **drink**, *Bar Barroca* in Carrapateira (daily 8am–midnight), the village's main café-bar, serves inexpensive snacks. It can also help with bus times. On Praia do Armado, *Café Praia do Armado* (April–Sept daily 10am–8pm), is where the surfers retreat for drinks and inexpensive snacks. For a more elaborate meal, *O Sitio do Rio* (Mon & Wed–Sun noon–10pm; closed Nov), 1km back from Praia do Bordeira towards Carrapateira, offers moderately priced Portuguese food using organic and free range produce.

ALJEZUR

The village of **Aljezur**, 16km north of Carrapeteira, is both the prettiest and liveliest town along the west coast of the Algarve. The main coast road passes through a prosaic, more modern lower town where you find banks, the post office and a range of cafés and restaurants. The more inter-esting **historic centre** spreads uphill beyond the bridge over the Aljezur river, a network of narrow cobbled streets reaching up through whitewashed houses to the remains of a tenth-century Moorish **castle**. It's a lovely walk with sweeping views over the valley. En route you can stop off at a motley selection of free museums. The first of these, the **Museu Municipal** (Tues–Sat 10am–1pm & 2–5.30pm), is set in the attractive former town hall, housing a distinctly average collection of historical artefacts gathered from the region: dusty farm implements, old axes and the like. Just uphill, the **Museu de Arte Sacra** (Tues-Sat 9.30am–12.30pm & 2–5.30pm), offers a dull collection of religious vestments tucked into the back of the attractive, eighteenth-century Misericórdia church. Finally, the more interesting **Casa Museu Pintor José Cercas** (Tues–Sat 10am–1pm & 2–5.30pm) displays the works and collections of local artist José Cercas, who lived in the house until his death in 1992. His well-observed landscapes and religious scenes are complemented by an attractive house with a pretty garden.

Practicalities

There are four **buses** daily to Aljezur from Lagos via
Bensafrim, continuing to Odeceixe. A further three buses
run daily from Lagos via Portimão to Aljezur, continuing
on to Lisbon. The **turismo** (Mon & Fri–Sun 9.30am–1pm
& 2–5.30pm, Tues–Thurs 9.30am–7pm; ⓣ 282 998 229) is
in Largo do Mercado, by the river and in front of the town
market. More and more surfers are making their way here
in summer, attracted by the local beaches and the turismo
does its best to help with private **rooms**.

There are also a couple of decent **guesthouses** in town.
The *Hospedaria S. Sebastião* is the most central, on Rua 25
de Abril, (ⓣ 933 264 943; ❷), at the eastern end of town
on the busy through-road. It offers decent-sized rooms with
showers, the front ones with balconies overlooking the
pretty valley opposite. One kilometre out of Aljezur in the
neighbouring village of Igreja Nova – just off the
Monchique road – the modern *Residencial Dom Sancho*, on
Largo Igreja Nova 1 (ⓣ 282 998 119, ⓕ 282 998 763; ❹),
sits just above the main church overlooking a pedestrianized
street. Rooms are large and comfortable and come with
bath and TV; price includes breakfast.

There are several inexpensive **cafés** and **restaurants** in
Aljezur, most of them along the main through-road, Rua
25 de Abril. *Pastelaria Mioto* (daily 6am–midnight), at number 63, is a neat, modern place tucked into the back of a
shopping centre. It offers a fine range of cakes and pastries,
but the main appeal is a superb terrace overlooking the verdant river valley behind. Just up from here, the *Primavera*
(Mon–Sat 8am–11pm) is a bar-café and restaurant offering
all-day food and drinks on a little outdoor terrace. The
well-priced *frango no churrasco* (chargrilled chicken) is recommended. At the tourist-office end of the main street,
Restaurante Ruth (Mon–Fri & Sun noon–3pm & 6–11pm;

Ⓣ282 998 534), is a highly regarded restaurant specializing in moderately priced regional dishes. Along with daily specials it has superb *arroz de tamboril com camarão* (monkfish and prawn rice).

ALJEZUR'S BEACHES

There are three superb beaches within a few kilometres of Aljezur. One kilometre south of Aljezur, a road heads down to the longest of these at **Arrifana**, 10km to the southeast. The beach is a fine sandy sweep set below high, crumbling black cliffs. A narrow road leads down to the beach, but in high season all car parking spots are usually taken which means parking at the top of the cliff, a steep five-minute walk away. The beach is popular with surfers and surf competitions are sometimes held here. The clifftop boasts the remains of a ruined fort, just up from a cluster of cafés and holiday villas.

From May to September, two daily buses depart from Aljezur to Arrifana and Monte Clérigo.

Heading north along the coast road from Arrifana, you pass the **VALE DA TELHA** tourist resort, an unattractive low-density complex of shapeless villas set amongst trees and unnecessary roundabouts. It is far better to head north the 4km to **MONTE CLÉRIGO**, a pretty little holiday village of pink- and white-faced beach houses. A cluster of café-restaurants face a superb, family-oriented beach tucked into the foot of a river valley. There is a campsite (see p.290), otherwise the best accommodation options are in Aljezur itself, 8km to the southeast.

A third, usually quieter beach, **PRAIA AMOREIRA**, is accessible off the main Aljezur-Odeceixe road some 5km northwest of Aljezur; the drive here down a broad river

A WALK FROM MARMELETE TO ALJEZUR

Part of the Via Algarviana (see p.175), this superb 18.5km walk passes through some of the western Algarve's most picturesque scenery, linking the mountain village of Marmelete, on the road to Monchique, with Aljezur, near the coast. Beginning in the wooded slopes of the Serra de Espinhaço de Cão, the walk descends through woodland following the valley of a small river, the Ribeira Paçil. It's a relatively undemanding downhill walk that crosses the river several times, so ask locally whether there's been heavy rain as the river becomes unfordable at times, and there can be rockfalls at certain points along the route.

A taxi from Aljezur to Marmelete (there are no buses along the 15km route) will cost around €15. A good starting point is the *Café Sol da Serra* (daily 9am–10.30pm), opposite the Petrofer filling station, just outside Marmelete on the Aljezur road. From here, head west along the road for 1.5km, where a wooden sign reads "Neveda, Rocha, Espigão" and a "No Overtaking" sign on the north side of the road marks the start of the walk. From here, a stony track descends steeply down to the Ribeira Paçil, and then follows the course of the river all the way to Aljezur, the route marked with blue blobs.

The initial descent twists and turns giving superb views of the Atlantic after about 1km. The first river crossing is reached after a further 3km, where stepping stones or a eucalyptus pole with handrail will help you across. Continue along the path for a couple more kilometres, through traditional farming country, with citrus trees, a piggery and some

valley is delightful. It's another fine sandy bay stretching north of the mouth of the Riba de Aljezur, backed by a handy seasonal beach café.

beehives, and you'll see a rural house and an old windmill on the southern bank of the river. Another 2km beyond the windmill (9km into the walk) you descend to the second river crossing, where you have to wade through ankle-deep water to reach a pleasant picnic spot surrounded by dragonflies and butterflies.

Heading up from the river (take care as there is loose shale above), you'll soon find yourself walking through sturdy oak woods, until, 3km beyond the second crossing, you'll reach the third river crossing, spanned by a concrete bridge.

From here on, the valley widens and the track stays close to the river. A kilometre beyond the concrete bridge, you'll arrive at a sharp bend: ignore two tracks to your right and continue straight on, the path climbing past a ruined building with a traditional bread oven on your left at the hilltop. After another three kilometres, you'll reach a small farming community where the track becomes tarmac.

It's now just a couple of kilometres to Aljezur. Ignore the road on the right leading to Vale da Nora das Sobreiras, and continue on the track which leads west, past a white house on the right bank. Look for a blue arrow on a right-hand lamp post. Here, climb up the steep bank as indicated, always keeping right, until you reach a T-junction at the ridge. Turn right, then left at the top of the hill onto another track, and you'll reach a ruined windmill. In front of you is the village of Igreja Nova. Head through the village and you'll see Aljezur capped by its castle, 1km to the west.

Practicalities

For **accommodation**, try the tourist office in Aljezur or enquire about the possibility of renting a room or villa at

ALJEZUR'S BEACHES

one of the cafés back from the beaches. In Arrifana, behind the *Brisamar Café* at the top of the cliff, at Rua João Dias Mendes 43a (☎ 282 9987 254, ⓕ 282 767 645; ❷), there are simple, clean **rooms** with TVs and small bathrooms. There are also two decent **campsites** in the region: *Camping Vale da Telha* at Vale da Telha (☎ 282 998 444; €2/person, from €2/tent), less than 1km from Monte Clérigo beach and around 4km from Arrifana. Further north, *Parque Campismo de Serrão* (☎ 282 990 220, ⓔ serrão@clix.pt; €3.50/person, €38/tent), is a large, tranquil campsite sitting among dense trees some 7km northwest of Aljezur. It has its own pool, supermarket and tennis courts. A rough track leads from the campsite through scrubland down to Praia Amoreira, around 4km away.

There are also several places to get a moderately priced **meal** or **drink** at all the beaches, though most places close out of season. Praia Amoreira has a superbly positioned café-restaurant facing the beach *Restaurante Paraíso do Mar* (May–Sept daily 10am–7pm), the perfect place for an early evening beer. It also does snacks and moderately priced grilled meat and fish. The best positioned of Monte Clérigo's café-restaurants is *O Zé* (daily 9am–10pm), with decently priced snacks, drinks and full Portuguese meals and tables out the back facing the beach.

ODECEIXE AND PRAIA DE ODECEIXE

Some 17km north of Aljezur, the town of **Odeceixe** tumbles down a hillside opposite the broad valley of the Odeceixe river below the winding, tree-lined main coast road. The last town in the Algarve – the neighbouring Alentejo district starts north of the river – it's a fairly traditional, attractive and tranquil place, at least outside summer. From June to September, however, it seems to attract just about every hippy and surf dude in the Algarve, drawn by the proximity of its superb beach along with some of the cheapest rooms in the region. If you hit town outside high season, though, it is very pleasant. Most of the action is centred round the main **square**, Largo 1º de Maio, from where the beach is signed to the west. Round here you'll find the post office, banks, supermarkets and plenty of places letting out **rooms**. Aside from the square the town's sights are limited to a small covered **market** and the **Adega-Museu de Odeceixe** (Wed–Sun 7pm–11pm; free), an old wine cellar that has been preserved in its traditional state, full of old barrels and cheap wine.

Reached down a verdant river valley, the beach – **Praia de Odeceixe** – lies some 4km to the west. It's a lovely walk following the river to a broad, sandy bay framed by low cliffs. It is one of the most sheltered beaches on this stretch of coast, offering superb surfing and relatively safe swimming, especially when the tide is down. A pretty cluster of traditional houses and cafés lie banked up to the south of the bay.

ACCOMMODATION

Restaurante Café Dorita

Praia de Odeceixe
ⓣ 282 947 581
Simple rooms, the best with sweeping views over the waves, are let out by the restaurant (see below) above the beach. One even has a terrace. Shared facilities only, but book ahead in high season. ❶

Hospedaria Firmino Bernardinho

Rua da Praia, Odeceixe
ⓣ 282 947 362
At the foot of town on the road out to the beach, this is the most attractive place in town. Spotless, modern rooms with small balconies and bathrooms, overlook the wide river valley. ❷

Residêncio do Parque

Rua da Estrada Nacional 11

ⓣ 282 947 117

Run by an eccentric welcoming owner, this huge house is probably the cheapest option in the Algarve. The rooms are a mixed bag – the best on the top floor with small balconies overlooking the valley; all are en suite with TVs. ❶

EATING AND DRINKING

Blue Sky
Largo 1 de Maio
Daily 8am–midnight. **Inexpensive**
Popular travellers' spot on the main square offering *petiscos*, pizzas, pasta and drinks. A good place to catch the last rays of the day.

Restaurante Café Dorita
Praia de Odeceixe
Tues–Sun 10am–10pm.
Moderate
On the road above the beach, this simple café-restaurant offers decently priced Portuguese food best enjoyed on the outside terrace overlooking the beach. It also lets out rooms (see above).

O Retiro do Adelino
Rua Nova 20
Daily noon–3pm & 6–11pm.
Inexpensive
Bumper portions of grilled chicken, fish with tomato rice and *feijoada* are served at this simple grill house with a little courtyard.

CONTEXTS

History

T he Algarve was the last region in Portugal to be recaptured from the Moors, who occupied the territory for around 500 years. In the fifteenth century, Algarve's ports became the main departure point for the great Portuguese navigators, but as a rural and agricultural region, the region's role in Portuguese history has been relatively subdued. Although Portuguese monarch's were crowned king or queen "of Portugal and the Algarve", the history of the region is essentially tied to that of the rest of Portugal.

Early settlers and the Romans

Scant remains of early **stone** and **copper age** cultures are still to be seen in the municipal museums of Albufeira and Lagos and the archaeological museums in Faro and Silves, but the earliest settlements of note were founded by the **Phoenicians** who formed fishing villages at various points of the Algarve including Lagos, Portimão and Tavira. There is evidence that Greeks and Carthiginians traded with Iberia from 500 BC onwards, attracted by its salt – a precious commodity in those days when salt was essential for preserving food – and tuna paste, a popular export to classical Athens.

The **Romans** swept into the Iberian peninsula in 210 BC, and though they met stiff resistance from Celtiberian tribes in the interior, by 60 BC, most of modern Portugal had been integrated into the Roman Empire under Julius Caesar. In 27 BC, Emperor Augustus divided Roman Iberia into two provinces, the western province of Lusitania stretching from the Algarve northwards up the coast to beyond the Douro (the eastern province, Baetica, corresponds to current day Andalucía). In the Algarve, a network of roads was laid out with major bridges at Silves (Silbis) and Tavira (Balsa).

By the second century AD, the Romans had developed the spas at Caldas de Monchique and had expanded most of the Phoenician trading settlements in the Algarve. Here they developed salt extracting plants to preserve fish, which can still be seen at Quinta da Marim (see p.107) and at the Cerra da Vila Roman complex in Vilamoura (see p.82). One of the most important Roman sites in Portugal is at Milreu, near Faro (see p.99), complete with remains of a temple and bathhouses.

Christianity and the decline of Rome

From around the third century AD, Christianity began to make inroads into the Portuguese mainland, mostly via Germanic tribes. From around 400, the Roman empire's hold on Iberia was diminishing. In around 585, a **Christian Visigoth** empire was established with its capital at Toledo in present-day Spain, with a major base at Faro, where a bishopric was established. The Visigoths were a heavily Romanized yet independent force who maintained rule over a unified Iberia for two centuries. By the end of the seventh century, however, internal divisions resulted in one faction seeking support from north Africa against a rival faction. In 711, the first wave of Moors crossed the straits into Spain and, meeting little resistance and only too happy to help out, happily took over much of the peninsula – within a decade they had spread up into most of Spain and Portugal.

The Moors

Many **Moors** settled in the warm south of the peninsula, mainly in the region they called al-Gharb, 'the west' – present-day Algarve. They established their capital at Shelb – modern Silves – and developed Lagos (Zawaya) into an important trading post. By the middle of the ninth century, al-Gharb had become an independent kingdom, separate from the great Muslim emirate of al-Andalus, which covered most of Spain.

Moorish rule had a stabilizing influence on the area. It was a peaceful era of religious tolerance with Jews and Christians free to worship and live by their own civil laws. Under the culturally sophisticated rulers the arts flourished, not least in the form of azulejos (see p.76) which have so influenced Portuguese design ever since. The Moors' construction and engineering skills built on what the Romans had left behind creating the advanced irrigation techniques, which can still be seen around the region. The Moors also introduced crops of cotton, rice, citrus fruits and almonds.

In 922, a Viking army attempted to attack Shelb, by then a flourishing city of some 40,000 people, but the army was forced back as it passed up the Rio Arade (then a major river). But the Moorish kingdom was shortly under threat again, this time by Christians who were to be more successful.

The birth of Portugal

In the north of Iberia, the Moors were slowly being driven out by Christian forces – first in Asturias, then León,

Galicia and 'Portucale', the area between the Douro and Minho rivers. By the eleventh century, Portucale was given the status of country by the kings of León and in 1073, Afonso VI came to the throne. Hard-pressed by subsequent Moorish invasions, the new king turned to **European crusaders** to help him protect the Christian kingdom. With the backing of the crusaders, Afonso's kingdom was able to expand south, taking in Lisbon by 1147. But despite countless attempts to conquer it, the Algarve remained under Moorish control for another century. In 1189, one of Afonso's successors, Sancho I, succeeded in taking Shelb with the help of Richard the Lionheart, only to lose it again the following year to the Moors under al-Mansur.

The Christian conquest

The Christians attacked the Algarve for around a century, with many towns passing into Christian hands only to be retaken by the Moors shortly afterwards. It was not until the thirteenth century that the Algarve was finally conquered, much of it falling to Sancho II (1223–1248) and **Afonso III** (1248–79), who took Faro in 1249 to establish a **united Portugal** with pretty much the same boundaries as we know today. Afonso adopted the title "king of Portugal and the Algarve", a title given to every monarch until the birth of the republic in 1910.

After Shelb was taken by the new Christian monarch in 1249, the great Moorish capital quickly fell into ruin. Most of the remaining Arabs were enslaved, forced to convert to Christianity or driven out of the Algarve altogether, though skilled artisans known as *Mudéjars* were allowed to stay on. The *Mudéjars* ensured that the Moorish influence on Portuguese architecture continued, especially in the decorative *azulejos* and the distinctive filigree chimneys of the Algarve.

The south of the new Christian country had previously flourished thanks to trade links with North Africa. However, this market had now collapsed and there were constant threats from hostile forces from what is now Spain to the east, so the rulers set about securing their hard won territory. The far-sighted king **Dom Dinis** (1279–1325), established a line of castles along the coast and the frontier with present-day Spain, including the one at Alcoutim in the Algarve.

Being sparsely populated, however, Dom Dinis divided the Algarve into parcels of land that were awarded to powerful groups that the king felt could be trusted to protect them. Much of the Algarve was therefore entrusted to noblemen, the Church and holy orders – notably the Order of Christ (see p.145). In 1319, this order established a base at Castro Marim near the Spanish border and they went on to become one of the most important financiers of the country's expansionist ambitions.

Maritime expansion

Throughout the fourteenth century, Portugal was intermittently at war with Castile but in 1386, João I signed the **Treaty of Windsor**, sealing a trade alliance with England that was further cemented by João's marriage to Philippa of Lancaster, John of Gaunt's daughter. As Portugal's position was politically and commercially strengthened, Castile was forced to sign a truce in 1411. Portugal then enjoyed an unrivalled period of peace and security which would see the country developing one of the most powerful maritime empires in the world.

Most of the early **overseas expeditions** departed from Lisbon and the Algarve – mainly Lagos and Portimão – and the region received an unexpected boost to its economy with the resulting discoveries, with merchants, spices and precious metals passing through its ports from the new trade routes.

João I's first target was north Africa: Ceuta was taken in 1415 and, under Afonso V, Tangier in 1471. The Portuguese moved south round the African coast and began a lucrative **gold trade** from Senegal and the Gold Coast. These new African colonies were to provide Portugal with another sources of wealth: in 1444, the first **African slaves** were sold in Lagos (see p.243).

Henry the Navigator and the great explorers

The third son of João I and Philippa of Lancaster, **Prince Henry**, was also Grand Master of the Order of Christ, and turned the order's vast resources towards marine development. He founded a School of Navigation on the desolate promontory of Sagres in around 1420 and staffed it with Europe's leading cartographers, navigators and mariners; Fernão de Magalhães (Magellan), Pedro Álvares Cabral and Vasco da Gama all studied at Sagres during the fifteenth and sixteenth centuries. As well as improving the art of offshore navigation, the school redesigned the caravel, making it a vessel specifically designed for long ocean-going journeys. From the beach at Belixe, new expeditions set off to penetrate the unknown world and bring back its treasure. Gil Eanes, who had been born in Lagos, was one of the first sailors to take advantage of the caravels, being the first to sail round Cape Bojador in 1434, a West African headland that at the time was believed to be the edge of the world.

By Henry's death in 1460, Madeira (1419), the Azores (1427), Cape Verde (1457) and west Africa as far as Sierra Leone had all been "discovered". With rural poverty commonplace in the Algarve and the neighbouring Alentejo district, many pioneering farmers set off in hope of a better life and settled in Madeira and neighbouring Porto Santo.

In 1487, Bartolomeu Dias, a knight of the Order of Christ, left Portimão with a commission from João II to find a sea route to India. He became the first European to round the southern tip of Africa, later accompanied Vasco da Gama at the start of his journey to India in 1498 and also sailed with Pedro Alvares Cabral, the discoverer of Brazil in 1500.

João II was courted by another explorer, Christopher Columbus, but João's advisers insisted that his suggested passage west to India was unfeasible. João died in Alvor in the Algarve in 1495, three years after Columbus – funded by the Spanish – arrived in America.

Manuel I and the maritime empire

Overseas expansion continued under the reign of **Manuel I** (1495–1521), whose reign led to a proliferation of construction in the so-called Manueline style (see p.216), where decorative marine motifs and carvings of fantastical creatures were inspired by tales from the New World.

In 1498, Vasco da Gama finally found a sea route to India, opening up the **spice trade** to the Portuguese monarch who was already doing well from African gold. Meanwhile, Spain was opening up the New World and in 1494, at the Treaty of Tordesillas, the two Iberian countries divided the world between them along an imaginary line 370 leagues west of the Cape Verde islands. This not only gave Portugal the run of the Orient but also, from 1500, Brazil. By the mid-sixteenth century, Portugal dominated world trade; strategic trading posts had been established in Goa (1510), Malacca (1511), Ormuz (1515) and Macau (1517). The revenue from the East was topped up by the increasingly large-scale trade in slaves between West Africa,

Europe and Brazil. But though Lagos became the centre for this slave trade, the main departure point for overseas exploration had moved to Belém near Lisbon from the beginning of the fifteenth century.

The Inquisition and Spanish domination

Despite the enormous wealth generated for Manuel I's court, very little of it filtered down through the system, and in the country at large conditions barely improved. The practice of siphoning off a hefty slice of the income into the royal coffers effectively prevented the development of an entrepreneurial class and, as everywhere else in Europe, financial matters were left very much in the hands of the Jews, who were not allowed to take up most other professions.

Portugal had traditionally been considerably more tolerant than other European nations in its treatment of its Jewish citizens (and towards the Moorish minority who had been absorbed after the reconquest). However, popular resentment of their riches, and pressure from Spain, forced Manuel – who had initially welcomed refugees from the Spanish persecution – to order their expulsion in 1496. Although many chose the pragmatic course of remaining as "New Christian" converts, others fled to the Netherlands. This exodus, continued as a result of the activities of the **Inquisition** (from 1531 on), created a vacuum which left Portugal with an extensive empire based upon commerce, but deprived of much of its commercial expertise. By the 1570s the economy was beginning to collapse: incoming wealth was insufficient to cover the growing costs of maintaining an empire against increasing competition, coupled with foreign debts, falling prices and a decline in the productivity of domestic agriculture.

In the Algarve, Lagos's position as an important port meant it was awarded the title of capital of the Algarve in 1577, and administrative jiggling also saw the bishopric moved from Silves – now a declining town – to the more important centre of Faro.

In the end it was a combination of reckless imperialism which brought to an end the dynasty of the House of Avis and with it, at least temporarily, Portuguese independence. **Dom Sebastião** (1557–78), obsessed with dreams of a new crusade against Morocco, set out from Lagos at the head of a huge army to satisfy his fanatical fantasies. They were crushed at the battle of Alcácer-Quibir (1578), where the Portuguese dead numbered over eight thousand, including Sebastião and most of Portugal's nobility. Sebastião has achieved a similar status to King Arthur, with many believing he never really perished and would one day reappear. The aged Cardinal Henrique took the throne as the closest legitimate relative.

The Cardinal's death without heirs in 1580 provided Spain with the pretext to renew its claim to Portugal. Philip II of Spain, Sebastião's uncle, defeated his rivals at the battle of Alcântara and in 1581 was crowned **Felipe I** of Portugal, inaugurating a period of Hapsburg rule which lasted for sixty years. In the short term, although unpopular, the union was good for Portugal's economy, but in the long run, Spanish control proved disastrous. Association with Spain's foreign policy meant the enmity of the Dutch and the British, Portugal's traditional allies, losing the country an important part of its trade which was never to be regained. In 1587, Lagos and Sagres were sacked by Sir Francis Drake. Nine years later, the English attacked the Algarve again and Faro was ransacked by the Earl of Essex. But it was not until 1640 that a small group of conspirators stormed the palace in Lisbon and deposed the Duchess of Mantua, Governor of Portugal. By popular acclaim and despite personal reluctance, the Duke of Bragança, senior member of a family which had long been the most powerful in the country, took the throne as **João IV**.

The House of Bragança

Under the **House of Bragança**, Portugal found that most of its previous trade routes had been taken from it by the new maritime powers (in particular the Dutch and British), its alliance with Britain was weakened and the threat from Spain remained. But, occupied by internal troubles and conflicts within its colonies, Spain finally acknowledged Portugal's independence in 1668. Shortly after this, **gold** and **diamonds** were discovered in Brazil during the reign of Pedro II (1683–1706), and the Portuguese crown was once again financially independent. When **João V** came to the throne in 1706, however, he squandered most of the riches on the lavish convent at Mafra north of Lisbon. The infamous Methuen Treaty of 1703 with Britain further weakened Portugal's economy; the treaty opened up new markets for Portuguese wine but helped destroy the native textile trade by letting in British cloth at preferential rates. Portugal was becoming financially dependent on Britain.

Pombal and the Great Earthquake

João's apathetic son, José I (1750–1777) allowed the total concentration of power to pass into the hands of his chief minister, the **Marquês de Pombal**, who set about modernizing all aspects of life in Portugal. He established a secular bureaucracy, renewed the tax systems, set up export companies, abolished slavery within Portugal and even abolished the powerful Jesuits, the religious order that had long dominated education and religious life in Portugal. But one event above all enabled Pombal to rebuild the country: the **Great Earthquake of 1755**.

On 1st November 1755 (All Saint's Day), an enormous earthquake flattened most of Lisbon and damaged virtually every town on the Algarve coast. A twenty-metre high tidal

wave added to the destruction, silting up previously naviga-
ble rivers at a stroke such as that at Silves. Tremors continued in the Algarve for the best part of a year, and hardly a
building in the region was unaffected. In 1776, the provincial capital moved from a ravaged Lagos to Faro.

Napoleon

Just as Portugal began to recover from the earthquake,
Napoleon began to threaten. Britain had managed to keep
Portugal's trade routes open, but when the Portuguese
refused France's demands to support their naval blockade of
Britain, Napoleon's troops, who already had control of
Spain, marched into Lisbon under General Junot in 1807.
The royal family fled to Brazil and the war was left in the
hands of the British generals Beresford and Wellington.

The local Algarve population did their utmost to resist
the occupation, especially with Napoleon's plans for an
Algarve Principality. A popular revolt forced out much of
the occupying force in 1808, though only temporarily. It
was not until 1811 that the French were finally forced back
into Spain by Beresford's and Wellington's forces.

Britain's reward for helping Portugal was the right to
trade freely with **Brazil**, which declared itself a united
kingdom with Portugal in 1815 (it announced complete
independence in 1822), fatally weakening the relationship
that had bolstered up the Portuguese treasury for so long.
Historical roles were reversed, with Portugal effectively
becoming a colony of Brazil (where the royal family
remained) and a protectorate of Britain, with **General
Beresford** the administrator. The Portuguese army, however, remained an active national institution and in 1820, with
Beresford abroad, a group of officers called an unofficial
government and drew up a new constitution. Inspired by
recent liberal advances in Spain, they called for an elected

assembly and the abolition of clerical privilege and the traditional rights of the nobility.

The king, forced to choose between Portugal and Brazil, where his position looked even more precarious, returned in 1821 and accepted their terms. But his queen, Carlota, and their younger son Miguel, refused to take the oath of allegiance to the new state and became the dynamic behind a reactionary movement that grew considerable support in rural areas, including the Algarve.

The Miguelite Wars

With João VI's death in 1826, a delegation was sent to Brazil to pronounce Crown Prince Pedro the new king of Portugal. Unfortunately Pedro had already been declared Emperor of the newly independent Brazil. Unable to perform both duties, he resolved to pass the crown to his infant daughter, with **Miguel** as regent provided he swore to accept the new charter, redrawn by Pedro and somewhat less liberal than the earlier constitution. Miguel agreed, but once in power he promptly tore up any agreement, abolished the charter and returned to the old, absolutist ways. This was a surprisingly popular move in Portugal and in particular in the Algarve, where pro-monarchists under José Joaquim de Sousa Reis, better known as **Remexido**, ensured the king's orders were obeyed. Remexido's forces attacked the liberals who had occupied many parts of the eastern Algarve and who had a base in Faro. Towns were fiercely fought over, and the liberal base at Albufeira was besieged by Remexido in 1833.

The pro-monarchists were not popular with the governments in Spain, Britain or France who backed the liberals, and finally, after Miguel's defeat in the battle of Evora-Monte in 1834, Pedro IV, who had been deposed in Brazil, was put back on the throne. But Remexido continued to be a scourge to the new regime. In 1836, his gang murdered sleeping soldiers at their barracks in São Bartolomeu de Messines and it was another two years before the rebel was tracked down to his mountain retreat. Remexido was finally captured and executed in Faro in 1838.

Death of the Monarchy

In the second half of the nineteenth century, the economy began to recover, with the first signs of **industrialization** and a major public works programme under the minister Fontes Pereira de Melo. Social conditions also improved, with **João de Deus**, an Algarvian from São Bartolomeu de Messines, developing a new form of nursery school, setting up some 30 schools round the country which ran on a similar line to Montessori schools – although de Deus was primarily known as a poet and was briefly the MP for Silves.

Much of the industrialization was achieved with British backing. Indeed the copper mines at São Domingos in the Alentejo were operated by a British company until World War I. The British even employed their own private police force to keep the local workers in check. The copper was transported down the Guadiana for export from Vila Real de Santo António, whose harbour was improved by the British for this purpose. The Lisbon–Faro railway line opened in 1889 as the population of the Algarve grew to almost quarter of a million, though its economy was still largely reliant on fish canning, cork and agriculture.

The Portuguese monarchy, however, was almost bankrupt and its public humiliation over possessions in Africa – Britain and Germany simply ignored Portuguese claims to the land between Angola and Mozambique – helped strengthen republican feelings. **Republicanism** took root particularly easily in the army and among the urban poor, fuelled by falling standards of living and growing government ineptitude. **Dom Carlos** (1898–1908) attempted to rule dictatorially after 1906, alienating most sectors of the country in the process, and was assassinated in Lisbon, along with his eldest son, following a failed Republican coup in 1908. Finally, on 5 October 1910, the monarchy was overthrown once and for all by a joint revolt of the army and the navy. Dom Manuel II went into exile and died, in Britain, in 1932.

The "democratic" republic

In the early twentieth century, divisions among the Republicans, the cyclical attempts at violent overthrow of the new regime by the monarchists, and the intrinsic weakness of the country's economic, social and political structures, kept the Republic in permanent turmoil. There were 45 changes of government in sixteen years and several military uprisings. By 1926 not even the trade unions were prepared to stand by the Republic, preferring to maintain "proletarian neutrality" in the face of what at first seemed no more significant a military intervention than any other.

Salazar and the "New State"

While the military may have known what they wanted to overthrow in 1926, they were at first divided as to whether to replace it with a new Republican government or a restored monarchy. From the infighting, a Catholic monarchist, **General Carmona**, eventually emerged as president (which he remained until his death in 1951) with the Republican constitution suspended.

In 1928 one **Dr. António de Oliveira Salazar** joined the Cabinet as Finance Minister. A professor of economics at Coimbra University, he took the post only on condition that he would control the spending and revenue of all government departments. His strict monetarist line immediately balanced the budget for the first time since 1913 and in the short term the economic situation was visibly improved. From then on he effectively controlled the country, becoming prime minister in 1932 and not relinquishing that role until 1968.

His regime was very much in keeping with the political tenor of the 1930s and while it had few of the ideological pretensions of a fascist state, it had many of the trappings. Opposition was kept in check by the PIDE – a secret police force set up with Gestapo assistance – which used systematic torture and long-term detention in camps to defuse most resistance. The army, too, was heavily infiltrated by PIDE and none of the several coups mounted against Salazar came close to success.

Salazar succeeded in producing the infrastructure of a relatively modern economy but the results of growth were felt by few and in the Algarve, the essentially agricultural economy was allowed to stagnate. Internal unrest, while widespread, was muted and seemingly easily controlled; the New State's downfall, when it came, was precipitated far more by external factors.

The growth of tourism

Salazar was an ardent imperialist who found himself faced with growing **colonial wars**, which proved costly and brought international disapprobation. India seized Goa in 1961 and at about the same time the first serious disturbances were occurring in Angola, Mozambique and, later, in Guinea-Bissau.

The regime was prepared to make only the slightest concessions to any dissenters, attempting to defuse the dissenting movements by speeding economic development at home. This included the wooing of the first **foreign**

tourists to the Algarve. Up until the 1960s, Salazar's regime had welcomed upmarket visitors to what was essentially a closed society, but had been reluctant to admit mass tourism, fearing that local workers would be influenced by the material wealth of lower-class tourists. However, the need for some sort of foreign income persuaded Salazar to open up the highly marketable Algarve. New international-style hotels appeared along the coast, Faro's international airport was opened in 1965 and the Salazar suspension bridge over the Tagus – later renamed the Ponte 25 Abril – linked the Algarve more directly to Lisbon.

The end of Salazar

The government's reign came to an undignified end in 1968 when Salazar's deckchair collapsed, bringing on a stroke. Incapacitated, he lived for another two years, deposed as premier – though the man imbued such fear that no one ever dared tell him. His successor, **Marcelo Caetano**, attempted to prolong the regime by offering limited democratization at home. However, tensions beneath the surface were fast becoming more overt. It was especially in the army stationed in Africa that opposition crystallized. There the young conscript officers increasingly sympathized with the freedom movements they were intended to suppress and resented the cost – in economic terms and in lives – of the hopeless struggle. From their number grew the revolutionary **Movimento das Forças Armadas** (MFA).

Revolution and the growth of mass tourism

By 1974 the situation in Africa was deteriorating rapidly and at home Caetano's liberalization had come to a dead end; morale, among the army and the people, was lower than ever. The MFA, formed originally as an officers' organization to press for better conditions, had become increasingly politicized and was already laying its plans for a takeover. Finally on **April 25, 1974**, the plans laid by Major Otelo Saraiva de Carvalho for the MFA were complete and their virtually bloodless coup went without a hitch, no serious attempt being made by anyone to defend the government.

The next two years were perhaps the most extraordinary in Portugal's history, a period of continual revolution, massive politicization and virtual anarchy, during which decisions of enormous importance were nevertheless made – above all the granting of independence to all of the overseas colonies.

Meanwhile, colonialists who no longer had a home overseas returned to Portugal, with many of them taking advantage of the new found opportunities in the Algarve. Throughout this period of political uncertainty hotels and restaurants continued to sprout up, luring foreign visitors and the wealthier urban Portuguese whose new-found freedom could be enjoyed in an Algarve that seemed to represent the outside world they had been denied under Salazar.

Democracy and Europe: The 1980s to the present

There were various if less dramatic changes of government over the next ten years, but the most significant event was Portugal's entry into the **European Community** in 1986, which brought with it the most important changes since the Revolution. With increased foreign investment and the help of a massive injection of funds to modernize infrastructures, Portugal enjoyed unprecedented economic growth, and despite pockets of deeply entrenched poverty, the Algarve's economy in particular took off, with wide-scale touristic development along its coastline.

The 1990s took Portugal into the second stage of its ten-year transition phase for EC entry and into its presidency of the European Community in 1992, the year when all remaining trade and employment barriers were removed and the EC became the EU. The country adopted its EU task with considerable imagination, and expense, developing among other things the east-west Algarve highway and a new bridge over the border to Spain just north of Vila Real.

General elections in October 1995 brought ten years of Conservative rule to an end and the moderate Socialists came into power under the enthusiastic leadership of **António Guterres**. 1995 also saw the establishment of the Parque Natural do Sudoeste Alentejano e Costa Vicentina, which offers protected status to much of the western Algarve.

Guterres and the Socialists returned for a second consecutive mandate – the first since the revolution – in 1999. But after a series of controversies involving local socialist councillors, and faced with the unenviable task of steadying Portugal's economy after the September 11 terrorist attacks in the run up to the introduction of the Euro, the Socialists were unexpectedly trounced in the local elections in December 2001. Guterres promptly resigned. The opposition PSD were voted into power under **Manuel Durão Barroso** in March 2002, promising tighter state spending and a possible hardening of drugs and immigration laws.

In the new millennium

Although the opening up of Eastern Europe has exposed Portugal to fiercer competition for trade and investment – in particular textiles – a **modernized infrastructure** and improved transport networks mean that Portugal continues to be attractive to foreign investors. The so-called Via do

Infante IP1 motorway is due to open in 2002, linking Vila Real de Santo António in the eastern Algarve with Lagos in the west, and the final stage of the Lisbon motorway is also due finally to connect the Algarve with the capital in the same year. By 2004, train passengers will be able to travel directly from Faro to Coimbra and Porto without the need to change in Lisbon, and there are longer-term plans to connect Faro to the high-speed trans-Europe network via southern Spain.

One of the main headaches for the government, though, continues to be the inefficiency of Portuguese **agriculture**, which employs nearly one-fifth of the workforce but produces only a fraction of the country's wealth. The opening in 2002 of the Alqueva dam – the largest man-made lake in Europe – in the Alentejo district, is a controversial attempt to bring agriculture to a previously barren area. The water should permit the farming of vegetables, but at the expense of millions of trees. Damming the Guadiana river also threatens the delicate ecosystems at the river's estuary around Castro Marim and Vila Real in the Algarve.

The next major development in Portugal's economy will be the reaction to the introduction of the **Euro** in January 2002. The persistent worry is that the euro might slowly push up prices in a country which still earns much less per capita than its more industrialized partners. A slightly alarming shift, too, has been the takeover of large areas of banking, real estate and the financial sectors by Spanish companies, while EU funds that have played a dominant role in Portugal's development will largely end in 2006.

Internationally, however, Portuguese self-esteem has been boosted by the country being chosen to host the European Football Championships in 2004, with the new Faro-Loulé stadium near Almancil being one of eight chosen venues. All of this should ensure that **tourism**, which accounts for nearly a tenth of the country's GNP and over a quarter of all foreign investment, will continue to flourish. Many people worry about the industry's all too obvious environmental side-effects, but at least some restrictions have finally been imposed to control the environmental impact of development. New golf courses have to use recycled water and leave fallow areas for wildlife to flourish, and low-density green resorts such as Vilamoura and Vale do Lobo are likely to form the blueprint for the Algarve's new holiday villages.

Wildlife

Despite widespread coastal development – and the continuing pressure on many of its natural habitats (see p.133) – the Algarve continues to support a diverse range of flora and fauna. From wild boar in the mountainous interior to rare wading birds and reptiles on the coastal mud flats, the Algarve's mild climate supports a surprising selection of creatures. Plant life is also varied, covering the ubiquitous cork, olive and citrus trees, plus more exotic species such as the Canary date palm and the North American Agave.

Much of the marine life of the Algarve is concentrated in the protected areas around the coastline west of Burgau and around the mud flats to the east of Faro. In addition to these national parks, the mountains of Monchique, the Guadiana, Alvor and Odelouca river valleys and much of the Serra do Caldeirão form part of Rede Natura 2000, which means they are classified as areas of natural importance by the EU – though unfortunately this does not necessarily guarantee protection from constructors.

Fauna

Algarve supports some unusual-looking animals found virtually nowhere else in Europe, notably the swamp-loving purple galinule – a stumpy bird – and the Mediterranean chameleon with a phenomenally long tongue.

Mammals, reptiles and insects

Most **wild mammals** survive in the more mountainous interior, away from the coastal development and the trigger-happy Portuguese hunters. Here, wild boar, otters, foxes and mongoose are all quite common. Sea otters are sometimes seen off Cabo de São Vicente, in summer.

Reptiles also flourish in the mild climate including geckos, snakes – including the poisonous Lataste viper and Montpellier snake – and scorpions, though the poisonous species keep to themselves and reports of bites are very rare. Tree frogs, viperine snakes, Montpellier snakes and pond terrapins are all common in the Parque Natural da Ria Formosa east of Faro. But the most bizarre reptile is the rare swivel-eyed Mediterranean chameleon, which – though common in North Africa – is only found in Europe in parts of the eastern Algarve, Spain and Crete. It is well adapted to survive in the marshy and scrubby coastal areas, around Castro Marim (see p.146), where it changes colour to blend in with the background. However, if you are interested in a closer look bear in mind that it hibernates from December to March.

The Algarve also supports around 300 species of **butterfly** and **moth**, including the emperor moth, hawkmoth, swallowtail, large blue butterfly, brimstone and red admiral, all of which are commonly seen especially when flowers first bloom in spring and early summer.

Birds and marine life

One of the most common, and most beautiful, visitors to the region are **white storks**, which nest on every available chimney, bell tower, or telegraph pole in early summer. The more wooded, mountainous **inland** Algarve shelters the eagle owl, buzzard, little owl and hoopoe. However, it is the coast that contains some of the most important areas for bird and **marine life** in Portugal – much of the terrain with protected status.

Cabo de São Vicente, the westernmost point of the Algarve, supports the highest concentration of marine and birdlife in the country, with rare birds such as Bonelli's eagles, ospreys, white herons, cattle egrets, kites and rock doves; most birdlife can be seen in the spring and autumn, when migrating birds stop off here. Some 22 species of wading bird can be seen in the **Quinta da Rocha** nature reserve near Alvor (see p.221). But it is east of Almancil that Portugal's most extensive wetlands are found. The salt flats in the Parque Natural da Ria Formosa (see p.108), enclosed by the sandspits between Ancão and Manta Rota in the eastern Algarve, shelter over 50 species of fish, including gilhead, bass, white bream, mullets and eels. Reptiles and sea horses also thrive here. This plentiful food supply helps support birdlife to rival that of the more famous Spanish Reserve of Doñana across the border in Andalucía, including pintails, pochard, purple herons, egrets and black-winged stilts, as well as waders such as the sanderling and the knot. The **Parque Natural da Ria Formosa** is also the only breeding ground in Portugal for the rare purple galinule – or swamp hen – a bluey-purple bird with red legs and a red bill. Once nearly extinct in Portugal, there are now around 30 pairs, mostly at Ludo between Quinta do Lago and Faro airport (see p.78). This is also the largest nesting site for the Little Tern, and forms the wintering ground for many northern European species including the wigeon, teal, bar- and black-tailed godwit, curlew and grey plover, as well as being the stopover point for birds migrating to Africa, such as the dunlin. Another important wetland area is the **Reserva Natural do Sapal de Castro Marim e Vila Real** (see p.146) near the Spanish border, which shelters white storks, spoonbills and, in winter, flamingos.

Flora

The Mediterranean-like climate encourages a huge array of plantlife to flourish in a landscape that is surprisingly verdant for much of the year. Native species include the holm oak and the yellowy or reddish cistus, or rockrose, which flower in early summer. Much of the vegetation found in the Algarve, however, was introduced from abroad.

The Romans and Moors introduced numerous crops, including **olive** trees, some of which are believed to be up to 1000 years old. Harvested in September, Algarve olives tend to be unsuitable for the production of olive oil, but are eaten widely, either green, black or purple depending on their ripeness. The **carob** tree looks similar to the olive and has also been grown since Moorish times. The brown pods are used to make chocolate or for a type of bread; the size and weight of the pods is so consistent that they were used to weigh gold, giving us the word *carat*.

The mild climate also supports various **fruit trees** introduced by the Moors – orange, with its superbly aromatic blossom, as well as lemon, figs, pomegranates, quince and the strawberry tree, which produces strawberry-like fruits used to make medronho (see p.41). One of the most spectacular trees is the **almond**, whose superb blossom in February has given it the nickname "snow of the Algarve" (see p.139). Other trees include the cork oak (see p.90), yellow-flowering mimosa, jacaranda, maritime pine and umbrella pine, which grows on sandy soil near the coast and offers shade to many of the Algarve's golf courses.

Other species were bought to the Algarve by early Portuguese navigators, including the Canary date palm, the Bermuda buttercup, the Agave, which came from America,

and the Japanese medlar. A more recent arrival is the eucalyptus, a fast-growing, sweet-smelling tree from Australia
which was an extremely popular import in the mid-twenti-
eth century. Originally seen as the perfect tree for paper
production, it is now realized that its capacity to extract
water and its proneness to forest fires can be highly damaging to the environment, which takes years to recover once
the trees have been removed.

One of the most important areas for botanists is around
Cabo de São Vicente, where there are several rare species
of plant including milk-vetch, cistus, sea pink, lavender and
narcissi. The **Ria Formosa** area is also known for its 50
species of plantlife including cord grass, which thrives in
brackish water; marram grass, which helps stabilize dunes;
sea holly, thrift, cotton-weed and the hottentot fig, whose
yellow or purple flowers eventually produce edible fruits.

Books

The Algarve has been covered very sparsely by British and American writers, and many of the works that do exist in English are out of print (o/p) and available only from libraries or specialist book dealers.

Where two publishers are given for the books listed below, they refer to the UK and US publishers respectively. Books published in one country only are followed by the publisher and UK, US or Portugal; if a book has the same UK and US publisher only the publisher's name is given.

General travel and guides

Marion Kaplan *The Portuguese: the Land and its People* (Penguin; Penguin, o/p). Readable, all-embracing volume, covering everything from wine to the family, poetry and the land. It's the best general introduction to the country available and includes lots of background information on Algarve's history and culture.

Rose Macaulay *They Went to Portugal, Too* (Carcanet, UK). The book covers British travellers to Portugal from the Crusaders to Byron, weaving an anecdotal history of the country in the process.

Anne de Stoop *Living in Portugal* (Flammarion;

Abbeville). A glossy coffee-table tome filled with beautifully evocative photographs of Portugal's sights and architectural gems, including a chapter on Algarve interiors and landscapes.

History and politics

David Birmingham *A Concise History of Portugal* (Cambridge University Press). Recommended for the casual reader; concise indeed, but providing straightforward and informative coverage from the year dot to 1991.

Peter Russell *Prince Henry 'the Navigator': A life* (Yale University Press, UK). Fascinating if academic biography of the fifteenth-century prince.

José Hermano Saraiva *Portugal: A Companion History* (Carcanet, UK). Accessible and concise history of the country written especially for non-specialist foreigners.

Fiction

Lídia Jorge *The Migrant Painter of Birds* (Harvill Press, UK). Lídia Jorge was born near Albufeira in 1946, and is one of Portugal's most respected contemporary writers. This beautifully written novel describes a girl's memories as she grows up in a small village close to the Atlantic, and in doing so poignantly captures a changing rural community.

Len Port *Bica the Portuguese Water Dog*, (Vista Ibérica, Portugal). Jolly if inconsequential story for young children based on the adventures of the water poodles from near Olhão (see p.108).

Mário de Sá Carneiro *Lucios' Confessions*, *The Great Shadow* (Dedalus, UK). Sá Carneiro was a contemporary of the more famous Pessoa and a regular visitor to Faro before he committed suicide at 26. *Lucio's Confessions* describes a ménage à trois which leads to a killing. In *The Great Shadow* is a series of short stories of stunning intensity.

José Saramago *All the Names, Baltasar and Blimunda, Blindness, The Year of the Death of Ricardo Reis, The Gospel According to Jesus Christ, The Stone Raft, The Tale of the Unknown Island* (Harvill Press); *Manual of Painting and Calligraphy* (Carcanet, UK). Saramago won the Nobel prize for literature in 1998 and is Portugal's most famous living writer. Highly prolific, he is both readable and experimental.

Poetry

Luís de Camões *The Lusiads* (Penguin, UK); *Epic and Lyric* (Carcanet, UK). *The Lusiads* is Portugal's national epic, celebrating the ten-month voyage of Vasco da Gama which opened the sea route to India. This is a good prose translation. *Epic and Lyric* includes extracts from *The Lusiads* together with other shorter poems.

Fernando Pessoa *A Centenary Pessoa* (Carcanet; Sheep Meadow). The avant-garde writer Pessoa was a regular visitor to Faro with fellow writer Mário de Sá-Carneiro. This superlative anthology of poems, prose, letters and photographs is the most comprehensive selection of Pessoa's output yet published in English.

Food and wine

Rainer Horbelt & Sonja Spindler *Algarve Country Cooking* (Vista Ibérica, Portugal). A series of regional recipes based round local anecdotes and the four seasons; well-translated from German and a charming insight into rural Algarve traditions.

Edite Vieira *The Taste of Portugal* (Grub Street, UK). A delight to read, let alone cook from. Vieira combines snippets of history and passages from Portuguese writers (very well translated) to illustrate her dishes. It includes several traditional Algarvian recipes.

Nature

Kevin and Christine Carlson *A Birdwatching Guide to the Algarve* (Chelmsford Arlequin, UK). Containing maps, photos and essential information.

Mary MacMurtine *Wild Flowers of the Algarve* (Kintore, UK). Colour pictures and glossary of the region's flora.

GA & RS Vowles *Breeding Birds of the Algarve* (Newent Centro de Estodos Ornithológicos no Algarve, Portugal). Details of the 154 species that breed in the Algarve.

Walking and golf

Brian and Eileen Anderson *Algarve* (Sunflower Landscapes, UK). Maps and small photos accompany twenty walks described in great detail; there are also car tours and some practical information.

Maurice Clyde and Esme Clyde *Algarve Silves Walking Guide* (Discovery Walking Guides). Map and booklet covering 20 walks in the Silves area, written by a Rough Guides contributor who has helped waymark the Via Algarviana (see p.175).

June Parker *Walking in the Algarve* (Cicerone, UK). Details of 35 walks around the Algarve, with sketch maps and cultural facts.

John Russell and Nuno Campos *Golf's Golden Coast*

(Vista Ibérica, Portugal). An attractive, illustrated guide for anyone interested in the Algarve's 18-hole clubs.

Julie Statham *Algarve: Let's Walk* (Vista Ibérica, Portugal). Covering over 20 walks throughout the region "for the casual, holiday walker".

Michael York, Jacqueline York *Algarve Loulé Walking Guide* (Discovery Walking Guides). Map and booklet covering 20 walks in the Loulé area.

Language

E nglish is widely spoken in most of the Algarve's hotels and tourist restaurants, but you will find a few words of Portuguese extremely useful if you are travelling on public transport, or in more out-of-the-way places. If you have some knowledge of Spanish, you won't have much problem reading **Portuguese**. Understanding it when it's spoken, though, is a different matter: pronunciation is entirely different and at first even the easiest words are hard to distinguish. Once you've started to figure out the words it gets a lot easier very quickly.

A useful word is **há** (the H is silent), which means "there is" or "is there?" and can be used for just about anything. Thus: "*Há uma pensão aqui?*" (Is there a pension here?). More polite and better in shops or restaurants are "**Tem**...?" (pronounced *taying*) which means "Do you have...?", or "**Queria**..." (I'd like...). And of course there are the old standards "Do you speak English?" (*Fala Inglês?*) and "I don't understand" (*Não compreendo*).

Pronunciation

The chief difficulty with **pronunciation** is its lack of clarity – consonants tend to be slurred, vowels nasal and often ignored altogether. The **consonants** are, at least, consistent:

C is soft before E and I, hard otherwise unless it has a cedilla – *açucar* (sugar) is pronounced "assookar".

CH is somewhat softer than in English; chá (tea) sounds like Shah.

J is pronounced like the "s" in pleasure, as is G except when it comes before a "hard" vowel (A, O and U).

LH sounds like "lyuh" (Alcantarilha).

Q is always pronounced as a "k".

S before a consonant or at the end of a word becomes "sh," otherwise it's as in English – Sagres is pronounced "Sahgresh".

X is also pronounced "sh"– caixa (cash desk) is pronounced "kaisha".

Vowels are worse – flat and truncated, they're often difficult for English-speaking tongues to get around. The only way to learn is to listen: accents, **Ã**, **Ô**, or **É**, turn them into longer, more familiar sounds.

When two vowels come together they continue to be enunciated separately except in the case of **EI** and **OU** – which sound like a and long ò respectively. E at the end of a word is silent unless it has an accent, so that *carne* (meat) is pronounced "karn", while *café* sounds much as you'd expect. The **tilde over Ã or Õ** renders the pronunciation much like the French -an and -on endings only more nasal. More common is **ÃO** (as in pão, bread – *são*, saint – *limão*, lemon, Olhão), which sounds something like a strangled yelp of "Ow!" cut off in midstream.

BASIC PORTUGUESE WORDS AND PHRASES

sim; *não*	yes; no
olá; *bom dia*	hello; good morning
boa tarde/noite	good afternoon/night
adeus, até logo	goodbye, see you later
hoje; *amanhã*	today; tomorrow
por favor/se faz favor	please
tudo bem?	Everything all right?
está bem	it's all right/OK
*obrigado/a**	thank you
onde; *que*	where; what
quando; *porquê*	when; why
como; *quanto*	how; how much
não sei	I don't know
sabe . . .?	do you know . . .?
pode . . .?	could you . . .?
desculpe; *com licença*	sorry; excuse me
aqui; *ali*	here; there
perto; *longe*	near; far
este/a; *esse/a*	this; that
agora; *mais tarde*	now; later
mais; *menos*	more; less
grande; *pequeno*	big; little
aberto; *fechado*	open; closed
senhoras; *homens*	women; men
lavabo/quarto de banho	toilet/bathroom
banco; *câmbio*	bank; change
correios	post office
(dois) selos	(two) stamps
Como se chama?	What's your name?
(chamo-me . . .)	(my name is . . .)
Como se diz isto em Português?	What's this called in Portuguese?

| *O que é isso?* | What's that? |
| *Quanto é?* | How much is it? |

* *Obrigado* agrees with the sex of the person speaking – a
woman says *obrigada*, a man *obrigado*.

Getting around

Para ir a . . .?	How do I get to . . .?
esquerda, direita,	left, right, straight ahead
sempre em frente	
Onde é a estação	Where is the bus station?
de camionetas?	
a paragem de	the bus stop for . . .
autocarro para . . .	
Donde parte o	Where does the bus
autocarro para . . .?	to . . . leave from?
A que horas parte?	What time does it leave?
(chega a . . .?)	(arrive at . . .?)
Para onde vai?	Where are you going?
(Vou a)	(I'm going to)
obrigado/a	thanks a lot
Pare aqui por favor	Stop here please
bilhete (para)	ticket (to)
ida e volta	round trip

Accommodation

Queria um quarto	I'd like a room
É para uma noite	It's for one night
(semana)	(week)
É para uma pessoa	It's for one person
(duas pessoas)	(two people)
Quanto custa?	How much is it?
chave	key

Eating and drinking
(for more food terms, see p.36–40)

Carne	Meat
Peixe	Fish
Ovos	Eggs
Pimenta	Pepper
Arroz	Rice
Sal	Salt
Legumes	Vegetables
Pão	Bread
Queijo	Cheese
Manteiga	Butter
Colher	Spoon
Faca	Knife
Garfo	Fork
Copo	Glass

Days and months

domingo	Sunday
segunda-feira	Monday
terça-feira	Tuesday
quarta-feira	Wednesday
quinta-feira	Thursday
sexta-feira	Friday
sábado	Saturday

Numbers

1	*um*	6	*seis*
2	*dois*	7	*sete*
3	*três*	8	*oito*
4	*quatro*	9	*nove*
5	*cinco*	10	*dez*

Numbers (continued)

11	*onze*	40	*quarenta*
12	*doze*	50	*cinquenta*
13	*treze*	60	*sessenta*
14	*catorze*	70	*setenta*
15	*quinze*	80	*oitenta*
16	*dezasseis*	90	*noventa*
17	*dezassete*	100	*cem*
18	*dezoito*	101	*cento e um*
19	*dezanove*	200	*duzentos*
20	*vinte*	500	*quinhentos*
21	*vinte e um*	1000	*mil*
30	*trinta*		

Common signs

Aberto	open
Fechado	closed
Perigo/Perigoso	danger/dangerous
Paragem	bus stop
Proibido estacionar	no parking
Saída	exit

INDEX

Visit us online
roughguides.com

Information on over 25,000 destinations around the world

- **Read** Rough Guides' trusted travel info
- **Share** journals, photos and travel advice with other readers
- Get exclusive Rough Guide **discounts** and travel **deals**
- Earn membership points every time you contribute to the
  Rough Guide **community** and get **free** books, flights and trips
- Browse thousands of CD reviews and artists in our **music** area

around the world

Alaska ★ Algarve ★ Amsterdam ★ Andalucía ★ Antigua & Barbuda ★ Argentina ★ Auckland Restaurants ★ Australia ★ Austria ★ Bahamas ★ Bali & Lombok ★ Bangkok ★ Barbados ★ Barcelona ★ Beijing ★ Belgium & Luxembourg ★ Belize ★ Berlin ★ Big Island of Hawaii ★ Bolivia ★ Boston ★ Brazil ★ Britain ★ Brittany & Normandy ★ Bruges & Ghent ★ Brussels ★ Budapest ★ Bulgaria ★ California ★ Cambodia ★ Canada ★ Cape Town ★ The Caribbean ★ Central America ★ Chile ★ China ★ Copenhagen ★ Corsica ★ Costa Brava ★ Costa Rica ★ Crete ★ Croatia ★ Cuba ★ Cyprus ★ Czech & Slovak Republics ★ Devon & Cornwall ★ Dodecanese & East Aegean ★ Dominican Republic ★ The Dordogne & the Lot ★ Dublin ★ Ecuador ★ Edinburgh ★ Egypt ★ England ★ Europe ★ First-time Asia ★ First-time Europe ★ Florence ★ Florida ★ France ★ French Hotels & Restaurants ★ Gay & Lesbian Australia ★ Germany ★ Goa ★ Greece ★ Greek Islands ★ Guatemala ★ Hawaii ★ Holland ★ Hong Kong & Macau ★ Honolulu ★ Hungary ★ Ibiza & Formentera ★ Iceland ★ India ★ Indonesia ★ Ionian Islands ★ Ireland ★ Israel & the Palestinian Territories ★ Italy ★ Jamaica ★ Japan ★ Jerusalem ★ Jordan ★ Kenya ★ The Lake District ★ Languedoc & Roussillon ★ Laos ★ Las Vegas ★ Lisbon ★ London ★

in twenty years

London Mini Guide ✶ London Restaurants ✶ Los Angeles ✶ Madeira ✶ Madrid ✶ Malaysia, Singapore & Brunei ✶ Mallorca ✶ Malta & Gozo ✶ Maui ✶ Maya World ✶ Melbourne ✶ Menorca ✶ Mexico ✶ Miami & the Florida Keys ✶ Montréal ✶ Morocco ✶ Moscow ✶ Nepal ✶ New England ✶ New Orleans ✶ New York City ✶ New York Mini Guide ✶ New York Restaurants ✶ New Zealand ✶ Norway ✶ Pacific Northwest ✶ Paris ✶ Paris Mini Guide ✶ Peru ✶ Poland ✶ Portugal ✶ Prague ✶ Provence & the Côte d'Azur ✶ Pyrenees ✶ The Rocky Mountains ✶ Romania ✶ Rome ✶ San Francisco ✶ San Francisco Restaurants ✶ Sardinia ✶ Scandinavia ✶ Scotland ✶ Scottish Highlands & Islands ✶ Seattle ✶ Sicily ✶ Singapore ✶ South Africa, Lesotho & Swaziland ✶ South India ✶ Southeast Asia ✶ Southwest USA ✶ Spain ✶ St Lucia ✶ St Petersburg ✶ Sweden ✶ Switzerland ✶ Sydney ✶ Syria ✶ Tanzania ✶ Tenerife and La Gomera ✶ Thailand ✶ Thailand's Beaches & Islands ✶ Tokyo ✶ Toronto ✶ Travel Health ✶ Trinidad & Tobago ✶ Tunisia ✶ Turkey ✶ Tuscany & Umbria ✶ USA ✶ Vancouver ✶ Venice & the Veneto ✶ Vienna ✶ Vietnam ✶ Wales ✶ Washington DC ✶ West Africa ✶ Women Travel ✶ Yosemite ✶ Zanzibar ✶ Zimbabwe

also look out for our maps,
phrasebooks, music guides
and reference books

Sorted

ROUGH GUIDES

100
Essential
CDs

Eight titles, one name

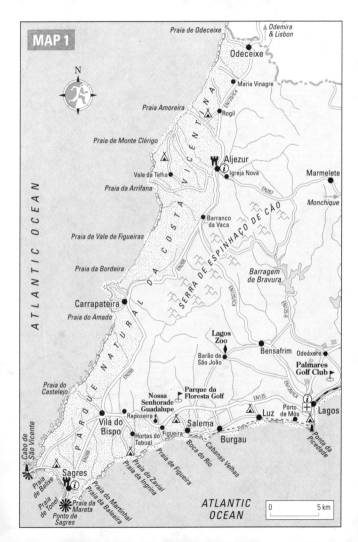

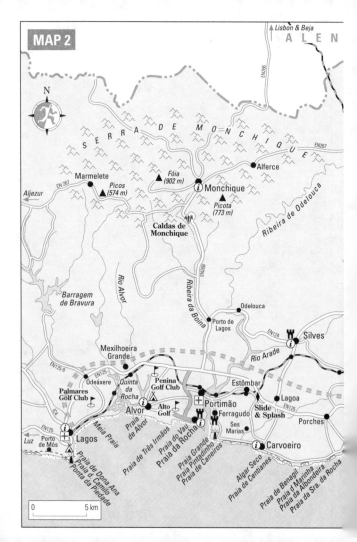

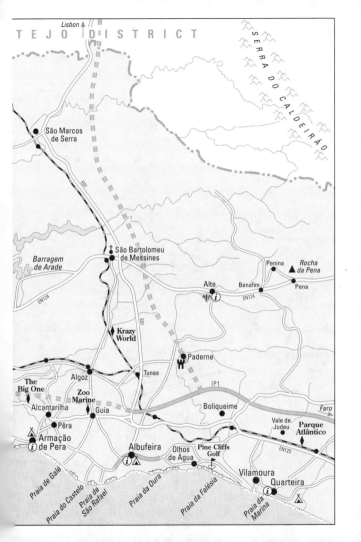

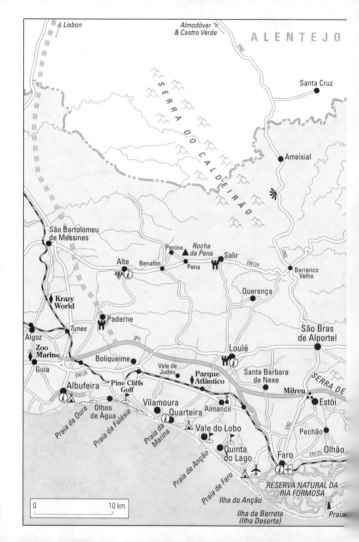

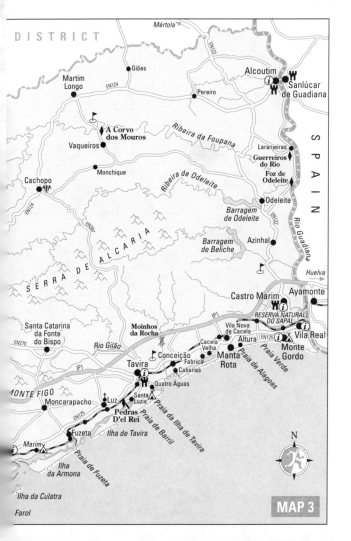

MAP 3